TEEN SPIRIT

TEEN SPIRIT

How Adolescence Transformed
the Adult World

Paul Howe

CORNELL UNIVERSITY PRESS   **ITHACA AND LONDON**

First published 2020 by Cornell University Press
Printed in the United States of America

Library of Congress Cataloging-in-Publication Data

Names: Howe, Paul, 1966- author.
Title: Teen spirit : how adolescence transformed the adult world / Paul Howe.
Description: Ithaca [New York] : Cornell University Press, 2020. |
    Includes bibliographical references and index.
Identifiers: LCCN 2019048953 (print) | LCCN 2019048954 (ebook) | ISBN
    9781501749827 (hardcover) | ISBN 9781501749841 (pdf) | ISBN
    9781501749834 (epub)
Subjects: LCSH: Adolescence—Social aspects—United States—History—20th
    century. | Adolescence—Social aspects—United States—History—21st
    century. | Adulthood—Social aspects—United States—History—20th century. |
    Adulthood—Social aspects—United States—History—21st century. |
    Emotional maturity—United States.
Classification: LCC HQ796. H745 2020 (print) | LCC HQ796 (ebook) | DDC
    305.2350973—dc23
LC record available at https://lccn.loc.gov/2019048953
LC ebook record available at https://lccn.loc.gov/2019048954

Contents

Figures and Tables

Figures

Tables

Acknowledgments

With a project such as this that crosses various disciplinary boundaries, it was sometimes challenging to know where to turn for input and guidance along the way. But there were several people whose support and counsel were indispensable. On the home front, Anna Cameron provided a valuable sounding board for varied thoughts and ideas, as well as love and encouragement at each step along the winding path from the project's initial conception to final conclusion. James Côté of the Department of Sociology at Western University offered incisive comments on an early draft of the work and consistent encouragement through subsequent stages of revision and review. Anonymous readers for Cornell University Press offered constructive critiques from diverse disciplinary perspectives that helped in shoring up different dimensions of the work, while Emily Andrew, my editor at the press, provided sharp-eyed editing advice as the finishing touches were being applied, as well as guiding the review and publication process with characteristic dispatch and good cheer. Financial support toward publication was provided by a grant from the Harrison McCain Foundation at the University of New Brunswick.

My thanks to all for their warm encouragement and support.

TEEN SPIRIT

ADOLESCENT SOCIETY, THEN AND NOW

Age, it is often said, is just a state of mind. You're only as old as you think you are.

Nowadays, it seems that many have taken this reassuring adage to heart. Individuals ages twenty to eighty seem little concerned about adhering to traditional adult norms, favoring instead the free and easy ways of youth. If Dick Clark was once dubbed the "world's oldest teenager," many of us these days appear to be vying for that title, hoping to remain forever young even as we move forward through the latter stages of life.

In some cases, this may reflect a deliberate effort to adopt a youthful frame of mind in an attempt to stave off the inescapable reality of growing older. But often an adolescent way of thinking and acting seems to come very naturally to people. Instead of consciously seeking to recapture their youth, they are simply doing and expressing what feels instinctively right, reflecting the fact that in some important sense they have never really fully grown up.

This, at least, is the way the phenomenon is often presented in popular culture. A case in point is the Adam Sandler movie *Grown Ups*, about a group of men who are clearly anything but, along with countless other forgettable films in which Sandler plays the stunted man-child to perfect effect. TV shows like *Arrested Development* and *It's Always Sunny in Philadelphia* follow a similar script, depicting characters who fall short of the adult mark in various ways with their erratic and self-absorbed behavior. Talk radio features outlandish hosts, such as shock jock Howard Stern, whose boorish broadcasts suggest an adolescent mentality hard at work, while reality TV includes shows like *Carpool Karaoke* where celebrities channel their teenage selves as they drive around town singing favorite pop songs at top volume.

If examples of adults acting like adolescents appear in many corners of the entertainment world, there are also signs of this same trend emerging in different avenues of real life. In our work, leisure, and personal pursuits, we sometimes act in a surprisingly impetuous manner, letting our impulses and emotions get the better of us rather than displaying adult qualities of balance and self-control. Some of us actively resist the trappings and responsibilities of adulthood throughout our twenties, our thirties, and even later, giving rise to widespread diagnoses of the so-called Peter Pan syndrome. For rest and relaxation, many adults these days prefer amusements—video games, superhero movies, comic books—designed first and foremost with teenagers in mind.

Clearly, these descriptions, and others like them, do not apply to everyone all of the time; but they encompass enough of us enough of the time to support the conclusion that a youthful spirit now holds considerable sway and has reshaped important elements of modern adulthood. We have entered what might be termed the age of adolescence, an era where there is an adolescent aura to much that adults think and do. It is, without doubt, an important social and cultural development that warrants closer investigation.

How Did We Get Here?

One way to gain insight into these changes is to look closely at teenagers themselves and their shared social setting—the subject matter of a classic sociological work from more than fifty years ago. In the late 1950s, James Coleman carried out a close study of ten American high schools, seeking to learn more about adolescents and their orientation toward schooling. He published the results several years later in *The Adolescent Society: The Social Life of the Teenager and Its Impact on Education*. What Coleman discovered through his research was that the social, not the educational, dimension of the high school experience was paramount. When gathered together in the high school setting, teenagers occupied a separate and distinct social space largely immune from adult influence, and with this came a tendency to "develop standards that lead away from those goals established by the larger society."[1] This adolescent society, as Coleman named it, was an inevitable by-product of the high school education system with the potential to decisively reshape the perspective and priorities of teenagers.

More than a half century later, the book continues to be a reference point for those who believe that herding teenagers together for several years in splendid isolation wasn't necessarily the wisest social experiment we've ever undertaken. "The child of high-school age," Coleman warned, "is 'cut off' from the rest of society, forced inward toward his own age group, made to carry out his whole social life with others his own age. With his fellows, he comes to constitute a small society, one that has its most important interactions *within* itself and maintains only a few threads of connection with the outside adult world."[2] In this insular world of the adolescent society, teenage traits and behaviors were free to flourish largely unchecked and unchallenged.

Coleman was mainly worried about the effects of this social cocooning on teenagers themselves. His principal concern, in other words, was with the impact of the modern adolescent experience on adolescents. My work focuses on another important impact of teen segregation. Spending critical formative years in a social setting dominated by like-minded peers not only shapes who we are as adolescents; it also promotes a more permanent etching of adolescent habits and characteristics, leading to their continued influence into the adult years. Some of our teenage ways may be cast aside as we move forward to adulthood, but an important residue remains, deeply ingrained in our personal inventory of embedded instincts, norms, and values. And so Coleman's phrase "adolescent society" no longer applies only to the realm of teenagers; it is also a fitting description of the larger society's gradual absorption of deep-seated adolescent qualities. Fifty years on, a new understanding of adolescent society is in order, along with a new book to explain its origins and significance.

We can glimpse the connection between these different conceptions of adolescent society in two classic television sitcoms. *Happy Days* was a show popular when I was young that depicted the lives of a group of typical American teens in the 1950s, offering a stylized portrayal of adolescent society around the time that Coleman was writing on the subject. *Seinfeld,* for the one or two of you who haven't heard, was set in the adult world of the late twentieth century, following the daily activities and diversions of four thirty-something adults living in New York City.[3] The parallels between the shows are telling. In both cases, the action revolves around four fast friends who spend a lot of time hanging out in diners— Arnold's burger joint in the case of Richie Cunningham and his pals on *Happy Days*, Tom's diner for Jerry Seinfeld and friends. There is a rough alignment of characters: each features a rebel who bucks convention (Fonzie and Kramer), a nerd who wants nothing more than to be accepted and well liked (Potsie and George), a smart aleck who delights in giving the nerd a hard time (Ralph Malph and Elaine), and an amiable lead character at the center of the action (Richie and Jerry). Their banter focuses on similar themes and preoccupations: relationships, social status, what they're going to do that weekend. They share a vague sense of being at an unsettled stage, trying to figure out who they really are and where they're going in life, though no one seems in any great rush to sort it all out. The overwhelming sense in both cases is of a group of people mainly preoccupied with themselves and the present. If TV shows provide a window of sorts into the spirit of the times, the affinities between *Happy Days* and *Seinfeld* hint at the way that adolescent ways of thinking, acting, and being have seeped upward into adult life.

The implications of this idea are many and varied. The adolescent fibers now embedded in the fabric of adulthood influence virtually every aspect of our lives: our relationships with family, friends, neighbors, and strangers; our sense of connection and commitment to our communities and the larger world; the actions we undertake, or sometimes fail to undertake, as citizens in a democratic society; economic choices around work, leisure, and consumption; the social norms and values we endorse; the cultural practices we embrace.

Citing examples of adolescent thinking and behavior in the adult world from the way Jerry and his friends live their lives would be like shooting fish in a barrel. I'll leave it to readers to conjure up their own examples—but just to get you started, recall George's squirming efforts to escape his engagement to Susan and his barely disguised relief when she succumbs to toxic glue on the cut-price wedding invitations he selected. Or if Seinfeld seems a bit passé, picture Phil from *Modern Family* collaborating on a video with his son Luke that involves gamely taking dozens of basketballs to the head (hoping one will ricochet into the basket) in fulfillment of his personal parenting ideal: "I've always said that if my son sees me as one of his idiot friends, then I've succeeded as a dad."[4] In real life, the effects are equally pervasive but a bit more subtle, and have crept up on us slowly over time as adolescent habits and manners have gradually worked their way into the adult realm. Most of the time, we barely notice them—and certainly don't recognize them as the product of an ascendant adolescent mentality.

Yet when we look at specific characteristics that are quintessentially adolescent, we can find in today's adult population widespread manifestations of comparable qualities, suggesting a connective thread. Or if we examine norms and practices common among adults of earlier decades and compare them systematically to those prevalent among adults today, we discover ample evidence that we now think and act differently from before—not just because the world has changed in so many ways, as common wisdom would have it, but because *we have changed* in so many ways. Our inner adolescent has been given freer rein, not quite to the point of taking full navigational control, but certainly having substantial influence over our everyday decisions and actions along with our larger life ambitions.

If this seems like a sweeping claim, the supporting ideas from which it flows are simple and uncontroversial. The core notion is this: many of our basic dispositions take shape in the early stages of life and are profoundly influenced by those around us. Part of this socialization process occurs, as it always has, when children are still under the close care of parents and are taught a series of basic skills, norms, and values necessary to human well-being and social functioning, some universal, others peculiar to their own culture and society. For many years of human history, the next step was for children to move out from under their parents' wing around the age of puberty and enter adult society—not as a separate cohort of "teenagers," but as the youngest members in an adult world marked by a relatively seamless age continuum. Here the finishing touches were applied. The prevailing norms of adulthood in a given society were firmly imprinted on each new generation through interaction between individuals of mixed ages in various work and social settings. The smooth and direct transition from childhood to the adult world allowed for the steady reproduction of existing norms and practices in each new generation.

About one hundred years ago, as part of a larger package of changes in countries experiencing economic and social modernization, the entry of youngsters into the world of adults was delayed. Now as we reached the stage where we were pulling away from parental influence and looking to others around us for guidance and direction in life, we no longer did so under the full influence of adult society. Instead, we did so primarily in the company of same-age peers, people more apt to reinforce than to challenge our youthful mind-set and temperament. There were still adults around, of course—parents at home, teachers in the schools, adult figures throughout the community—but as Coleman observed, the focal point of the teenager's world became the adolescent society and its prevailing norms and ideals. Instead of being shaped by adults, young people now were being primarily molded by peers, a change in the socialization process with ramifications both immediate and far-reaching.

This book tells the tale of that transformation, surveying the events and developments that led to the consolidation of the adolescent stage of life, as well as the social and cultural ripple effects that followed in its wake. The first half of the twentieth century witnessed changes in the adolescent realm that produced early rumblings of social change that proved to be the precursor of greater upheavals to come. At the heart of this account is the power of peer influence not just as an interesting phenomenon in the here and now, but as a social force capable of catalyzing long-term historical change.

Why Should We Care?

The relevance of all this to our lives today becomes quite apparent when we consider how our increasingly adolescent outlook and disposition have infused contemporary adult society—a second key theme in the chapters that follow. In part, this analysis echoes that vein of current social commentary that highlights and decries wide-ranging problems of the present. The concerns are voiced in different ways, but the overarching lament is that our society has become more discordant and dysfunctional, that we as individuals have grown more impulsive and shallow, less thoughtful and conscientious—less adult, if you will. One prominent critic, political philosopher Benjamin Barber, goes as far as to accuse us of "infantilization" in his 2007 book *Consumed*, employing rhetorical hyperbole that probably pushes things a bit far back in the developmental timeline.[5] Rather than infantilization, the behaviors and attitudes that Barber and others decry should properly, and quite literally, be seen as the manifestation of an ascendant adolescent mentality—which still implies we need to grow up, but is not quite as scathing an indictment. Moreover, it hints at an important upside that is often overlooked in the lament literature. The emergence of our adolescent character, if harmful to certain types of mature conduct, has been a tremendously liberating change as well. We have become, in the manner of teenagers everywhere, more open, free-spirited, and adventurous. Perhaps the pendulum has moved too far in the direction of youthful abandon, but this doesn't mean we should now seek the other extreme—to become stern, unbending adults devoid of any adolescent exuberance. Our adult and adolescent selves offer different virtues worth cultivating, and there is a balance to be struck between the two.

Alongside this shift in the general tone of modern society, there are also many specific examples of our increasingly adolescent character in contemporary attitudinal and behavioral trends. On the downside, the rise of an adolescent mind-set can be seen, for example, in a general decline in civility and rise in rule-breaking behavior, including cheating, lying, and other forms of self-serving action. Episodes such as the college admissions scandal of 2019—in which affluent parents, among other schemes, bribed coaches to "recruit" their college-bound offspring for sports they had never played—are only the tip of the iceberg. There is likewise something decidedly adolescent about many impetuous behaviors, from excessive consumption to erratic commitments in the working world and personal relationships, that are common among adults nowadays and often detrimental to both the individuals involved and those around them. A profusion of less-than-adult attitudes and actions can be seen in contemporary politics as well, among citizens and political leaders alike, in both the erosion of venerable principles of civic duty and responsibility and in the rise of brazen and boorish behavior that sometimes goes so far as to threaten basic democratic norms (yes, I mean you, Mr. Trump). Yet not to be discounted, again, is the positive side of the adolescent coin. The growing influence of youthful sensibilities helps explain our gradual evolution into a more tolerant and open society, more receptive to the interests and rights of marginalized groups—not perfect, by any means, but undeniably moving in the right direction over the long haul. A related example is our transition from a society that places a premium on conformity to one that values creativity and difference, a development that has benefited individuals and society alike through the unbottling of innovative potential in economic endeavors and other areas. The influence of adolescent qualities on adultdom is not the entire explanation for all these disparate long-term developments (which are described in greater detail in later chapters). It is, however, a substantial contributing factor and a common denominator that reveals how many features of modern life normally treated in isolation are in fact diverse manifestations of our increasingly adolescent character.

In seeking to capture something important about the tenor and direction of modern times, this work shares common ground with others that have tackled this sweeping theme while also staking some original claims. Certainly there are many who have suggested that salient problems of the present—from social fragmentation, to impulsive and rash behavior, to declining civic engagement—can be seen as the unfortunate consequence of the steady erosion of traditional adult norms and practices over the course of time. Barber says we have developed infantile responses—a preference for that which is easy, simple, and fast—across many aspects of our lives, a sentiment echoed by journalist Paul Roberts, who claims that impulsiveness has become endemic in today's society. In a similar vein, sociologist James Côté decries the widespread problem of "arrested adulthood" in Western society and its unfortunate implications for individual growth and identity development; US Senator Ben Sasse laments what he calls perpetual adolescence and the "vanishing American adult"; while cultural historian Gary Cross contends that today's men often think and act like overgrown boys.[6] But while these kindred works all point to a stubborn immaturity that has become more prevalent in recent times, this is often little more than an evocative description of the phenomenon. The current study presses further, by developing a more fully elaborated theory connecting peer influence in adolescence to long-term trends in character development and social change, and by suggesting that adolescent qualities have, quite literally, refashioned many dimensions of contemporary adulthood.

This work also differs from studies that point to other social sites and different time periods as the wellsprings of social change. Most focus their attention on the postwar years, seeing this as the period when the ground started to shift and social changes connected to the erosion of traditional conceptions of adulthood began to unfold. Barber, for example, contends that commercial capitalism in its recent incarnation—driven forward by manipulative advertising designed to generate superfluous consumer wants (new iPhone, anyone?)—is to blame for turning us into infantile, impulsive, unreflective consumers. Robert Putnam, focusing on the steady decline in one critical benchmark of adulthood, civic engagement, famously identified the roll-out of television in the 1950s as a kind of anti-civic "X-ray" that stole our time and zapped our motivation to participate in community life.[7] In contrast to these works, this study searches for root causes further back in time, to the earlier years of the twentieth century when adolescence first became a more clearly demarcated stage of life; and it emphasizes the subtle escalation and diffusion of adolescent character traits over the course of many decades, rather than a more rapid transformation in social values occurring in the postwar period.

In short, if the common view is that external forces have been chipping away at our adult assets over the past few decades, this study suggests a transformation at once more subtle, gradual, and profound. Through an inversion of the traditional socialization process, adults no longer impose themselves on youth to ensure conformity to prevailing norms of adulthood; instead, youth have been afforded a separate and secure social space to develop by their own lights and through that vehicle have slowly but surely reshaped adulthood in their adolescent image. This isn't something that has recently begun, but is instead a process of great depth and duration that has become fully entrenched over the past one hundred years. If we are concerned about some of the effects of ascendant adolescence—a concern I would share, while also underlining that there are beneficial as well as baleful consequences to be considered—we need a full understanding of the phenomenon in order to design effective remedies.

Twists and Turns

While the rising tide of adolescent qualities in the adult population is the principal story line in the pages that follow, there are also some important side stories to consider. One intriguing twist lies in the fact that the creation of our adolescent society went hand in hand with another critical change of the twentieth century: a massive increase in education levels across all sections of society. The fact that the two unfolded concurrently is hardly a coincidence, since it was the introduction of universal secondary education that created adolescent society— both the high school enclaves where teens interact intensively with one another, and the adult society that has gradually absorbed a diverse range of adolescent qualities. This adolescent infusion is a factor little considered when evaluating the effects of enhanced education on our social evolution over time.

Yet consider it we should. For what is intriguing and more than a little ironic is that the positive ends education was meant to serve—to make us more thoughtful and competent adults—have in some instances been undermined by the inadvertent nourishing of adolescent qualities working against those same outcomes. The *educational effects* of greater schooling for one and all have played out largely as expected—individuals with higher levels of education are, on the whole, more enlightened and adept in a host of different ways—but the broader *social effects* were quite unanticipated and have undermined at least some of the ambitious goals of the vast educational enrichment project we have undertaken over the past one hundred years. In this way, the story behind the emergence of today's adolescent society is one of both momentous change and major unintended consequences.

Yet there are also circumstances where the educational and social effects of schooling do not work at cross-purposes, but instead serve as allied agents of social change, working in concert with one another to generate more potent and positive social transformation than might be achieved by educational edification alone. Such synergistic effects are especially apparent in areas of social change connected to openness, innovation, and creativity, qualities reflecting a youthful outlook that are reinforced by educational experiences that serve to promote an inquisitive and curious mind-set. In short, education and adolescent qualities in tandem can be a potent combination for cultivating the open mind and leading us in exciting new directions both individually and as a society.

If the intimate link between education and ascendant adolescent qualities over the past century represents one important nuance to the argument, another is connected to more recent developments—in particular, an intriguing U-turn that has taken place since roughly 1990. Some of the trends that reflect the rise of the adolescent society, which appeared to be moving inexorably in one direction over time, have slowed or even reversed themselves in the past quarter century. This more recent inflection hasn't turned back the clock completely, but there are signs of change popping up everywhere, especially among today's younger generation, who in many ways appear to be more adultlike in their habits and behaviors than young people of the past—more serious and conscientious, less given to impulse and whimsy, more likely to stay on the straight and narrow path as they make their way to adulthood. For every young person whose parents might have paid off a sports coach or built a new library wing to get them admitted to the Ivy League, there are many more who have studied, volunteered, and achieved relentlessly over their teenage years to achieve that same outcome. It can frankly seem quite exhausting and daunting for those of us who grew up at a time when high school was more about friends and fun than painstaking preparation for the future.

Again, I am hardly the first to make such observations, as the serious and steadfast nature of the millennial generation has caught the attention of many observers.[8] Yet their emergence remains something of a surprise and a puzzle. Later on, we'll see that this development may not be such a surprise after all but can instead be seen as part of the larger evolutionary arc of the adolescent society. In its more settled and established phase, it makes sense that we would see a countervailing trend of stronger adult inclinations emerging among rising generations—for reasons explained at greater length below. This more recent turn of events raises questions about our future social trajectory and prompts reflection on ways we might seek to steer that trajectory in desired directions.

How Did I Get Here?

In the course of developing this wide-ranging argument, I have strayed far from my academic home base, political science. But the work did originate with a classic issue of concern to political scientists: voter turnout. Like others in my discipline, I started to research voter participation as turnout took a sharp decline over the past number of years, particularly in some of the long-standing democracies. In searching for reasons why, one relevant clue that popped up in my research was a change in the character of nonvoting: instead of people missing the occasional election for practical reasons (too busy to vote, out of town that day), it was becoming increasingly common to abandon voting altogether, thereby rejecting, so it would seem, one of the traditional adult responsibilities normally respected by citizens in a democracy. The emergence of these "electoral dropouts," representing a sizable minority of the population, wasn't something that had happened overnight. On closer inspection, it was clear this was a problem that had crept up over time through steady erosion in political engagement among rising generations for a number of years, even decades.

The problem, as I saw it, was twofold. It was partly a matter of youth being immersed in their own social space and disconnected from the adult world, and therefore failing to develop some of the habits and motivations that underwrite democratic participation. Yet it was also a problem of adults who failed to advance beyond this youthful condition as they graduated from their teenage years, continuing to be politically disengaged and disconnected even as they moved into their twenties, their thirties, and beyond.

Out of this simple observation, the larger theme came into focus. A youth-oriented society with a clearly defined adolescent stage of life doesn't just alter the texture of teenage life. It has more general effects on society as a whole, as people move forward to adulthood with their youthful traits, habits, and instincts more fully intact. Stated this way, it was clear the idea could be applied to many facets of our lives, not just our participation or nonparticipation in democracy. The impact of adolescent ways on the adult world would have implications for all kinds of individual actions and decisions, as well as larger social, cultural, and political trends. This then shaped my research agenda going forward: to learn more about teenagers and the social dynamics of adolescence, and to trace the wide-ranging impact of rising adolescent traits across diverse sectors of modern life.

Learning about these subjects meant venturing into new academic territory. Research from various disciplines was discovered to be relevant and has been brought into play in the pages that follow, including substantial doses of psychology and sociology, modest measures of economics and demography, and even a dash of neuroscience. Working across a wide range of fields meant it was sometimes necessary to draw upon seminal and synthetic works to help distill essential conclusions. The end result is a work favoring breadth over depth; much of the originality lies in connecting the dots, making linkages between established ideas and insights across diverse disciplines that have not previously been pulled together in one place. Evidence is also widely drawn, from both the serious world of social, political, and cultural analysis and the more vivid and immediate realm of popular ideas and culture. This method of research and presentation best serves my overarching goals: to provide a cogent narrative describing the emergence and consolidation of our adolescent society and to develop a persuasive argument demonstrating how this perspective both complements and challenges other prominent theories on the theme of social change.

If the academic scope of the work is wide, the geographic range is more limited. Much of the research, and many of the examples, are taken from the American case, in part for the simple practical reason that there was more evidence available for the United States that proved helpful in developing the ideas and arguments. But the theory of ascendant adolescence is not meant to be limited to just one place. Anywhere that adolescents are encouraged to congregate and cluster there will be a tendency for adolescent qualities to become more deeply entrenched and to exert greater influence on the norms and mores of adulthood over time. And so all those countries where universal secondary education has become the norm—in other words, countries throughout the industrialized world—have seen the development of their own adolescent society (in both senses of the term). The effects do incubate slowly and have emerged at different speeds in various places, but the same forces of change have now been set in motion in many different countries. That said, there are grounds for thinking that the United States, more than anywhere else, has provided particularly fertile soil for the processes I describe and has therefore been something of a forerunner in the emergence of the adolescent society—for reasons I'll expand upon later. This is why much of the analysis in subsequent chapters is built around the American case, which serves as the bellwether model for explaining and illustrating many of the arguments. At the same time, examples and evidence, where available and relevant, are also taken from Canada and Western Europe.

Readers coming at this work from other places—other research traditions, other countries—may not agree with all I have to say about the adolescent society. But I do believe the core idea provides a new and useful conceptual prism, one that extends our understanding of the origins and evolution of some of the most important social changes of the past century that have so deeply influenced who we are and how we live today.

1

THE CHARACTER OF ADOLESCENTS

The first part of the story behind the emergence of the adolescent society is straightforward enough. If it matters that young people have come to spend critical formative years primarily in the company of adolescent peers, it is because those peers are so different from the adults that used to exert the greatest influence during that period—different in their perspective and priorities, their feelings and sensibilities, their temperament, personality, and values.

I say this is straightforward simply because most people who have spent any substantial time with teenagers would probably accept the idea without further argument or evidence. Those on the front lines—the parents, teachers, and others who interact with adolescents on a daily basis—could all provide their own stories about the sometimes bewildering, and certainly distinctive, behavior of the teens in their lives, along with speculation about the psychological features of adolescence responsible for that behavior.

Many of these typical adolescent qualities carry negative overtones. The irascible and irresponsible teenager is a venerable cliché emerging out of a long tradition of teen denigration. The classic study that set the tone more than a century ago was Stanley Hall's two-volume work, *Adolescence: Its Psychology and Its Relation to Physiology, Anthropology, Sociology, Sex, Crime, Religion and Education*, published in 1904.[1] Hall's core idea was that adolescence is inevitably a period of "storm and stress" attributable to deep-seated turbulence in the adolescent psyche—something to be weathered by those in its clutches and endured by those around them, until receding, slowly but surely, as adolescence gives way to adulthood.

12

The storm-and-stress perspective remains influential to this day. A popular book from a few years back about the shortcomings of adolescents bore the ominous title *The Primal Teen*. Yet not everyone accepts this characterization. In fact, some go so far as to reject the idea that there are any intrinsic differences between adolescents and adults whatsoever.

The viewpoint is expressed most forcefully by research psychologist Robert Epstein, in his 2007 book, *The Case against Adolescence*. Epstein strenuously objects to the notion that adolescents suffer from any kind of innate storminess. Their restive character is instead a reaction against the unreasonable treatment they have been subjected to in modern times. In making his case, Epstein catalogs a series of social, economic, and legal constraints introduced since the late nineteenth century that keep adolescents tightly in check—and a hefty catalog it is. Adolescents cannot sign contracts, vote, or buy or sell property. They are not permitted to refuse or consent to medical treatment. They cannot marry or enlist in the military without parental consent. Their right to work is severely restricted, and they must attend school full time, normally until at least age sixteen. When he tallies it all up, Epstein estimates that today's teenagers are subject to about twice as many restrictions as active-duty marines or jailed felons.[2]

To Epstein's way of thinking, there is nothing natural or normal about these constraints. Like a group of innocents unjustly incarcerated who eventually start to bang their cups on the bars or lash out at the guards, adolescents are a socially restricted group clamoring for the same freedoms enjoyed by everyone else, nothing more, nothing less. The solution, he tells us, is to remove age-based restrictions and let people of any age take on adult responsibilities—voting, driving, owning property, and so on—based solely on demonstrated competence. Dispense with the *idea* of adolescence, along with the rigid framework of laws and norms built around the idea, and adolescent behavior will adapt to meet our changed expectations.

The argument set out in these pages presumes that Epstein is both right and wrong. He is wrong in supposing that adolescents, beneath the social labels and barriers we have created, are just as mature and capable as adults—that all we have to do, as the subtitle of his book recommends, is to "rediscover the adult in every teen." If there are some exceptional individuals who prove themselves capable of adult ways of thinking and acting early on, this is normally not the case. The developmental trajectory from child to adult is typically incomplete by the teenage years. Deep-rooted differences on a wide range of personal qualities—some consistent with Hall's stormy stereotype, others reflecting more positive attributes—separate the average teen from the average adult.

At the same time, Epstein is right to point out that important consequences flow from taking a certain category of individuals, branding them with a common label, and penning them together in social settings where their main source of influence is one another. Under these circumstances, whatever natural differences might exist between the segregated group and the larger society are apt to be intensified and exaggerated.[3] When this social segregation extends over several years, the effects are likely to be rather profound—so profound that they not only influence teenagers as teens (Epstein's primary argument), but also retain influence into adulthood and thereby have implications for society as a whole (my principal contention).

In the end, it is hard to say precisely how much the distinctive character of adolescents reflects a natural stage in the human maturation process and how much is the result of the intensive interaction with other teens that has become the norm in modern times. The safest bet—and my presumption throughout these pages—is that it is a bit of both.[4] With that framework in mind, I first consider the distinctive qualities of teenagers that can reasonably be connected to the natural trajectory of human development, viewing this from a number of complementary vantage points; and then, in chapter 2, I turn my attention to the social setting of adolescence, where, as Epstein rightly points out, these teenage qualities have been given the opportunity to flourish and take root as never before.

The Personality Traits of Teenagers

To assess the general nature of adolescents, a fruitful starting point is to consider their personality traits; and the best framework for doing so is the Big Five classification system widely used in the psychology discipline. At the core of this system is the idea that all important human personality traits can be captured under five broad headings: openness, conscientiousness, extroversion, agreeableness, and neuroticism, summed up in the aptly expansive acronym OCEAN. Unlike some academic jargon, these terms correspond pretty closely to how they are used in everyday life—which is not surprising, since they were partly developed by canvassing the English language for adjectives that capture core personality traits. So when personality researchers describe someone as extroverted, they mean someone who is outgoing, gregarious, and excitable. When they say someone is agreeable, they mean a person who gets along well with others, someone who is cooperative and considerate. And when they call someone open, they mean a person who enjoys new encounters, experiences, and ideas. Of course, none of these personality traits is an either-or proposition. People possess them in varying degrees, so all are measured by numeric scales taking on a range of different values.

While differences across age groups have been a subject of considerable interest in the Big Five research literature, relatively little attention has been given to the distinct personality profile of teenagers. In part this may reflect a key practical barrier: many surveys are limited to respondents eighteen years of age and older and therefore do not include teenagers of high-school age in their samples. However, a handful of studies probing personality traits—including ones from the United States, Britain, and Canada—do include respondents from this age range, and they offer significant insight into the personality profile of the typical teenager.

Conscientiousness

The Big Five trait that probably offers the most predictable example of adolescent distinctiveness is conscientiousness. The image of the lackadaisical and unruly teenager, caring little for social rules and niceties, was front and center in Stanley Hall's classic study of adolescence and has become a staple of contemporary popular culture in characters of the Beavis and Butthead variety. This long-standing stereotype is at least partly confirmed when we look at differences between adolescents and adults in a more systematic fashion.

For example, the British Household Panel Study used three questions to assess conscientiousness, asking more than fourteen thousand respondents whether they were someone who "does a thorough job," someone who "does things efficiently," and whether they "tend to be lazy" (with those saying they are *not* lazy obviously receiving higher conscientiousness scores). The results reveal clear differences between adolescents and adults on each of these measures. Nearly two-thirds of respondents (64 percent) in the thirty-to-sixty age range say they are someone who does a "thorough job" (rating themselves 6 or more on a 7-point scale). Only 42 percent of respondents age fifteen to seventeen say likewise.[5] Similarly, 53 percent of the older group say that they do "things efficiently," compared to 36 percent of teens. And when it comes to being lazy, results for the two groups are reversed: only 29 percent of those thirty to sixty admit to being somewhat lazy (placing themselves on the upper half of the scale), compared to 61 percent of the adolescent respondents.[6]

Personality researchers normally summarize their results using standardized scores, specifically T-scores. For any given personality trait, the average T-score for everyone combined is set to 50. A difference of 2 points for any given age group—an average T-score of 52 or 48—represents a small departure from the norm. A 5-point gap is considered a medium difference, while 8 points is deemed to be large (while individuals may deviate more, it is rare to see any group average below 40 or above 60). In this case, British adolescents have a T-score of 44.9 on the conscientiousness scale, 5.1 points below the average T-score of 50 and 6.7 points below adults in the thirty-to-sixty age range—differences in the moderate to large range.[7]

Another study—this a web-based project based in the United States, where researchers have invited more than one million visitors of all ages to fill in a Big Five questionnaire—reinforces these findings. It uses the same questions as the British study, but adds others that pick up on other aspects of conscientiousness, asking whether respondents "tend to be disorganized," are "somewhat careless," are "easily distracted," and whether they "persevere until the task is finished." With this fuller set of questions, adolescent respondents stand out even more. Their average T-score falls a shade under 43, which puts them a full 10 points below older adults; in the world of T-scores, this is a very sharp contrast indeed.[8] Figure 1.1, reproduced from this study, traces conscientiousness scores across the full age spectrum from 10 to 65 and reveals the dramatic dip that occurs during the adolescent period. The early teenage years, roughly ages thirteen to seventeen, look to be about the worst, just when teenagers are in the high school setting, mixing and mingling primarily with same-age peers.

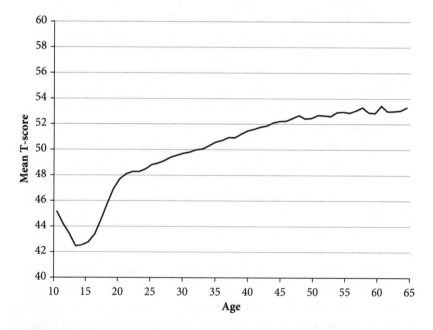

FIGURE 1.1 How conscientious are teens?

Source: Soto et al., "Age Differences in Personality Traits from 10 to 65," 337 (data for males and females averaged and combined). N = 1,267,218.

From these initial results, we start to gain a sense of the potentially decisive impact of the adolescent experience on the character-building process in modern times. First of all, adolescents aren't just somewhat different from adults; in certain respects, they are vastly different. It is worth repeating that this (and other adolescent-adult gaps) may not reflect intrinsic differences alone. Whatever the "natural" divide between adolescents and adults, it has likely been amplified by the intensive peer interaction in segregated social settings that is a defining feature of modern adolescence. Be that as it may, this second important observation remains: with differences like these between teens and adults, the company of adolescent peers represents a social setting profoundly different from one populated by people of diverse ages. Teenagers who spend the bulk of their days surrounded by fellow teens inhabit a social environment where conscientiousness is in relatively short supply, a developmental experience that is likely to have some impact on their own developing character and thereby have potential influence on their adult mind-set down the road.

A whimsical example of this particular teenage trait finding expression in the contemporary adult world lies in the founding of a new religion in 2005: Dudeism. Formally known as the Church of the Latter-Day Dude, this spiritual movement takes its inspiration from the 1998 film *The Big Lebowski* and its central character Jeff "the Dude" Lebowski—an unemployed, middle-aged, genial slacker played by Jeff Bridges, who, the film quickly reveals, is decidedly deficient in all the qualities that make up the conscientiousness scale. In the opening scene of the movie, for example, we see the Dude shuffling around his local supermarket in a gray bathrobe and slippers, paying for his sixty-nine-cent purchase with a postdated check. Reportedly nearly five hundred thousand people inspired by his example have now been ordained as Dudeist priests (via the internet) and take spiritual guidance from Dudeist scripture outlined in the *Abide Guide: Living Like Lebowski*.[9] Whether these believers follow Dudeism faithfully is not clear, and doing so would, in any event, go against the grain of the movement. But the cultlike following that the film and the character have inspired since the movie's release more than two decades ago suggests a certain contemporary affinity for a mind-set and a manner of living—rejecting rules, structure, and social niceties— that traditionally would have been linked primarily to the teenage stage of life.

Extroversion

Distinctive adolescent qualities, with similar implications for processes of character formation and developments in the adult realm, are also evident for another of the Big Five personality traits: extroversion. But here we have to dig a bit deeper to uncover the most interesting patterns. Extroversion is a broad personality trait encompassing many finer distinctions, and it is only on some of these that adolescents truly stand out.

To most people, the term "extrovert" suggests first and foremost someone with a sociable, friendly, and outgoing personality. On the 2005 British Household Panel Study, the three questions used to measure extroversion all speak to this sociability dimension, or what is sometimes referred to by personality researchers as gregariousness. Respondents were asked if they were someone who is "talkative," if they were "outgoing and sociable," and whether they were "reserved" (with lower scores on this question obviously meaning higher levels of extroversion). The T-score result for adolescents is 3.7 points above the average score of 50—a more moderate difference from what we saw for the conscientiousness results above. Adolescents do sit above the norm on the outgoing and sociable qualities linked to extroversion, but this is not as strong and salient a feature of the adolescent character.

The American web-based study covers similar ground in its array of questions in the extroversion category, but adds some that probe traits relating to energy and activity (whether individuals are "full of energy" and whether they "generate a lot of enthusiasm"), and others that tap into assertiveness (whether they have an "assertive personality"). This expanded focus makes little difference: the adolescent gap on this study is even more muted than on the British one. Adolescents rank slightly higher on the activity measures, but there is little difference on the assertiveness component of extroversion.

In some respects, then, adolescents are simply not exceptionally extroverted. But there are other components of this broad personality trait that are more revealing. One important aspect of extroversion that is not picked up by the questionnaires on either the British or American studies is excitement seeking. Again, there is no mystery here with research jargon—the phrase simply refers to the tendency to seek out activities and experiences that are exciting and stimulating, everything from gambling to lively music to skydiving. This is the dimension of extroversion that has been most closely linked to conscientiousness in prior studies, where those who are the least conscientious are the most apt to be excitement seekers.[10] Knowing what we do about conscientiousness levels among adolescents, we would probably expect to see some more fizz in our results when we focus on this dimension of extroversion.

A series of earlier Canadian surveys posed relevant questions that effectively probed this important dimension of extroversion. They asked respondents whether they agree with these statements: "From time to time, I like to do things which are dangerous or forbidden, just for the sake of the risk and sensation," and "I get pleasure of letting myself go along with an impulse or passing emotions." As the first of these questions suggests, the willingness to accept risk is a behavioral implication flowing from a penchant for thrills and excitement. Further questions from these surveys speak directly to risk attraction and aversion: "In order to get what pleases me, I would be prepared to take great risks in life"; and "I am willing to try things I have never done before, even if it may not lead to a successful outcome." Based on these measures, teenage respondents are far more extroverted than the norm. The excitement-seeking and risk-taking T-scores for adolescents (ages fifteen to seventeen) lie in the 56 to 57 range, about 8 points higher than scores for adults in the thirty-to-sixty age range.[11]

Daniel Nettle is a British professor of psychology who has written a compact but compelling book on the Big Five personality traits, *Personality: What Makes You the Way You Are*. His work deepens our understanding of the underlying motivations that shape the extroverted personality and is helpful in trying to make sense of some of these results. Rather than averaging personality scores across large numbers of research subjects, Nettle uses case studies of individuals to try to get at the essential core of each of the Big Five traits. Through his analysis of the passions, pleasures, and vices of various individuals who fit the extroverted label, Nettle concludes that it is a person's responsiveness to "positive emotion" that fuels the extroverted personality. This positive emotion can derive from interactions with other people—hence the outgoing and sociable nature of the extrovert—but it can also come from exciting activities, risk taking, and other sources of external stimulation. The defining feature of extroversion is not special regard for that which is pursued, but rather the exhilaration derived from its pursuit and attainment. As Nettle puts it, what extroverts really crave is "the *buzz* of company, excitement, achievement, adulation, and romance."[12]

Seen in this light, the sociable nature of extroverts—their desire to meet and mingle with others—is not so much a reflection of a desire for amiable social relations as it is a drive for personal stimulation. It is telling, Nettle points out, that those high in extroversion generally do a good job of meeting new people but do not necessarily have stronger or deeper friendships.[13] Extroverts are drawn by the excitement of new connections but show no special capacity to develop warm, lasting relationships.

This distinction helps us make sense of further results from other questions on the Canadian surveys. These ask people whether they agree with the statements "I like being in a large crowd" and "I like sharing major events (public and social events, gatherings, etc.) with the largest number of people possible." The emphasis here is clearly not on any kind of special intimacy with others, but rather the buzz and excitement that come from interacting with people on a large scale. And it is on these kinds of "sociability" measures that adolescents stand out sharply, with a T-score of 57, nearly 9 points greater than the score for older adults.[14]

A similar pattern appears when people are asked on the Canadian surveys about pleasure as a general principle. These include questions that are abstract and general: whether respondents agree that "in the future, I would like to enjoy all the pleasures in life," and how important they feel it is "to take advantage, without restraint, of the good things in life." They also include questions that focus on material pleasures and gratification: one asking whether they agree that "to spend, to buy myself something new, is for me one of the greatest pleasures in life," another how important it is to them "to make more money and be better off than most people around me." Again, these are areas where adolescents register well above the adult norm, with average T-scores in the mid-50s, 5 to 7 points higher than the scores for older adults.[15]

What we see then is that some of the positive features of extroversion—the outgoing and sociable qualities—can mask a more self-oriented trait that is really all about living life to the fullest in the pursuit of positive emotion or the "buzz" that Nettle identifies. The extroverted and gregarious individual is not necessarily someone who places special value on other people. That individual may simply be someone who relishes being in the social spotlight. As one of Nettle's extrovert cases reports of his own experiences: "I love standing in front of people and talking, telling them how beautiful life can be. . . . My greatest success was a speech I gave for 250 people at a business congress and to hear them applauding afterwards. It still rings in my ears."[16]

From examples like this, it is apparent why high levels of extroversion have often been linked to narcissism,[17] the self-focused, attention-craving syndrome that some fear has become an epidemic in modern society.[18] Examples of narcissism-run-amok in today's world are not difficult to find. The popularity and influence of the Kardashian clan come to mind, their narcissism exemplified by Kim's book of selfies published under the title *Selfish* and its unabashed follow-up, *Selfish: More Me!* Just how far the problem extends in modern society is a subject for later chapters; but certainly we can see how narcissism would find a nourishing seedbed in the extroverted character of adolescents.

In the end, then, extroversion is a fairly complex personality trait. It does involve elements of sociability but is more fundamentally a reflection of the drive for positive emotion, which is essentially a self-focused orientation geared toward personal stimulation, gratification, and attention. And it is in this area of extroversion that adolescents score especially high—as high on their extroversion scores as they are low on the conscientiousness scale.

Agreeableness

The Big Five personality trait more clearly and closely tied to pro-social attitudes and amiable human relations is agreeableness. People who score high on this trait are, Daniel Nettle tells us in his concise overview of the Big Five traits, cooperative and trusting, tendencies linked to a generally pro-social nature.[19] It is clearly an important trait in the human population, essential to harmonious relations on a personal level and a larger societal scale. How do adolescents fare on this important quality?

Agreeableness is typically measured by a variety of questions gauging the warmth and cordiality of our relations with others. Nettle argues that a key underlying driver is our concern for others—how "other-regarding" we are—which in turn rests on our ability to empathize. Some of the questions from the Canadian surveys tap into this empathetic capacity, asking whether someone agrees that "I like to put myself in another person's shoes and to imagine how I would have felt in her/his place," and whether or not someone feels close to "people who are almost unaffected by the reactions of others" (empathizers obviously being those who do not relate to such cold fish). On these two questions, adolescents are just about average, scoring neither higher nor lower than adult age groups in their empathetic capacities.

A different aspect of agreeableness is more revealing of the distinctive shading of the adolescent character. It taps into what personality researchers call "compliance"—the component of agreeableness that captures whether people tend to express and act upon feelings of anger, frustration, or contempt, rather than suppressing them for the sake of social harmony. Several questions from the Canadian surveys ask about aggressive behavior in different contexts: "The best way to get something from someone is by putting your foot down"; "It's acceptable to use physical force to get something you really want. The important thing is to get what you want"; and "When a person can't stand it anymore and feels like he/she is about to explode, to be a little violent can relieve the tension."

Most people on the surveys reject these strong statements, especially the last two, which allude to the use of physical force and violence. Only about 10 percent agree with them. But among adolescents, the rate of agreement is three times that level, at roughly 30 percent. The overall difference is captured by T-scores, which reveal a sharp nosedive in compliance levels among teenage respondents: the average T-score is 43.5 for adolescents, about 9 points below that of adults ages thirty to sixty.[20] In short, teenagers may be just as empathetic as adults, but they are more likely to react with anger when provoked or agitated—and, as many parents can attest, it often doesn't take much to provoke or agitate their "teenage time bomb."[21] Anger management is not generally their strong suit.

None of this should come as a great shock. Given what we have seen about the impulsiveness that is characteristic of adolescents—an impulsiveness that manifests itself in their excitement-seeking and risk-taking behavior and in their relatively low levels of conscientiousness—it is no great surprise to learn that they are more likely to lash out in anger on occasion. There are clear connections here across the Big Five dimensions of personality.[22]

The fact that it is more behavior than disposition that makes adolescents less agreeable than adults is somewhat reassuring. It suggests that deep down adolescents are just as pro-social and empathetic as the rest of us; they just don't always manage to show it or apply it in certain situations. At the same time, actions are important, and we might ask what effect these teenage behavioral tendencies are likely to have in the context of intensive adolescent interaction. If many around us are quick to fly off the handle in tense situations, what impact might this have on our ideas about our fellow humans and the prospects for trusting and cordial relationships? We might remain agreeable in theory but in practice start to approach others with some reserve and caution, perhaps even suspicion, which is hardly conducive to warm personal relations. In thinking about the adolescent character and its larger effects, we have to consider not only the direct impact of particular personality traits, but also how those traits influence social dynamics as young people interact with one another—and how this social atmosphere in turn shapes norms and expectations that might be carried forward to adulthood.

Openness

To this point, we have encountered a number of personality traits that cast adolescents in a fairly negative light. They are, on average, less conscientious than adults, showing diminished regard for rules, order, and self-discipline; they are extroverted in ways that suggest a self-focused emphasis on personal stimulation and gratification; and they are, relatively speaking, quick to anger.

The last of the Big Five traits that clearly distinguishes adolescents from adults carries more positive overtones, though it may well spring from a common source. The same lack of inhibition that weakens respect for social norms, promotes the pursuit of positive emotion, and results in the freer expression of agitation and anger also favors a Big Five trait normally seen as more salutary: openness.

At the core of openness is the idea of possessing an open mind and spirit. Open to what? Well, openness implies taking a broad perspective on that question. So the list of areas that are considered part of this personality trait is fairly extensive, covering most basic aspects of human experience. Among the questions sometimes used to probe openness are ones that ask respondents whether they are receptive to that which is new and novel in the realms of ideas, actions, feelings, values, and aesthetics.

Because of the challenges in measuring openness across such a wide spectrum, previous studies have not always done a good job of uncovering the nuances of the adolescent character. The problem lies in the specific areas probed on personality questionnaires. The British Household Panel Study, for example, asks respondents just three questions that concentrate on openness in the areas of aesthetics and ideas: whether they "value artistic, aesthetic experiences," are "original and come up with ideas," and if they have an "active imagination." Adolescents do score slightly higher on these measures than older adults, but they certainly don't stand out from the crowd in the same way they do on other personality attributes. The average T-score for those fifteen to seventeen years old is 51.6, just above the overall average of 50; for those in their twenties it is slightly higher than for teens. There is then a small drop-off among older adults, but no dramatic differences overall.

There is likewise nothing remarkable about levels of openness among teens on the US web-based study of personality traits. The general focus of the questions is the same as in the British study. In addition to the same three questions used on that study, the American one adds a few further items, asking, for example, whether respondents consider themselves "sophisticated in art, music or literature." The general thrust is the same, however, concentrating on openness in the areas of ideas and aesthetics, and the results are unchanged. In fact, the American study actually finds slightly lower levels of openness among teenage respondents than older adults (with a T-score sitting around 48).

A possible conclusion—one that others have drawn—is that adolescents are simply not much different from the rest of us when it comes to the trait of openness. But Daniel Nettle's insightful analysis of the defining qualities of core personality traits raises important questions about how we go about measuring this particular quality. He starts by pointing out an interesting quirk: across many studies, education levels are found to be strongly linked to openness. For the British Household Panel Study results just cited, for example, there is a T-score difference of almost 10 points between those with the lowest and highest levels of education—people with university degrees are much more open than early school-leavers.

What is odd about this is that openness is the only one of the Big Five traits to show this kind of relationship to education. As I learned from my earliest social science training (courtesy of *Sesame Street*), when one of these things is not like the others it usually signals that it belongs in another category altogether. Nettle certainly interprets it this way. He suggests that some of the preferences and tendencies normally slotted under openness—in particular ones that focus on ideas and aesthetics—are not actually measures of personality. Instead they reflect intellect, which is a combination of both cognitive capacity and a taste for certain kinds of intellectual activity.[23] Like personality, intellect may be partly innate. But it also can be cultivated through educational experiences in a way that basic features of personality and temperament are not. A question asking whether someone is "sophisticated in art, music and literature"—I can readily imagine Frasier Crane, the pompous psychologist from the '80s sitcom *Cheers*, vigorously agreeing—has an undeniably erudite ring to it and appears a better fit with the intellect category than the personality trait of openness.

The link between education and intellect probably helps explain why adolescents sometimes have appeared unexceptional on measures of openness on prior studies. Virtually all adolescents have not yet had the opportunity to attend postsecondary education, where intellectual pursuits are encouraged and cultivated, and so they are not assessed as being overly open when asked about intellectual interests and inclinations. However, they certainly can be enthusiastic about that which is new and different—but less so in the manner of Frasier Crane, and more along the lines of Ferris Bueller on his famous "day off," when he ventures to the city in a borrowed sports car for fun with friends, new experiences, and unpredictable adventure.

Unlike the American and British studies, the Canadian surveys contain openness questions à la Ferris Bueller that have little intellectual baggage and seem more like clear-cut expressions of personality—and here the distinctiveness of adolescents pops out as before. The general categories (ones widely recognized by personality researchers as key components of openness) and the specific questions are as follows:

- *Experiences (sometimes called actions)*: How important is it to "try new products, new places for vacation, new foods, just for the pleasure of novelty?" How often do you "have the desire to meet people who are very different from you, who will stimulate you and make you change?"
- *Feelings*: "I should like to experience new emotions every day"; "I like to let my moods vary with my surroundings."
- *Fantasy*: "I am especially interested in those aspects of reality which remain mysterious and unexplained"; "I am interested in everything that science cannot explain."

The T-scores for adolescents in these three areas range from 54 to 55, while the gap compared to adults ages thirty to sixty runs between 5 and 6 points—close to the differences seen for other Big Five traits where teenagers stand decisively apart from adults.[24] The other relevant finding that emerges from the Canadian surveys is that across these three areas of openness, the connection to education is either relatively weak (experiences) or nonexistent (feelings and fantasy). People who spend more years in school and university are no more drawn toward emotion, feelings, and fantasy than others, presumably because these qualities are not cultivated in the culture of higher learning in the way that intellectual openness toward ideas and aesthetics is. When the latter factor is taken out of the equation, the openness of adolescents becomes more evident.

The conclusion suggested by these findings is that openness is, in fact, a distinguishing trait of adolescents. It joins several other Big Five traits as a notable feature of the adolescent character and is consistent with the more general image that has emerged from this review of adolescent personality traits. The broad conclusion, simply put, is that the key dividing line separating adolescents from adults is their disinhibited and free-spirited nature. While this comes with certain challenges, such as unruly and tempestuous behavior, it also means that teenagers are more open and adventurous than the norm, which has more favorable implications. And so the overall assessment of the adolescent personality mix is that there are both negative and positive features to be found therein, something we will keep in mind in later parts of the book when analyzing the impact of rising adolescent qualities on adult society. Before pushing on, however, it's worth looking at how teens differ from adults from a couple of additional angles—ones that give us a more complete understanding of the adolescent character and offer further clues to its widespread manifestations in today's adult world.

The Teenage Brain

While work done in the field of personality psychology helps us better delineate what is different and distinct about adolescents, researchers in other fields have also been actively pursuing this question and generated compelling findings of their own. These further perspectives can help expand our understanding of the contours of the adolescent character and its underlying drivers.

The most prominent of these additional perspectives comes from the realm of hard science, specifically neuroscience. Since the early 1990s, ongoing advances in neural imaging technology have allowed researchers to track brain activity and function in live subjects with increasing precision. What they have discovered are important differences in the basic structure of the brains of adolescents and adults. We used to believe that neural development was largely complete before puberty, but we now recognize that the teenage brain is still very much a work in progress. Not only are teenagers as a group possessed of a distinctive bundle of personality traits; they are also, quite literally, wired differently.

The response to these scientific findings has been a flurry of books and articles highlighting the connections between the neurological condition of adolescents and their general character and behavior. "Teens' Brains Key to Their Impulsiveness," one story announces.[25] Another carries the headline, "The Teenage Brain: Why Adolescents Sleep In, Take Risks and Won't Listen to Reason."[26] A popular book on the subject bears the ominous title *The Primal Teen*, its first chapter proclaiming that teenagers are "Crazy by Design," while another bills itself as a "A Neuroscientist's Survival Guide to Raising Adolescents and Young Adults."[27]

Some of the language is a bit over the top, but these works do roughly reflect the essential findings from the recent wave of teen brain research. The parts of the brain that produce strong emotions and drives are well developed by this stage of life, while the frontal cortex, which facilitates coordination of thought and contemplation of consequences—tasks usually referred to as executive function—is still relatively underdeveloped. As one of the leading authorities on the subject, Laurence Steinberg, puts it, teenagers have acquired a well-developed accelerator but only a partly developed brake to stop them from acting on the many powerful feelings and impulses their developing minds and bodies are producing.[28]

These findings from the field of neuroscience are generally consistent with much of what we have already seen about the personality leanings of adolescents. Lack of inhibition is a common theme running through the various traits adolescents display: a weak sense of conscientiousness, the headstrong pursuit of positive emotion, their sometimes intemperate behavior, their craving for new feelings and experiences. In his book *Age of Opportunity*, Steinberg lists a similar array of behavioral tendencies stemming from the teenage brain, noting that adolescents are "more easily excited, emotionally aroused, and prone to getting angry or upset."[29] They are also, he adds, very sensitive to rewards, especially immediate rewards, and more inclined to take risks to achieve them. The overarching issue, Steinberg suggests, is impulse control and the lack thereof, which leads adolescents to exercise poor judgment and to engage in various forms of risky and intemperate behavior. The idea that there is a neurological basis to these features of adolescent character and behavior reinforces my prior observations and offers an interesting extension of the argument.

Yet there is also an apparent challenge presented by teen brain research. It seems to suggest, at first blush anyway, that teenagers eventually outgrow their adolescent ways as a simple matter of course. As teenagers mature into adults, their teenage brains become adult brains, developing the fully operational braking mechanisms associated with development of the frontal lobe and enhanced executive function. So their stormy ways and disinhibited personality traits are presumably left behind. The notion of adolescent qualities being carried forward to adulthood, the central idea in this book, makes little sense if brain development is the ultimate driver of adolescent (and adult) character and behavior.

The recent work of Steinberg and other leading neuroscientists—while not necessarily designed with this purpose in mind—effectively dispels such notions. The core idea is that the development of the teenage brain into the adult brain does not follow a set trajectory but is instead a more open-ended proposition. A critical feature of the adolescent brain, Steinberg emphasizes, is its neuroplasticity—that is, its susceptibility to modification as a result of experience. Neuroplasticity is a pervasive phenomenon, explaining why, for example, London taxi drivers who spend their days shuttling passengers around that notoriously Byzantine city have more highly developed networks of neurons in the brain region responsible for geographic memory (as was found in a 2005 study); or why the brains of musicians differ substantially from the norm in the auditory, motor, and visual-spatial areas of the cerebral cortex (as has been seen in many studies).[30] As Steinberg describes the phenomenon, "the very connections between neurons that allow us to do something—think a particular thought, feel a particular feeling, perform a particular act, remember a map of city streets—are strengthened each time we do it."[31] Neuroscientists have a catchy phrase to describe this dynamic process: "neurons that fire together wire together." While neuroplasticity can be observed in people of all ages, the brains of teenagers are particularly plastic and therefore highly susceptible to modification as a result of experience.

Experimental lab work carried out by Steinberg and colleagues demonstrates that *peer interaction* is one important feature of adolescent experience that can substantially influence the wiring of the teenage brain. In a 2011 study, they found that the presence of peers not only caused teenage subjects to engage in more risky behavior when playing a driving-based video game, running yellow lights to get to their virtual destination more quickly; they also discovered (using fMRI) that peer presence stimulated greater activity in those areas of the brain connected to reward mechanisms. So sensitive were teens to this influence that peers did not even have to be in the same room for these effects to be observed; it was enough that those engaged in the driving exercise were aware that adolescent peers were in an adjacent room watching them perform. Since neurons that fire together wire together, the researchers drew the further conclusion that their teenage research subjects would "subsequently [be] sensitized to respond to the potential rewards of risky choices"—in other words, that there would be a lingering effect from peer-induced neural stimulation.[32] If we can imagine similar effects occurring outside the lab setting across countless peer interactions, we start to see how immersion in the adolescent social setting for a period of several years could have a considerable influence on the brain of the developing teen.

As Steinberg summarizes matters in *Age of Opportunity*, "The developing brain is sculpted by both passive exposure and by active experience. That means that before our brain has fully matured, we can be affected, in potentially permanent ways, by every experience, whether it's positive or negative, whether we understand it or not—in fact, whether or not we're even aware of it."[33]

These and related findings lead Steinberg toward his principal conclusion: we must pay close attention to ensure teens have appropriate exposure to experiences and social settings that encourage the fullest possible development of executive function. He notes that "adolescence is a key time to develop self-regulation"[34] and that the development of "higher level cognitive functions, like making complicated decisions . . . can be *forever* shaped by our adolescent experiences."[35] While prefrontal development and enhancement of executive function during adolescence is to some degree "preprogrammed" and therefore common to all, it is also "dependent on experience," which explains why some teens "improve more than others."[36] At the neurological level, there is no single fixed path of maturation from adolescence into adulthood that we all automatically follow.

Other neuroscientists have proposed similar ideas, drawing connections between youth experiences and adult outcomes at the level of brain circuitry. Tomas Paus, a leading neuroscientist at the University of Toronto, put it this way when interviewed for the documentary film *Generation Boomerang*: "If you put a young teenager into an adult role, it's very likely that it's going to change his or her brain. That brain is going to start shaping up in the adult way much faster than the brain of today's teenager who is not put into those adult roles."[37] The same idea is further developed in an article Paus cowrote with Howard Sercombe, a social scientist at the University of Strathclyde in Scotland. "There is," Paus and Sercombe tell us, "a serious road-building programme going on" in our neural circuitry in the teenage years. As a result of our actions and experiences, key decisions are being made about "which circuits will be confirmed and which ones bypassed according to the imperatives of [our] environment." It is, they suggest, "an active process in which young people are consciously or unconsciously selecting preferred pathways for action and response, confirming favoured templates for life from the smorgasbord of ways of being generated through the process of childhood." Most critically, they suggest that the effects are long-lasting: "the environment in which young people live while those decisions are being made is critical in determining the mind-set of the adult."[38] Neural pathways etched in adolescence run deep and have the potential to remain active and influential in adulthood.

These are intriguing ideas and findings that provide a very different perspective on what it is that makes teens tick. The principal takeaway for present purposes is to acknowledge the neurological underpinnings of teen personality and behavior, but also to underline that this does not lead to the conclusion that teen-agers simply shed their adolescent ways like a pair of old coveralls as they gradu-ate to adulthood and become possessed of "adult" brains. If social scientists have long believed that experiences in youth can shape the kind of adults we become, neuroscientists seem to be edging toward the same conclusion—all which sug-gests a more open-ended process of individual development (and social evolu-tion) than was implied by earlier models.

Back to the Social Sciences: Adolescent Values

From this point on, I'll leave the neuroscience aside and stick to the more com-fortable terrain (for this researcher certainly) of the social science account of adolescent society. Part of that account draws on the findings above from the field of personality psychology, focusing on core personality traits that are prominent among adolescents. When teens interact heavily in the social environment of adolescence, these traits are apt to flourish and take deep root. Given the impor-tance of the teenage years as a period of socialization on the cusp of adulthood, this experience has the potential to leave a substantial residue of adolescent per-sonality traits that remain active and influential in the adult years.

To the Big Five personality traits I would now add another dimension of ado-lescent distinctiveness that has also taken hold in the seedbed of adolescence and subsequently come to flourish in society at large. This second component, more closely linked to the work of social scientists in fields such as sociology and politi-cal science, is the distinctive *values* to which adolescents adhere.

It's really not much of a stretch to add values to the mix, since personality traits and values are so tightly interwoven. It only stands to reason that our tem-perament and personality would affect the priorities and principles we feel are important for ourselves and for society. The title of this first chapter—the *char-acter* of adolescents—is deliberately chosen in order to convey an expansive sense of the array of personal qualities that sets teenagers apart from adults.

The intimate connection between personality traits and values can be seen in the survey questionnaires sometimes used by personality researchers. One long version of the Big Five questionnaire uses forty-eight different items to measure each of the Big Five traits—240 questions in all. On it, we find statements such as the following used to gauge people's level of openness to experience: "I believe that laws and social policies should change to reflect the needs of a changing world"; "I believe that the different ideas of right and wrong that people in other societies have may be valid for them." On the same questionnaire, we find the statement "I don't take civic duties like voting very seriously" used as a barometer of conscientiousness; and we see "Political leaders need to be more aware of the human side of their policies" serving as a measure of agreeableness.[39] Most people encountering such statements without any prompting would likely assume they were designed to assess people's values, not aspects of their personality. The fact that researchers feel they are valid measures of Big Five traits only underscores the intimate link between personality traits and the core values to which people adhere.

Looking at some of these examples, and thinking back on the various personality patterns that distinguish teenagers from adults, there is a general label that seems to capture the overarching value orientation of adolescents: individualism. Individualism implies a focus on the self and a preference for self-directed action that manifests itself in a wide variety of values and attitudes, most of which can be linked back to one or another of the Big Five traits.

One way in which adolescents display individualistic values is in their skepticism toward abiding social norms and concepts of obligation and duty, a reflection of their generally low levels of conscientiousness. Another individualistic value of teens is the premium placed on the pursuit of personal pleasure, a hedonistic tendency that can include a strong penchant for materialist values. This, we have seen, can be readily connected to the extroverted nature of adolescents and a powerful craving for the "buzz" that comes from enjoying life to the fullest. Teenagers also display a focus on the self, and disregard for others, when they lash out in frustration or anger from time to time; their tempestuous nature is linked to values and behaviors that involve putting the self before those around them. Finally, on a more positive note, the elevated levels of openness that adolescents exhibit imply adherence to values that involve respecting individual difference and an appreciation for human diversity. If adolescents seek to guard their own individuality and personal freedom to do as they please, they also are inclined to extend that same respect to others.

In short, there are two distinct, yet intertwined, dimensions that contribute to the distinctive character of adolescents: the prominence of key personality traits that reflect their relatively disinhibited and free-spirited temperament; and the salience of various individualistic values that naturally flow from these traits. These foundational qualities find clear expression both in individual teenagers and in the culture of the adolescent society they form together.

Individualism and Social Sensitivity

Before moving on, there is one final issue to address, a wrinkle in the argument that needs to be ironed out. The general idea is that modern society has become more "adolescent" because of important changes in individual character brought about by immersion in a society of peers during the teenage years. Surrounded by fellow teens, we are influenced to the point that it has a substantial impact on the adults we eventually become. But if the hallmark of adolescent character and culture is an emphasis on *individualism*, shouldn't adolescents be largely immune to these sorts of *social* influences on development of the self?

To make sense of this entails drawing a clear distinction between two types of outside influences: those resisted because they are perceived as external impositions and those we feel drawn to because of their attractiveness to us as free-thinking and free-acting individuals. The first type includes what we might call the "givens" of life—the roles and responsibilities that are handed to us and often presented as obligations we are expected to follow without question. These can include expectations of the family we are born into or tenets of the religion pressed upon us from the earliest age. Those who are highly individualistic in their thinking will treat these ties and obligations with caution, if not outright suspicion, because they prefer to make their own choices about how to live their lives—to decide for themselves the attachments and commitments they will embrace, the rules and regulations they will follow.

At the same time, in searching for ways of being aligned with their own inner compass, these individualists do not make their choices in a social vacuum. They don't conjure up all the alternatives for themselves. Instead, they look around at how others live their lives and choose what seem the most appealing options—which, often enough, means following what others are doing. As the sociologist Eric Hoffer once remarked, "When people are free to do as they please, they usually imitate one another."[40] Interestingly, this conformist behavior doesn't seem to compromise people's sense of individual autonomy. As long as they feel a particular choice was a freely chosen alternative—be it a change of career, a new car, or a different hair color—their sense of individuality is not compromised.

All of this helps make sense of the individualistic culture that has flourished in the realm of adolescence and, by and by, in society at large. Teenagers, in the name of personal autonomy, are inclined to reject certain norms, specifically those that are seen as heavy-handed ones bearing down from above, so they will resist what parents, teachers, or society tells them they *must* do. Yet they exhibit a great deal of conformity, almost a herd mentality, as they clamor to imitate one another—wearing the same clothing, adopting similar expressions, immersing themselves in a shared youth culture.

Important psychological mechanisms linking individualism and social sensitivity in teens were identified in an influential 1967 article by David Elkind on the topic of adolescent egocentrism.[41] Part of that egocentrism, Elkind argued, is the teenager's belief that they are at the center of others' attention, that they are the focal point of an "imaginary audience" scrutinizing their every move. This renders teenagers highly self-conscious and anxious to fit in by shaping their behavior in accordance with the norms and expectations of this imaginary audience; they are highly responsive to social cues, especially those coming from peers watching closely from the front row. At the same time, many teens are buoyed in their sense of individuality by a second feature of adolescent egocentrism identified by Elkind, the "personal fable." This refers to the feeling, common among teens, that their own life story, defined primarily by their inner thoughts and emotions, is unique, even if the external trappings of their lives—the clothes they wear, the music they listen to, and so on—are virtually identical to those around them. The richness and complexity of their inner life balance the conforming tendencies in their external selves. Through the psychological mechanisms of the imaginary audience and the personal fable, adolescents manage to be at once highly individualistic and intensely social.

In short, social influence remains important despite the individualistic values that have come to flourish in the age of adolescence. As a general principle, we are deeply influenced by those around us, taking cues and guidance from others even as we seek to solidify our personal identity and forge our own life path. For teenagers, this means the social circles that define their day-to-day existence, the peers with whom they are so closely connected on a daily basis. It's time now to take a closer look at this social environment that James Coleman called the adolescent society: how it came into being and how it has come to leave a deep and lasting imprint on those who have experienced its powerful conditioning effects over the past century.

2

THE CRUCIBLE OF ADOLESCENCE

Social influence is a formidable force operating across many arenas of human experience. While we like to believe that we think for ourselves, the reality is that much of the time, in both our immediate thoughts and enduring dispositions and values, we are deeply influenced by those around us.

A vivid example of these processes at work is provided by Arthur Miller's play *The Crucible*, which dramatizes events taking place in and around Salem, Massachusetts, in 1692. The play begins with accusations of witchcraft being leveled at a black slave discovered dancing in the forest with a handful of young girls, one of whom falls mysteriously ill. Rumor and innuendo start to circulate around the town, and the accusations quickly accumulate. "Witches" point the finger at other "witches" to deflect attention from themselves. Others jump on the bandwagon and denounce their enemies in the village as agents of the devil. Those who come forward to defend the innocent against these groundless charges themselves come under scrutiny and suffer terrible consequences.

Talk about storm and stress, especially for those on the receiving end of the accusations! While the lesson from these events—and from the persecution of communists under Senator Joseph McCarthy in the 1950s that inspired Miller's allegorical play—is to be vigilant against groupthink and the suspension of rational thought, they also highlight just how powerful mutual influence can be in tight social quarters. Someone outside the situation can recognize certain thoughts and actions as excessive and unwarranted, but for those wrapped up in the events and reinforced in their convictions by those around them, they appear entirely reasonable.

The crucible metaphor is not only used to highlight cases of irrationality and persecution run amok, however. It also captures more edifying processes of mutual influence and movement toward common ground. A synonym for crucible is "melting pot," the phrase long used to describe the forging of a common set of American values among immigrants hailing from far-flung corners of the world. The term was first introduced by playwright Israel Zangwill near the start of the twentieth century, when he described America as "God's Crucible, the great Melting Pot, where all the races of Europe are melting and re-forming."[1] For people of diverse backgrounds arriving in a new land, social fusion of this sort has been seen as an essential prerequisite to the development of a well-functioning society and the shaping of a common national identity.

The forging of a common mind-set through intensive interaction with those around us is a pervasive part of the human experience, with potential effects both good and bad. We don't always appreciate the range of these effects, nor do we fully recognize how adolescence, since the early years of the twentieth century, has become one of the most critical social sites where these forces of convergence are at play.

The Origins of Adolescence

To describe adolescence as a crucible is to think about it not only as a particular phase of life between the ages of thirteen and nineteen, but also a social milieu where intense interaction has powerful effects on people's ways of thinking, acting, and being. Even as teenagers are engaged in a deeply personal process of self-discovery over the adolescent period, they are profoundly influenced and shaped by those around them.

The effects are powerful because they occur in an insular arena, one that operates according to its own internal rhyme and reason. As James Coleman wrote in *The Adolescent Society*, "the child of high-school age . . . is 'cut off' from the rest of society, forced inward toward his own age group, made to carry out his whole social life with others his own age. With his fellows, he comes to constitute a small society, one that has its most important interactions within itself, and maintains only a few threads of connection with the outside adult world."[2]

The creation of these teenage enclaves started long before Coleman identified them as a significant problem in 1961. The key catalyst was extension of the years of public schooling to include the adolescent period. The change came about gradually though the provision of free secondary education for one and all, alongside the legal requirement that everyone had to attend. The first state to introduce mandatory school attendance laws was Massachusetts in 1852; at that point, students ages eight to fourteen were required to be in the classroom at least three months of the year. The idea didn't catch on right away, but gradually other states followed suit. From 1867 through to the early 1900s, all adopted similar regulations.[3] The number of years of mandatory schooling was gradually extended over the same period, so that by 1920 there were thirty-one states with a school-leaving age of sixteen. By the late 1930s, 90 percent of states had adopted this provision.[4]

Enforcement was patchy at the start, but as these provisions took hold in the first decades of the twentieth century, near universal enrollment of adolescents in high school became a reality. Over just a fifty-year period, there was a dramatic sea change that many would say effectively created adolescence as a new stage of life, more sharply marked off from both childhood and adulthood than ever before. In the late 1800s, fewer than 5 percent of Americans ages fourteen to seventeen attended high school. By 1910, the figure was nearly 15 percent, by 1925 over 40 percent, and by 1940 it had reached about 72 percent.[5] By that point, virtually all fourteen- and fifteen-year olds were attending school, as were the majority of slightly older teens. The length of the school year was slowly increased over the same period, so that by 1940 it was more or less of the duration it is today. Adolescents were now spending a large proportion of their waking hours, for many months of the year, in the educational setting surrounded by teenage peers.[6]

This was a dramatic change from a past where, historian Howard Chudacoff observes, "age did not play an important role in the structure and organization of American society."[7] In the nineteenth century, especially in rural areas where working the family farm was the top priority, teenage life was lived primarily within the "strong, intertwined family," with the consequence that "intergenerational association generally prevailed over peer-group socialization."[8] Likewise, community associations and activities, whether religious, fraternal, or social in nature, generally engaged both youth and adults across a broad age spectrum, while most workplaces "provided another setting in which different age groups mingled."[9] There were then a variety of social sites where the sharing of knowledge and imparting of norms from one generation to the next was a steady and implicit part of daily life. "Older persons explained, demonstrated and commanded; younger persons watched, listened, asked and practiced. Most teaching took place within the context of everyday life, not in classes that grouped together unrelated children and professional instructors."[10]

The introduction and spread of mandatory high school attendance disrupted this long-standing arrangement. As several years of high school for young people became the norm over the first decades of the twentieth century, the lives of adolescents, as well as the character of the educational institutions they attended, underwent dramatic changes. Back in the day when only a privileged minority remained in school beyond the elementary level, secondary education had a clear streaming and grooming purpose. Students came mainly from well-to-do families and were being prepared to take their places in the upper echelons of society, in the professions, in business and industry, in government. As high school became a mass experience in the first part of the twentieth century, the grooming of society's elite shifted to the university level, which would continue for a number of decades to be a bastion for a privileged minority. With the high school doors flung open wide, secondary education no longer served to divide teens into the elite and the masses but instead became a uniting experience. The society they formed was a more *complete* society, an adolescent society, as Coleman called it, representing teens from all walks of life.

As this expansion occurred, the sharply defined mission of secondary schooling was blunted. Adolescents now brought a wider range of ambitions and expectations to their secondary schooling experience—or in the case of students who were only there because they had to be, no ambitions or expectations whatsoever. The needs of this diverse student population were gradually accommodated, and high schools came to have a more diffuse focus, no longer dedicated to academic enrichment and social refinement of the upper crust, but providing more general life preparation for a wider clientele. The responsibilities have mounted over time, and it now seems as though schools, in addition to the three Rs, are expected to provide young people with all manner of basic know-how they might not otherwise acquire, everything from sex education to financial literacy through to cooking skills and drivers ed.

As the number of students swelled, the social dimension of high school life also assumed greater significance. The changes occurred early on and were identified in a classic study published in the late 1920s. The book's title, *Middletown*, was the fictional name given to Muncie, Indiana, by the husband-and-wife research team of Robert and Helen Lynd. In 1924–1925, the Lynds spent a year and a half in Middletown engaging in cultural anthropology as they immersed themselves in different aspects of community life to gain a better understanding of American society at a micro-level. The method, more commonly used to study tribal peoples in other parts of the globe, was innovative, the book's findings revealing—particularly those relating to the texture of adolescent life in the 1920s.

Through conversation and observation, the Lynds discovered how greatly the atmosphere in the high schools of Middletown had changed in the space of just thirty years. Since the 1890s, there had been a significant "widening of the school's function," with a proliferation of all sorts of additional activities that had not previously been part of the educational agenda.[11] The priorities of students had shifted in lockstep, so that there was now "relative disregard" for "teachers and for the content of books" and an "exalted position of the social and athletic activities."[12] The latter activities—and the school community more generally—clearly had become the focal point of adolescents' lives in Middletown: "The high school, with its athletics, clubs, sororities and fraternities, dances and parties, and other 'extracurricular activities,' is a fairly complete social cosmos in itself, and about this city within a city the social life of the intermediate generation centers. . . . The school is taking over more and more of the child's waking life. . . . [It] is becoming not a place to which children go from their homes for a few hours daily but a place from which they go home to eat and sleep."[13]

A government-sponsored study from around this same time put a more precise estimate on this trend. Based on a survey of three thousand families, it was found that the average urban teenager was spending four to six nights a week in activities with peers rather than spending quiet nights at home with the family.[14] Later, when James Coleman visited ten American high schools in the late 1950s, he would find much the same pattern. Students were deeply connected to peers and immersed in their schools, with nonacademic pursuits of primary importance, a state of affairs he found most troubling. Even schools more academically inclined were affected by this mind-set, with students seeing academics as secondary to other pursuits and diversions. But it was an inevitable transition, less the result of any overt anti-intellectualism and more a reflection of the changing nature of high schools and their development into relatively self-contained adolescent societies.

This transformation has reached symbolic culmination in the Canadian province of Quebec, where one high school in the Eastern Townships region has formally adopted the label "city-school"—a place that "welcomes students from the surrounding communities, sometimes as far away as 50 km, and integrates them into what looks and functions like a real city."[15] Our institutions of secondary learning have enthusiastically embraced the idea that their job is to provide an all-encompassing experience and sense of community for students.

The intended goal of these efforts is to foster a sense of belonging and cohesion, which in itself is a laudable objective. But it may be at odds with what is normally understood to be the ultimate goal of secondary schooling: to get young people ready for the adult world. As one observer archly notes: "Ironically, schools institutionally isolate youth from adults in order to prepare them for adult roles."[16] The heavy interaction among peers and the lack of youth-adult interaction means that their sense of attachment to one another comes at the expense of their connection to the larger society.

Teachers reading these statements might reasonably chime in at this point, given their prominent role in the high school setting. There they are, the adults at the front of the classroom, doing their level best, day in day out, to help prepare their young charges for the adult world. But the heavy burden placed on them as the sole adults present in the system only underlines the shortfalls of the arrangement. Not only are teachers meant to educate; they are also expected to guide, advise, mentor, and inspire—in short, to act as role models and illuminate the path to adulthood in ways that teenage peers cannot possibly do. Occasionally it works this way, but more so in the movies than in real life. Robin Williams as the exuberant and dedicated teacher in *Dead Poets Society* comes to mind, inspiring his impressionable young charges with his exhortation to "seize the day." Typically, their impact is more limited. One study found that when a group of sixteen- and seventeen-year olds were asked about the significant adults in their lives, only 7 percent of those mentioned were teachers.[17] And when teachers do get a mention, it is mainly from the more enthusiastic learners who are thinking primarily about influence and inspiration in academic matters.[18] Guidance on the life well led normally comes from elsewhere.

High schools were, and remain to this day, the hub of adolescent life, and so the decision to make secondary schooling mandatory was the crucial catalyst in promoting the development of the adolescent society. But other factors have also been at work encouraging more intensive teenage interaction in the last one hundred years. There were, in the first place, various background motivations that led to the decision to establish mandatory secondary education in the first place. One was the increasing demand for workers with the necessary literacy skills to fill the burgeoning white-collar occupations of a modern economy. There was also a growing aversion to child labor, which is certainly something we can appreciate and applaud. Greater levels of economic prosperity made it possible to imagine an economy that didn't require the toil of children to make ends meet.

On top of this, there were rising concerns about teenage gangs and youth hooliganism, especially in the urban slums that were multiplying in the late 1800s in places like Manhattan.[19] This particular problem was fodder for the "storm and stress" perspective that would be popularized by Stanley Hall's classic book on adolescence in 1904 and became an important argument for keeping young people in school longer. The rightful aim, many believed, was not just to educate adolescents but also to ensure their acceptance and observance of the norms of "civilized" society—though this didn't work out precisely as envisaged by stern overseers of the moral order, given the challenges of stringent character development in an environment where teenagers vastly outnumbered adults.

Other changes taking place around the turn of the twentieth century contributed to more intensive social interaction among adolescents and reinforced the core dynamic produced by the high school experience. The steady migration from rural to urban areas meant there were fewer teens who had to stay home in the planting and harvesting seasons or to leave immediately at the end of the school day for the long trek home and thereby miss out on extracurricular activities. The urban environment also provided diverse settings where young people could congregate outside school hours. Coleman wrote in the late 1950s about their numerous "habitats," including "the halls and classrooms of the school, the teen-age canteens, the corner drugstore, the automobile and numerous other gathering places."[20] New venues have emerged over time—the shopping mall, for example—while technology has provided further opportunities for teens to remain in intimate contact at a distance. The home telephone used to be the technology of choice for staying in touch, but now it's mostly briefer updates via texting and social media. The wired teenagers of today are rarely out of touch with their circle of friends and in this way are subject to their constant nudging and influence.

Even without the added dimension of virtual connectedness, adolescents were already spending large portions of their day in one another's company. Back in 1977, two University of Chicago professors interested in probing the lives of teenagers used the Experience Sampling Method to find out how they occupied their time. This involved asking a sample of teens to record what they were doing and with whom whenever they received a signal on an electronic pager—a much more effective way of capturing how people spend their time than asking them to remember details later on. Their findings were revealing. "Teenagers spend much of their time in locations supervised or structured by adults, but they spend relatively less time actually involved in adult-oriented activities. . . . The self-reports indicate that students are seldom in the company of adults."[21] More precisely, one-fifth of their waking hours were spent with family, though only a small portion of this with parents alone. Time with other adults apart from parents accounted for only another 2 percent of their day. One-quarter of their time was spent in solitude. But most significantly, fully half their waking hours were spent with peers, more of it outside the classroom than within. "In terms of sheer amount of time," the researchers wrote, "peers are by far the greatest presence in an adolescent's life. It is with them that a boy or girl spends the most time: talking, joking, experimenting, getting feedback on who he or she is."[22]

Concerns about this situation emerged early on, as it became clear adolescents were more attuned to one another and their adolescent society than to the larger world. This was certainly true when the Lynds visited Middletown in the mid-1920s and found teens enjoying a relatively insular and carefree existence. It remained true in later periods, even as cataclysmic events rocked the adult world, including the deep economic depression of the 1930s and global warfare in the first half of the 1940s. While individual youth were clearly affected in many ways by these devastating events, the adolescent society they formed together was largely untouched. Certainly, in sheer numbers, it held fast: secondary education enrollments climbed substantially during the Depression (from 4.7 million students in 1929 to 6.2 million in 1934)[23] because there were few jobs for anyone, let alone young people thinking about leaving school early to enter the workforce; and they dipped only slightly during the war years, given the formal enlistment age of eighteen. Nor did the world of teenagers lose any of its social cohesiveness. The Lynds revisited Middletown in the mid-1930s and wrote again about the thriving adolescent society they encountered: "One got the impression in 1935 of a more self-conscious subculture of the young in Middletown. Adult-imposed restraints of obedience to parents, school, and public opinion have weakened further as the adult world has crumbled under the depression. . . . It is our impression that no two generations of Americans have ever faced each other across as wide a gap in their customary attitudes and behavior as have American parents and children [since the first World War]."[24]

Historians have documented similar patterns in other countries where there was a surge in the number of young people attending high school during the interwar period. In Canada, for example, where "most provinces raised the age of school-leaving to fifteen or sixteen during the 1920s, keeping the majority of young Canadians within the school's confines at least during the critical formative years of early adolescence,"[25] there opened up "a perceived generational divide of such breadth that it made children and parents, young and old, more estranged and 'alien' in their relations than had been any previous generations."[26] As this new social structure took hold in Canada, adolescent "values, much like activities, were being increasingly defined by the newly important peer group."[27]

The same trend continued on both sides of the forty-ninth parallel as the decade of economic depression came to a close and the world entered into a period of devastating warfare—or so suggests evidence from a sociological research project, similar to the Middletown studies, conducted from May 1941 to December 1942 in "Elmtown" (another fictional name for a small midwestern town, the true name never disclosed, to the best of my knowledge). The book coming out of that study, *Elmtown's Youth*, found high-school students much more concerned with the preoccupations and priorities of the teen environment than the problems of the outside world. One telling indicator was the reading habits of the young residents of Elmtown:

> Reading of newspapers, magazines, and books is not an important trait in the students' leisure hour activities. A youngster who is known as a "reader" is looked down upon by the non-readers, and in a sense pitied, for he is left out of the group activities which form such an important part of "life" in this age group. The front page of *The Bugle* is scanned hastily, the reader often reads nothing more than the headlines and local

> news of personal interest, but the comic page is read carefully. To be
> well informed, a high school boy has to know the standing of the major
> league baseball teams in the summer and fall, the major college teams
> in October and November, and the basketball scores in January and
> February. . . . Girls read the women's page and the society column with
> almost as much relish as the boys read the sports page. Their concern is
> focused upon clothes, cosmetics, hair styles [and] publicity on motion
> picture stars.[28]

This preoccupation with diversions popular with other teens sounds very
familiar to modern ears and suggests that the major crises of the 1930s and
1940s did not make much of a dent in the adolescent crucible. Teenagers, for the
most part, remained in the school setting, where they interacted primarily with
peers and continued to focus their attention largely on the priorities within their
immediate social environment.

Of course, the teenage experience was not identical for everyone through this
period. In fact, the principal focus of the Elmtown study was the way in which
social class affected adolescents and their passage through the school system,
as well as their experiences and opportunities in the larger community. Some
students were in vocational streams channeling them toward manual occupations and the trades, others in academic courses geared toward college admission.
Those in part-time employment were exposed to the working world at an earlier
date than their peers and could not partake of the full slate of extracurricular
activities open to the unencumbered teen. Gender was another abiding division:
as the reading habits of Elmtown youth suggested, teenage boys and girls inhab-
ited distinct, if overlapping, social worlds defined by preoccupations and activities considered to be the proper preserve of males or females alone. Race likewise
was a deep fault line among teenagers (as in the larger society), with the black
minority taught either in separate schools or "encouraged" to keep to themselves
in mixed school settings—hardly an incidental feature of the adolescent experience for members of the ostracized minority.

A fuller history of adolescence, seeking to capture this diversity in the world
of teens and variations in the adolescent experience connected to class, race, and
gender, would have to explore these issues in much greater detail, as any number
of prior studies have done.[29] In this briefer review, the key point to underline is
that despite these important differences and divisions, there was a general pattern
emerging of more frequent and intimate peer interaction as high school education
became the typical experience for teens from all social backgrounds. Moreover,
if some were less affected than others—less influenced by peers, quicker to move
from adolescence to the adult world, shaped in their worldview and individual

character by other important aspects of their early, formative experiences—it was sufficient that many were strongly influenced by the new social configuration of adolescence for this shift in the socialization process to make its impact both deeply and widely felt as time wore on.

Around the time that the Elmtown study appeared, there was another seemingly minor development that had greater effects down the road than anyone would have imagined at the time and which underlined the commonality of the adolescent experience: the invention of the word "teenager." The term was first coined in the late 1930s and became the preferred lingo with both marketers and the general public from the 1940s on.[30] The fact that adolescents lacked a snappy label prior to this time says something about the more nebulous character of adolescence in earlier periods. The acquisition of the new title both reflected and reinforced the solidifying boundary between adolescence and adulthood and contributed to a burgeoning group identity. If teens needed any further encouragement to establish themselves as a group apart, this was it: christening by society at large that gave official recognition to the teenage years as a unique stage of life.[31]

As the world moved on from years of economic depression and devastating warfare, as postwar prosperity took hold in the 1950s, there was little doubt that teenagers had come to inhabit a world all their own. In the field of popular culture, teenage icons and styles abounded, from James Dean to Elvis Presley to bobby sox and rock 'n' roll, while their everyday lives remained firmly embedded in the adolescent setting where peer influence continued to work its quiet but steady influence. The adolescent crucible was fully formed, its origins lying in the first decades of the twentieth century when its principal physical embodiment, the modern high school, opened its doors to one and all.

Of Parents and Peers

These changes in the lives of young people in the first half of the twentieth century gave much sharper definition to the stage of life we call adolescence. It was meant to be a step forward, providing young people with the knowledge and skills necessary to succeed in the modern workforce, along with more general preparation for the challenges of the adult world. The effects, however, were anything but straightforward, as the social milieu of adolescence and the powerful effects of peer influence on the adolescent character took us in directions no one had quite anticipated.

Some might find this description exaggerated, taking the view that peers matter to a degree, but that adults remained, and still remain, the most influential people in the lives of young people. One set of adults in particular looms large in the lives of most: parents. Beaming at us on arrival, parents remain front and center in our lives for a good number of years, providing protection against harmful influence and guidance in matters both momentous and mundane. The parenting guides that weigh down the shelves of bookstores everywhere would seem to suggest that what parents do matters a great deal in determining the kind of adults children become. If parents read the books faithfully and do their job right, common wisdom holds, children will follow their lead right through to leaving the nest and beyond. It is only parental neglect and indifference that sometimes see children falling prey to excessive peer influence and venturing down the wrong path.

On the face of it, there seems to be considerable evidence for the powerful effects of parental nurturing: the offspring of well-adjusted, happy, and successful parents are themselves often well-adjusted, happy, and successful, while the offspring of neglectful parents are more likely to make bad life choices and suffer the effects of various misfortunes and tribulations. The correlation is far from perfect, and no one's destiny is set in stone, but there are undeniable parallels between parental character and that of their offspring, suggesting parents do, in fact, have powerful molding effects.

There is one key problem with this line of thinking, however. The point is driven home most forcefully by Judith Harris in her iconoclastic 1998 book, *The Nurture Assumption*. Harris acknowledges that the apple typically doesn't fall far from the tree, recognizing that there is a good deal of similarity between parents and their offspring across a host of behavioral and dispositional measures—to put it more plainly, as she often does, that "pleasant, competent parents tend to have pleasant, competent children."[32] But this doesn't mean parents make a difference in the way it is normally understood, according to Harris. The common wisdom fails to take into account the fact that children end up a lot like their parents simply because of the genes they share. Parents pass on not only height, eye color, and shoe size, but also basic temperament and personality traits, and these in turn strongly influence many life choices and outcomes.

The evidence for her claims comes from a wide range of research studies based on the standard methods used to measure genetic effects. These include studies where identical twins (who share 100 percent of their genes) are compared to fraternal twins (who share 50 percent): identical sets are substantially closer in core personality traits than fraternal twins. This holds true even in cases where twins have been raised in separate households because of early adoption: identical twins end up more alike despite being brought up by different parents. Other studies reveal that adoptive siblings raised by the same parents, but obviously sharing no genes in common, are hardly more alike in temperament than two strangers. The more genetic material two people share, the more alike they are in personality, regardless of whether they were raised in the same household. Based on these studies, the rough estimate is that genetic inheritance accounts for about 50 percent of Big Five personality traits such as extroversion, conscientiousness, and agreeableness.[33] These ingrained personality traits, in turn, have an impact on virtually every aspect of our lives.

The striking claim of Judith Harris in *The Nurture Assumption* is that once we take this 50 percent genetic effect into account, there is not really much need for any further explanation of parent-child similarities. Shared genes *alone* explain why kids end up a lot like their parents. So parents do make a good deal of difference to how their children turn out, but this is mainly because of who they are, genetically speaking, not because of what they do, parenting-wise.

Naturally, this argument has sparked a lot of controversy. One recent review of personality research calls it "a stunning finding" that is "probably the most important discovery in psychology in recent decades."[34] Others temper their enthusiasm. While conceding that Harris has a point, they feel she takes the argument too far in suggesting that the nurturing influence of parents is essentially nil[35]—or, in her own zestful language, that "parents count zilch."[36]

Certainly, the argument is one that many parents will resist. Most of us don't want to think that our careful nurturing of our progeny is largely immaterial and we might as well be pursuing our careers full tilt or sipping margaritas poolside for all the difference it will make to little Ethan or Emily's basic character. To reassure parents everywhere, Harris does make a few concessions to the benefits of sound parenting in her scathing attack on the nurture assumption. Outright abuse of children, she allows, can leave lasting psychological damage and affect the character of offspring.[37] It is only within a fairly broad range of "normal" parenting methods that the ministrations of parents matter little. And certainly, Harris allows, there is a role for parents in providing life opportunities for their children and fostering the cultivation of specific skills and talents: kids don't learn how to play the piano without music lessons, parental encouragement, and a keyboard to practice on.[38] Perhaps most importantly, the way parents treat their children has one effect that most would consider significant: the quality of their personal relationship with their child.[39]

This, however, is quite different from the kind of person their child becomes— in other words, the personality and character traits he or she displays in interactions with the world at large. On that point, the science is quite conclusive: the similarities that exist between parents and offspring largely reflect the genetic transmission of key personality traits. The active contribution of parents to our character development, if not quite zilch, is considerably less than outward appearances would suggest.

None of this is to say that people's character is not shaped by environmental influences, since genetic inheritance only goes about halfway in explaining the kind of person we become. What it does mean, however, is that parents figure less prominently on the environmental side of the equation than we normally think. It follows that *other people* in our social environment matter more than was assumed in the past. This finding—a logical corollary to the powerful genetic transmission of personality traits—is also critical for the field of personality research, though the implications are not as immediately obvious.

Those implications start to emerge when we consider the other key point that Judith Harris emphasizes in her study of child development. The people that really matter in shaping children, she tells us, are other children, since youngsters spend much of their waking hours in the company of same-age peers. Children are little attuned to the adult world, instead focusing their attention on the social setting that matters most at that stage of life. "A child's goal," Harris writes, "is not to become a successful adult, any more than a prisoner's goal is to become a successful guard. A child's goal is to be a successful child."[40]

Harris focuses primarily on the earlier years of childhood, but her argument applies quite naturally to adolescence as well. As the period of peer immersion has been extended upward to include the teenage years, her reasoning can be extended to say that a teenager's goal, when immersed in the adolescent setting with other teens as primary reference points, is to be a successful teenager. Phrased this way, the idea seems hard to dispute. Even Robert Epstein, who is skeptical of the idea that teenagers are constitutionally different from adults, nonetheless acknowledges that the social environment of adolescents can skew their behavior to meet the norms and expectations of peers. "If you're fifty, it's unlikely that driving fast or smoking marijuana will impress your friends; in other words, reckless behavior probably won't be of much 'value' to you. But when you're fifteen ... reckless behavior might have great value, and the benefits received by impressing your friends might easily outweigh some possible negative consequences of the behavior."[41]

Epstein's example of risk taking is perhaps the first that springs to mind when we hear the phrase "peer influence" in the context of adolescent interaction. But we shouldn't let this example limit our understanding of either the mechanics or scope of mutual influence among teens. In the first place, influence does not always require overt pressure. The example of risky behavior may conjure up the image of a quivering teen being pressured by a circle of friends to do something she really does not want to do, but the reality is that it often doesn't require a lot of arm-twisting. Teenagers are keen to fit in with the crowd and actively seek to emulate what their peers are doing. Moreover, much of the inclination to do the things they do—whether it's engaging in risky behavior or some other predilection—derives from within, from their own adolescent impulses and desires. Peer influence in this situation remains important, but primarily as a mechanism of validation and reinforcement. As one writer on adolescence observes, "feedback from friendships and the peer group provides not only support but also a mirror for the self" as teens test and explore new behaviors.[42]

These processes of social convergence occur not just within adolescent society as a whole, as James Coleman emphasized in his study of American high schools in the late 1950s. Later researchers have paid considerable attention to the smaller subgroups or cliques that subdivide adolescent society and bring smaller pockets of teenagers together.[43] Commonly described by labels such as jocks, druggies, or goths, these cliques involve young people joining together with like-minded individuals who share similar interests and proclivities, but they can also be seen as embodying different shades of the adolescent character, the clustering process serving to deepen that shading in members of particular cliques. Extroverts who enjoy being part of the crowd at the heart of the action, for example, will be front and center at school events, football games, and parties, coming together with others who are likewise inclined. Those with a rebellious streak will together engage in rule breaking and thrill seeking, reflecting their less than conscientiousness character. Teenagers who score high on openness to experience may migrate toward alternative subcultures that embody unconventional ways of thinking and acting.

These sorting dynamics were evident in one study of cliques carried out over a two-year period in a high school in the Midwest. The research focused on a small group of about twenty students who moved out of the large "headbanger" group to form a smaller "hippie" cluster. In addition to embracing new tastes in clothing and music (more Grateful Dead, less Metallica), these young students started to more fully express the personality trait of openness. This was evident in their emotional warmth with one another, their interest in new social and political issues they were learning about, and their efforts to be open-minded and friendly with others who were not part of their newly formed group—to be a clique that wasn't quite so cliquey.[44] It was partly on the basis of similar personality traits that these teens set out to create their own subgroup; and once created, it provided a social venue for the further reinforcement of those traits. In this way, the varied experiences of teenagers during their adolescent years lead to the reinforcement of a diverse assortment of character attributes in different individuals.

At same time, there are some who stand out within adolescent society as central players whose influence transcends their personal circle. These alpha teens are those who are the most popular in the high school setting—"popular" referring not to those well liked by fellow teens necessarily, but to those able to command attention and control through a mix of charisma, looks, money, and willfulness.

One author has used the term "queen bee" to describe the female archetype of the popular teenager, an image that effectively conveys the power and sense of entitlement typically displayed by these central figures in the teenage hierarchy.[45] It all points to elements of the narcissistic personality syndrome, suggesting the queen bee is not necessarily the best role model; but her influence is undeniable, as many around her are "wannabes" who aspire to join the royal circle and to emulate her brash and self-assured manner. Those further on the fringes may develop more by their own lights yet still absorb a certain image of the type of individual who rightfully belongs at the center of social attention.

None of these ideas and observations are entirely novel, as the power of peer influence and the diverse mechanisms through which it operates in the various branches of adolescent society are widely understood. As one review of this field of research says, "It is nearly axiomatic in the adolescent development literature that peers play an increasingly important role in the lives of adolescents." But that same review goes on to note that "few studies have examined how peer experiences shape personality."[46] Instead much of the research concentrates on how peers sometimes lead teenagers astray, into the perils of drug use or other risky behaviors—research that is obviously valuable in helping us better understand these particular problems, but which may inadvertently contribute to a limited appreciation of the dynamics of peer influence in adolescence. We can miss seeing the broader effects on character development as teens form their own society and smaller subsocieties where they imitate, emulate, and learn from one another—effects that influence not only those who fall off the prescribed path into risky behaviors, but instead all who pass through adolescent society on their way to adulthood.[47]

I'm an Adult Now

Given the power of peer influence to shape who we are, extending the period of intensive youth interaction in the first half of the twentieth century to include the adolescent years was a portentous development. More than a simple extension, it represented a major shift in the developmental process because of important differences between childhood and the teenage years.

The crucial difference lies in the way children and teens relate to adults and adulthood. Younger children may be highly peer oriented, but they have a keen awareness of the adult world in one critical way. Children understand that their current desire to flourish in their peer environment—to be a successful child, as Judith Harris puts it—is *not* the same thing as being a successful adult. They may not say it aloud, may not consciously think it, but children are quietly aware that their current phase of life, revolving around playing, eating, sleeping, going to school, and doing as they're told (sometimes), is not the end point of their personal development. Adulthood lies ahead, distant and quite bewildering at present, but clearly understood to be an inevitable part of their future. So children don't mistake their current definition of "success" and the kind of person they want to be for their final destination.

Teenagers, on the other hand, do. A key priority at this stage of their personal development is to assert themselves as independent agents. They are grappling with the question of personal identity, famously identified by developmental psychologist Erik Erikson as the fundamental preoccupation of the teenage years; they are sifting through different ideas and possibilities to sort out what they truly believe in and the kind of person they wish to be.[48] This isn't seen as a temporary project to be set aside once adulthood arrives, but instead a more permanent agenda.

The distinctive mind-set of adolescents is evident in one simple indicator: how old they feel. One of the first studies to look at this question found that adolescents' subjective ages were, on average, several years older than their actual ages. This tendency, the same study suggested, is "consistent with the view that this life stage marks the transition from childhood to adulthood, during which time individuals strive toward a self-definition as independent, autonomous and self-reliant."[49] As teenagers grapple with the fundamental question of personal identity, they feel older than their youthful years, seeing themselves as nascent adults rather than older children.

Reflecting this same mind-set, teenagers strongly resist the idea that adults have any special insight into the norms and values that should guide a life well led. If their own preferences differ from those of adults, it is not because they themselves have yet to come of age. They are more likely to believe that adults have lost their way, becoming unduly preoccupied with mundane matters—mortgages and meetings, keeping the dandelions at bay—and losing sight of what is important in life. To them, adults' priorities are misplaced, their ideals insincere. Adults are, as the teenage narrator Holden Caulfield pegged them in that famous 1950s tale of adolescent contempt for the adult world, *The Catcher in the Rye*, a bunch of "phonies"—a sentiment that has resonated over the years with so many young readers of J. D. Salinger's classic work.

The adolescent perspective is further revealed in studies that focus on a concept researchers call the "ideal self"—the actual person or type of person someone would like to be. One such study carried out in Norway in the late 1990s asked a sample of teenagers a simple question: "Who would you most like to be like?" Given the young age range of those included in the study (thirteen to seventeen), the expectation was that most would cite older role models—either

THE CRUCIBLE OF ADOLESCENCE   49

people known personally or prominent figures from some area of public life. A good number did give such responses, with many, predictably enough, from the world of celebrity—movie stars, models, and sports heroes. But what surprised the researchers was the number who offered an off-kilter response: myself. Many others answered "nobody," which the researchers felt amounted to much the same sentiment—young people in need of no role models were presumably content with themselves as is. About one-quarter of teenage boys and one-third of girls gave one of these two responses.[50]

A particular advantage of this study was that it was a follow-up to another conducted fully eighty years earlier. In 1914, a sample of Norwegian teenagers was asked the same "ideal self" question. The results from the earlier period offered a stark contrast, not only in the role models cited (more historical figures, fewer supermodels), but also in the absence of any "myself" or "nobody" answers. As the researchers on the later study reported, such responses "were almost unknown in 1914. The present study shows that this is, for contemporary Norwegian adolescents, a common and natural response, even if the question clearly asks them to name concrete others."[51] An important shift in the adolescent mind-set had occurred over the course of the twentieth century.

The Norwegian study is not the only one to stumble upon this finding. Researchers in the UK who asked teenagers the same ideal-self question likewise found sizable numbers rejecting the premise of the question and reporting that they were quite content with themselves as is, thank you very much.[52] Teenagers used to look unfailingly to the adult world for some idea of who they would like to become. Now, these studies suggest, even when explicitly pointed in the direction of the adult world, many seem to feel they have already arrived.

All of this underlines the special importance of peer influence in the adolescent years. Younger children and teenagers may be alike in that both are inclined to adopt their peer group as a reference point for "success"—in this sense, the goal of the teenager is simply to be a successful teen. The difference is that, for teens, being a successful teenager is not a temporary objective to be replaced in due course by the aim of being a successful adult. To be a successful teen is, quite simply, to be a successful person.

This is not to suggest that nothing changes as we move from adolescence to adulthood, that we remain frozen in our teenage view of the world and of ourselves. A maturation process takes place in the transition from adolescence to adulthood that leads to some updating of the values, ideals, and ambitions that were predominant in adolescence. But the adolescent years remain influential as the period in which a provisional sense of adult self takes shape. This initial conception, forged in the company of like-minded peers, provides the foundation on which our evolving sense of personal identity is constructed.[53]

One sign of the ongoing influence of this early sense of who we are is that even as we mature and lose some of our most conspicuous adolescent qualities, a yearning for youth is experienced by many. The same studies that find teenagers reporting they feel older than they are show that after the mid-twenties or thereabouts, people start saying they feel *younger* than they actually are.[54] The idealization of youth is nothing new, but it has become especially acute in the age of adolescence. It used to be that youth looked up to adults around them as role models and looked forward to adulthood as the next step in the natural progression of life; now many teens feel entirely content in their own skin, while many adults look backward wistfully to locate their ideal self rather than fully embracing their current stage of life.

The special significance of teenage experiences to the adult sense of identity is captured in a recent car commercial. The ad first shows a teenager learning to drive in the family sedan. We then witness his progressive vehicle choices as he ages from teenager, to young adult, to newlywed, to middle-aged dad—deciding at that point to buy a convertible reminiscent of the sportster he drove in his youth. According to the voiceover, this new purchase allows him, after many years, to reconnect with his authentic self: "Now in the garage, something new, [that] reminds you of when you were you."[55] The message is clear: the adolescent self from years ago is more true and real than the crimped and compromised adult of middle age.

The car commercial resonates because it reflects a genuine psychological phenomenon known as the "reminiscence bump." Adults of all ages recall events from their teenage years and early twenties with greater frequency and clarity than those from any other period of their lives. Moreover, these memories from youth, imprinting themselves in the period when a sense of personal identity is starting to crystallize, are, in the words of Dan McAdams, "especially rich in emotional and motivational content."[56] The episodes they recall are felt to represent "symbolic messages, originating events, anchoring events and other self-defining memories" that serve as an important touchstone for the present.[57] The reminiscence bump phenomenon underscores the continuing influence adolescence exercises on the psyche of modern-day adults, highlighting important psychological mechanisms that have lent special salience to teenage sensibilities and ideals through later stages of life.

Early Imprints, Lasting Effects

The education reforms of the first half of the twentieth century that saw young people attending high school in ever-increasing numbers simultaneously created a new social structure that bore significant implications for the future. Teenagers henceforth came of age in a social setting dominated by same-age peers whose steadfast influence served to embed adolescent qualities at a pivotal stage of life when questions of personal identity—who am I, who do I want to be?—are first being raised and answered in a serious way. These adolescent qualities include an array of personality traits reflecting the exuberant, willful, and impulsive nature of adolescents, along with a variety of norms and ideals reflecting an individualistic set of core values—the precise mix varying from individual to individual, the aggregate effect for all adolescent traits to become more prevalent and prominent in younger generations. As a result of this social imprinting, adolescent character traits have slowly found their way into the adult realm, lending the phrase "adolescent society" an entirely new meaning over the course of time.

It is to this latter proposition and central theme of this book that we now turn, taking a closer look at various social patterns and trends that offer wide-ranging evidence of the changing character of rising generations over the twentieth century. As the story edges toward the present, we also start to reflect on some of the consequences of these developments for who we are today—both as individuals and as a society—and to ponder what it means to be an adult in a contemporary world suffused with adolescent norms and sensibilities.

A CENTURY OF CHANGE

It was in the early years of the twentieth century, as adolescence emerged as a defined life stage marked by intensive peer interaction, that adolescent qualities started to overflow the boundaries of adolescence proper, seeping upward into the adult world. Changes in the first half of the twentieth century mark the starting point of a process that continues down to the present day.

Demonstrating the rise of the adolescent character over this long stretch of time involves various methods and sources of information. For the earlier years, systematic studies of personality and character traits were uncommon; evidence of the growing salience of adolescent attributes must rest primarily on a blend of historical and anecdotal evidence along with hints of emergent trends from scattered polling results. After the war, social science research flourished, and systematic, large-scale studies became more common, providing the foundation for more rigorous trend analysis. This mixed bag of evidence points to a steady rise of adolescent qualities over the decades, incubating first in the intimate circles of the adolescent realm and gradually moving outward and upward to find a home in society at large.

The Early Years

One recent popular book that captures the spirit of the early period, offering suggestive evidence of the initial upsurge in adolescent qualities, is Susan Cain's *Quiet*. The book is first and foremost about introverts and their underappreciated qualities, as the book's subtitle proclaims: *The Power of Introverts in a World That Can't Stop Talking*. Lawyer-turned-author Cain is a self-confessed introvert herself, not always easy for someone whose legal career demanded she be a forceful voice in courts and corporate boardrooms. But she survived, indeed thrived, in this intimidating environment by drawing on the hidden strengths of introversion. Cain describes both the intrinsic virtues and tangible benefits of a more cautious, conscientious, and contemplative way of being.[1]

In mounting her defense of introversion, Cain provides a fascinating account of how its opposite number, extroversion, came to be dominant over the course of the past one hundred years, and in doing so describes developments that reflect the gradual revelation of the adolescent personality. Drawing on the seminal work of cultural historian Warren Susman,[2] Cain describes how the traits most widely admired and cultivated back in the nineteenth century were those that emphasized the individual's relationship to society, such as duty, honor, and citizenship, traits that implied a healthy measure of self-restraint and conscientiousness. In the early years of the twentieth century, there was a decisive shift toward a focus on the self and the cultivation of a more "magnetic" personality. Character guides emphasizing "inner virtue," a mainstay of the nineteenth century, were replaced by self-help manuals advocating "outer charm." Americans were quickly seduced by an extroverted ideal preaching the merits of an outgoing, gregarious, and confident personality.[3]

The new era was epitomized, Cain suggests, by the success of Dale Carnegie, author of the classic manual on self-presentation, *How to Win Friends and Influence People*. Hailing from the Midwest, Carnegie was intrigued as a teenager by those who could captivate a crowd with their engaging words and forceful manner. He gradually overcame his own inhibitions to develop a popular public-speaking program that taught people the techniques of effective presentation and self-promotion. Starting in 1912 with night classes delivered through the YMCA in New York, Carnegie quickly became the Pied Piper of self-promotion, with thousands flocking to his courses and millions reading his best-selling book. Carnegie's rise marked the start of the self-help industry that has grown exponentially over the years, providing guidance and hope for the aspiring masses seeking to perfect their own extroverted selves.

Looking around at contemporary society through the interpretive lens provided by Cain reveals widespread evidence of the subtle but pervasive bias in favor of extroversion. I can't say I read a lot of advice columns, but one I sometimes peruse is by David Eddie, a Canadian columnist more attuned to contemporary sensibilities than more traditional dispensers of homespun wisdom. After reading Cain's book, one particular column caught my eye. The letter-writer asked for Eddie's advice on how to avoid frequent family functions marked by incessant mundane chatter. "The boredom is killing me," the letter-writer complained. Eddie's advice was straightforward enough—invent a recurring excuse that would prevent attendance at future family snooze fests whenever a break was needed. It was the follow-up advice that was telling. The letter writer was advised not to feel the least bit guilty about his deceit, given the manifest shortcomings of the relatives in question. "Life's too short," Eddie advised. "Remember, it's everyone's individual *duty to be interesting*—a duty your relatives have clearly shirked."[4] It's a safe bet that the "duty to be interesting" was not one of the personal responsibilities emphasized in the character guides of the nineteenth century, and that respect for family, imperfections and all, likely was. In today's extroverted world, charisma and magnetism are deemed essential virtues, trumping valued character traits of earlier times.

In describing the changing contours of character in modern society, Cain identifies a diverse set of attitudinal and behavioral changes connected to rising extroversion and other traits reflective of what I would term our adolescent character. She describes the heightened confidence and assertiveness displayed by extroverts, but also cautions that this often shades into brash, even abrasive, behavior. She laments the lack of self-restraint exhibited all too often nowadays and outlines a penchant for risk taking and the pursuit of personal pleasure, warning that these tendencies don't always serve individuals well (nor those around them).[5] Cain's observations echo my own: there has been a decisive shift toward more disinhibited character traits and personal behavior over the course of time, a societal sea change so enveloping that we often see it as the natural and preferred default, rather than stepping back to probe its historical origins or question its merits.

Though Cain (like cultural historian Susman) draws no linkage between the ascendance of this brasher personality type and the impact of adolescence on people's ways of thinking and acting, the timing certainly fits: it was in the first decades of the twentieth century that extroversion and allied qualities started to become the popular norm, just as masses of young people were passing through the adolescent crucibles of high schools across the land. Instead, she offers other ideas about how and why extroversion became the dominant way of being. The "rise of industrial America" around the turn of the century meant that more and more people were making the move to large urban centers where social interaction was more fleeting and anonymous than it had been back on the farm. An outgoing personality was a way of making connections and getting ahead in these challenging new circumstances. The same qualities were demanded of those who wanted to advance in the thriving world of business, not least in the advertising and marketing divisions that were driving the new era of mass consumerism. "Americans responded to these pressures," suggests

Cain, "by trying to become salesman who could sell not only their company's latest gizmo but also themselves."[6]

Yet there are some suggestive connections between the new emphasis on "salesmanship" in both business and personal relations and the rising influence of adolescent dispositions. People's concerns about self-presentation were, Cain tells us, driven by heightened sensitivity to "how others perceived them."[7] Wily marketers picked up on this and devised "new personality-driven ads [that] cast consumers as performers with stage fright from which only the advertiser's product might rescue them." The marketing concept was strikingly akin to the imaginary audience idea that grips the adolescent psyche. Ads deploying the strategy, Cain notes, were far from subtle: "'ALL AROUND YOU PEOPLE ARE JUDGING YOU SILENTLY,' warned a 1922 ad for Woodbury's soap. 'CRITICAL EYES ARE SIZING YOU UP RIGHT NOW,' advised the Williams Shaving Company."[8] If Americans were becoming more sensitive to how they appeared to others, more preoccupied with superficial features of the external self, there seems some likely connection to the peer-dominated social environment in which young people were coming of age from the 1920s onward.[9]

Other pieces of evidence suggest a connection between the changing character of Americans in the first decades of the twentieth century and the deepening imprint of the adolescent experience on younger generations. One trend Cain cites as evidence of the shift in favor of extroversion is the rise of celluloid celebrities. "It was no coincidence that in the 1920s and 1930s, Americans became obsessed with movie stars. Who better than a matinee idol to model personal magnetism?"[10] To Cain's observation, I would add the important point that it was a particular demographic segment of the American public most taken with this new entertainment form and its extroverted icons. Movies were embraced first and foremost by the younger generation; a 1937 national survey by Gallup found that 89 percent of those under age thirty had been to the movies in the past month, compared to only 39 percent of those over age fifty.[11] The same year another Gallup poll asked Americans if they gave more attention to the "story" or the "stars" in deciding which movies to see.[12] Twice as many young adults indicated they were drawn by the name on the marquee. A couple of years later, in January 1939, Gallup pushed further on this line of questioning, probing the views of the nation on the choice of Vivien Leigh to portray Scarlett O'Hara in the film version of Gone with the Wind. With war clouds on the horizon in Europe, many people had weightier matters on their mind than the casting decisions of Hollywood. Only 20 percent of those fifty and over managed to muster up an opinion, whereas 40 percent of young adults had a view to share (for the record, she was favored by a majority of those who actually answered the question).[13] If stars of the silver screen were the most obvious symbols of a society starting to embrace the extroverted ideal, their rise to the top was very much propelled by the sensibilities of younger generations.

Other behavioral differences picked up by pollsters also suggest a generational dividing line in the rising tide of extroversion and allied qualities. In 1937, Gallup put this proposition to a representative sample of Americans: "If someone paid your expenses, would you like to go by airplane to Europe and back?" The question speaks to the positive emotion or "buzz" that extroverts derive from new and exhilarating experiences. It's not clear if it was deliberate or just an unfortunate coincidence that the survey took place only a few days after Amelia Earhart had disappeared somewhere over the South Pacific on her attempted solo flight around the world; but presumably this news would have dampened the enthusiasm of less venturesome souls for the prospect of an airborne expedition across the Atlantic. Only 21 percent of those fifty and over found the prospect of flying to Europe appealing, whereas 56 percent of those under age thirty were still up for the adventure.[14] When another Gallup poll in 1939 raised the bar higher by asking people if they would like the chance to learn how to *fly* a plane, the generational gap was greater still: only 24 percent of the older group said they would take up the opportunity, compared to 66 percent of those under age thirty.[15] In this early period, choices and preferences reflective of an open and extroverted personality type were far more common among younger Americans.

Further examples appeared in the realm of culture and consumption, where young people marked out new preferences and passions throughout the 1920s and 1930s that collectively came to be identified as an emergent youth culture. In addition to Hollywood films, young people latched onto new musical trends— jazz in the 1920s, swing in the 1930s—and thereby reshaped "music produced for multi-generational audiences into an identifiable teen culture."[16] Likewise, teenage girls took it upon themselves to explore new trends in cosmetics and fashion that appealed to their youthful sensibilities and claim them as their own. Eventually commercial interests caught on to this developing pattern and started to target products toward the "teen market," but in the first instance it was teenagers themselves who were responsible for creating a new youth culture through spontaneous attraction to products and trends that appealed to their adolescent sensibilities.[17]

Other social trends likewise sprang forth among younger generations in the interwar period as the character traits of youth were given freer rein. Attitudes toward traditional taboos changed rapidly over this period, reflecting young people's increased propensity for risk taking and pleasure seeking, coupled with a diminished concern for social consequences. One study, for example, found college students to be increasingly open to betting, smoking, flirting, and divorce, as well as "extravagance" and "silliness"—for each of these, the percentage who disapproved dropped by a sizable 20 to 35 percentage points over the short ten-year interval from 1923 to 1933.[18] Another study of American youth, covering the years 1929 to 1939, found rising antisocial tendencies, including increased tolerance for "habitually failing to keep promises," "using profane or blasphemous speech," "driving an automobile while drunk but without accident," "being habitually cross or disagreeable to members of one's own family," and "keeping overchange given by a clerk in mistake"[19]—measures of disinhibition and deception implying a significant erosion in respect for social norms and the weakening grip of the traits of conscientiousness and agreeableness on young people's behavior.

Manifestations of a new generational mind-set became evident among the college set, a select group of young people who had experienced the close company of peers during their high school years and now found themselves in a similar peer-dominated setting for several more. Developments mirrored and reinforced what was happening at the secondary school level, as tensions emerged between the academic mission of the postsecondary institution and the social dynamics of the campus. In her study of American youth in the 1920s, Paula Fass observes that "on the [college] campus of the 1920's, the emphasis was elsewhere than on booklearning—on extracurricular activities that demonstrated allegiance to peer pursuits and on sociability that mediated peer relations."[20] Fraternities and sororities, Fass notes, became a focal point in this period, indeed the hub of campus social life, helping to "redefine college work and redirect energies from an adult-controlled classroom to a peer-controlled campus."[21] These organizations embraced the prevailing extroverted ideal, choosing their initiates on the basis of their "agreeable exterior and slick sociability,"[22] thereby setting the standard and tone for the campus environment at large. They also provided the social setting where students began experimenting in large numbers with previously taboo behaviors. None of this represented any conscious realignment or concerted youth rebellion, but was instead simply a manifestation of emergent youth energies coursing through the student population as never before. Fass quotes one undergraduate from Ohio State University who declared that there was no "air of ultra smartness" in students' enthusiasm for newly favored activities such as "smoking, dancing like Voodoo devotees, dressing decolleté, 'petting' and drinking." "We do these things," continued the student, "because *we honestly enjoy the attendant physical sensations. . . .* The real enjoyment lies in the thrill we experience."[23] As these sensation-seeking attitudes and actions started to become the norm among youth, there was little that alarmed college administrators or anyone else could do to stem the tide of social change.

Concerns naturally started to arise about where this was all headed. As one observer wrote in 1943, shifting norms across many sectors were adding up to a profound change in the "general tone or climate of life"—with good reason, the same author believed, to think that "changes in the next 20 years [would] probably be yet greater."[24] Later events would prove him right, as early signs of adolescent traits on the rise were eventually followed by their more full-throttled expression in the tumultuous 1960s and their widespread acceptance in the laissez-faire decades that followed. The specific behavioral manifestations of growing disinhibition have varied widely through different periods, but the general trend of youthful character traits exerting greater influence over social and cultural behaviors has been a continuous and steady development.

Just as there was a generational dividing line in the rising tide of adolescent traits and behaviors, there was also a generational dynamic to their ongoing reproduction and amplification. As time wore on, younger generations embodying adolescent qualities grew up and became part of adult society; they then played an important role in encouraging the fuller expression and deeper retention of adolescent traits in generations to follow. Parents set the tone through the messages they conveyed to their offspring. In her analysis of the rise of the extroverted ideal over the course of the twentieth century, Susan Cain writes, "Well-meaning parents of the midcentury agreed that quiet was unacceptable and gregariousness ideal for both girls and boys. . . . Introverted children were often singled out as problem cases."[25] Parents who themselves had been subject to the social influence of teenage peers during adolescence were, not surprisingly, more amenable to the expression of adolescent qualities in their offspring. The same point about intergenerational reinforcement is made by Cynthia Comacchio in her study of Canadian youth. While the "inaugural generation of 'flaming youth' in the 1920s" had established that "the young were indeed a different species than their parents and elders," further reinforcement arrived in "midcentury . . . [when] 'flaming youth' themselves became the parents of adolescents."[26] If the parents were no longer burning quite so brightly themselves, the embers were still strong enough to generate considerable sympathy for the passions of their teenage offspring.

Further evidence of obliging and accommodating parenting styles among parents who had themselves grown up under the influence of the adolescent society crops up in television sitcoms of the 1950s. Gary Cross, in his insightful study of generational changes in ideas of male adulthood over the course of the twentieth century, offers the example of Ward Cleaver, the iconic father figure from the show *Leave It to Beaver*. Mr. Cleaver appears on the surface to be the epitome of the traditional, straitlaced parent: serious, responsible, steady as a rock. Yet when we look more closely, Cross says, we are struck by the progressiveness embodied in his efforts to accommodate the foibles and missteps of his two sons, Wally and Beaver. In many ways, Ward Cleaver was actually the harbinger of the "modern dad"—a parent, as Cross puts it, "understanding and wary of following in the harsh and unfeeling footsteps of his own father, forever calling to mind the stresses (and pleasures) of his own youth and willing to see the world from his sons' viewpoint. . . . Far from being traditional and patriarchal, these fathers who 'knew best' were really permissive and progressive, tolerant bemused guides of children who would doubtless find their way."[27] This sympathetic viewpoint of midcentury parents offered greater room for the expression of adolescent qualities, allowing them to establish deeper roots in the next generation—until eventually, by century's end, Phil Dunphy of *Modern Family* could abandon any notion of parental tutelage with his heartfelt declaration: "I've always said that if my son sees me as one of his idiot friends, then I've succeeded as a dad. If he wants to go the wrong way on the escalator, then I'm on board. If he wants to go into a restaurant and pretend we're Australian, then g'day mate."[28]

Additional evidence of a long-term shift in parenting styles reflective of the preferences and priorities of youth can be found in a research project that directly compared attitudes in the 1920s and 1970s. The study took advantage of the Middletown research, which had included a survey of 141 mothers in Muncie, Indiana, asking them what qualities they felt were most desirable to cultivate in children. It also drew upon a follow-up survey conducted in 1978 that went back to Muncie to ask the same questions of more than three hundred mothers. The study revealed that parental priorities had changed quite dramatically over the span of half a century. In the original study in 1924, 45 percent had chosen "strict obedience" as one of the top three qualities they felt important to promote in their offspring; loyalty to the church and good manners were also heavily favored. By 1978, only 17 percent placed strict obedience in the top three, whereas 76 percent selected "independence" as a key trait to instill—far and away the most popular choice in the later period, and three times the number who had chosen it back in 1924.[29]

As a result of these changes emanating from below, adolescents and adults have moved ever closer in sympathies and outlook over the course of time. One newspaper writer a few years back produced a column with the headline "I Like to Hang Out with My Teenager—What's Wrong with That?" Her analysis of relations between teens and their parents was spot on, identifying a powerful trend of convergent sensibilities. "Since the entire culture is defiantly refusing to grow up, parents and children are all now approximately the same age. We've got the same music on our iPods. We go to the same movies and read the same magazines. The mothers I know don't wear 'Mom jeans' but the same skinny cult labels as their daughters. . . . If the end result of our stubborn immaturity is that there is no longer a real generation gap in terms of mutual respect and understanding between ourselves and our children, isn't this actually a positive development?"[30] The writer is not alone in her embracing of adolescent ways and chumminess with her teenage daughter. A 2004 survey of one thousand parents in the US, UK, and Canada found that fully 43 percent said they wanted to be their child's best friend.[31] Though there are no surveys from eighty years ago to measure this against, it's a safe bet to say it represents a significant change from the way things used to be. Adults now appreciate and nurture adolescent ways because they resonate deeply within their own psychological makeup.

The initial catalyst of the major changes in character traits and social values that have marked the past century was the creation of adolescent crucibles where young people started to rub off on one another to an unprecedented degree and to form their own ideas of what an adult should be. This has given rise to successive waves of generational change as adult society has gradually become more adolescent in disposition and outlook and increasingly receptive to the proclivities of teenagers.

The Postwar Period

For the first half of the twentieth century, the evidence suggesting an upsurge in adolescent traits—rising extroversion and openness, diminishing conscientiousness and agreeableness—is somewhat scattered, lying in a smattering of behavioral trends, illustrative anecdotes, and research papers stored away in the dusty archives section of the library. After the war, relevant research started to be carried out in a more systematic way, laying the groundwork for recent studies that have made use of this gradually accumulating body of data to trace changes in aggregate levels of personality traits over the past several decades.

The researcher who has done the best job of assembling hard numbers on the relevant trends and recognizing them as changes in personality on a society-wide scale is Jean Twenge. Twenge is a social psychologist at San Diego State University who has written two popular books describing this evolving social landscape. The first, *Generation Me*, described the rampant individualism that has taken hold of many Americans in recent years, with a special focus on its deep entrenchment among young Americans born since the 1970s. The second, *The Narcissism Epidemic* (cowritten with fellow psychology professor W. Keith Campbell), focused on some of the worst excesses of an individualistic society, describing and decrying the excessive exhibitionism, materialism, and self-focused superficiality that pervade society nowadays. The books are backed up by Twenge's scientific papers, which present detailed findings on trends in personality linked to these patterns, including rising extroversion levels and significant changes in other Big Five traits.

Twenge and her colleagues are not the first to highlight these developments. Writer Tom Wolfe famously dubbed the 1970s the Me Decade for its conscious turn toward a focus on the self in all its glorious and not-so-glorious forms,[32] while social critic Christopher Lasch gained widespread attention for his 1979 book, *The Culture of Narcissism*. But Twenge's recent works are notable for a couple of reasons. First, they highlight the continued encroachments individualism has made over the past forty years, seeping quietly into virtually every sector of modern life, where the doctrine has become so pervasive and unimpeachable that it often passes undetected. And secondly, she has gone further than others in systematically tracking the evolution of the underlying personality traits connected to this trend. Poring through psychology journals of the past several decades, Twenge identifies samples of subjects (often university students) administered the same standard personality tests at different times and compiles the results to assess changes in key personality traits over time. Her analysis goes beyond conjecture and anecdote to provide concrete evidence of a changing personality profile among rising generations—and thereby society at large—over the course of several decades.

The following are some of the more notable findings from Twenge's scholarly papers:

- In one article, she reports substantial increases in average extroversion scores over the period 1966 to 1993. This particular study focuses on the "Eysenck Personality Inventory," a personality questionnaire used on thousands of samples of individuals over many years. Questions probe a wide range of areas designed to assess whether respondents are excitable, impulsive, restless, sociable, outgoing, lively, and so on—a series of classic extroverted traits. Conscious of the fact that trends for men and women might differ over this period, given that the women's liberation movement was actively encouraging women to be less passive and demure, Twenge looks at the two groups separately. But the results are consistent: large increases for both men and women in extroversion scores from 1966 to 1993. Based on a 24-point scale, average scores rose from 11.36 to 15.27 for males and from 11.82 to 15.70 for females.[33]

- It's well established that extroverted qualities, when taken too far, start to shade into narcissism. The Narcissistic Personality Inventory is a standardized questionnaire that assesses whether people have moved beyond healthy levels of self-esteem and self-confidence to have what Twenge calls an "inflated view of the self." Items in the inventory include "I am more capable than other people"; "I really like to be the center of attention"; "I will usually show off if I get a chance"; and "I find it easy to manipulate people." In a study published in 2008, Twenge and colleagues found that average narcissism scores (based on a 40-point scale) increased from 15.06

in 1982 to 17.29 in 2006. The change is bigger than it sounds when you consider that almost two-thirds of subjects studied in 2006 were above the average score from the early 1980s.[34] Over the longer haul, changes on the narcissism front are almost certainly greater still. In *The Narcissism Epidemic*, Twenge and coauthor Campbell cite this striking statistic: the percentage of teenagers agreeing with the statement "I am an important person" went from 12 percent in the 1950s (boys and girls combined) to 80 percent for girls and 77 percent for boys in 1989.[35]

- In another paper, Twenge and coauthor Charles Im demonstrate a substantial decline in the need for "social approval" over the period 1958 to 2001. The study draws on another widely used personality instrument, the Marlow-Crowne Social Desirability Scale. Social desirability, as captured by this scale, primarily bridges two Big Five traits. Some questions speak to conscientiousness or the lack thereof ("I am always careful about my manner of dress"; "There have been times when I felt like rebelling against people in authority even though I knew they were right"), while others tap into agreeableness ("I have never deliberately said something that hurt someone's feelings"; "There have been occasions when I felt like smashing things"). The overall finding is that scores on the scale decreased substantially from 1958 to around 1980, leveling off after that point. Twenge and Im's conclusion: "Younger generations are less concerned with being polite, conventional, and acceptable to others."[36]

- Twenge has not done a detailed long-term study of another important Big Five trait connected to adolescence—openness to experience—but she does devote a chapter of her 2006 book *Generation Me* to related changes that have taken place in the area of social and political attitudes. Younger generations, Twenge observes, show greater support for the rights of various groups that have suffered oppression and lack of equal opportunity in the past, including ethnic minorities, members of the LGBTQ community, and women. She draws a link between these more open attitudes and the decline among younger generations in the need for social approval: "GenMe may have left behind some of the good social rules about politeness, but . . . we have also left behind some of the bad social rules about everyone living life in the same way, and minorities and women staying in their 'place.'"[37] Other leading personality researchers draw a direct connection between attitudes of tolerance and the Big Five trait of openness to experience.[38] So the rise in tolerance that Twenge describes is suggestive of a society becoming gradually more accommodating as a result of burgeoning levels of openness to experience—a very positive development in the eyes of many, Twenge included.

Supporting Twenge's findings, another study from a different country establishes that these are not uniquely American trends. A 2010 Swedish study examined changes in personality over a thirty-six-year period by comparing a sample of women ages thirty-eight and fifty from 1968, with another sample of women of the same ages in 2004. The research identified sharp increases in traits associated with extroversion (such as exhibitionism and dominance), combined with a downward turn in agreeableness (evident in stronger tendencies toward aggression and irritability) and conscientiousness (a decrease in the felt need for order, cleanliness, and planning).[39]

The general pattern across these results is clear and compelling. *Personality traits and allied qualities known to be elevated among adolescents are the same ones that have become more pronounced in rising generations and society at large over time.* This includes several of the broad Big 5 personality domains (higher levels of extroversion and openness to experience, lower levels of conscientiousness and agreeableness), as well as more specific syndromes (such as rising narcissism). The adolescent society James Coleman described, formed through youth segregation in the high school setting, has slowly reconfigured personality dispositions and values to create a new kind of adolescent society in the adult world.

Age or Generation—or Both?

These findings, which imply seismic shifts in the character of our society driven by steady generational change, have naturally attracted a lot of attention. Findings that receive a lot of attention usually attract a good number of critics, and these are no exception.

The most basic objection is quite simple. Twenge's studies focus primarily on today's younger adults, people born in the 1970s and onward ("Generation Me," as she calls them), who are presented as the current vanguard of generational change on a variety of important personality traits and basic values. But the patterns she has uncovered, the critics say, have nothing to do with generational change. Instead they simply reflect persistent differences between younger and older people. If today's young Americans tend, on average, to be more extroverted, narcissistic, disagreeable, and skeptical of social norms, it is because young people have always been more extroverted, narcissistic, disagreeable, and skeptical of social norms.

To emphasize the point, critics like to cite observers of youth from long ago. In ancient Greece, Aristotle remarked that "the young are prone to desires and inclined to do whatever they desire . . . they are impulsive and quick-tempered and inclined to follow up their anger. . . . Like those drinking wine, they are heated by their nature."[40] American commentators from nearly a hundred years ago can be found complaining that the young had no "sense of shame, honor or duty . . . they don't care about anything except pleasure."[41] Two of Twenge's most persistent detractors take up this line of reasoning, arguing that "there is insufficient evidence to support the conclusion that the personalities and self-beliefs of today's young people are dramatically different from previous generations of American youth."[42]

Critics also point out that predictable changes take place in people's personalities over the course of their lives and that these readily account for the differences we see between younger and older Americans today. Leading researchers in the field argue that age differences in personality reflect "intrinsic, biologically based, and universal maturational processes."[43] The biological maturation viewpoint is at odds with the generational change perspective, which presumes that personality is at least partly socially constructed and therefore more open-ended, allowing for significant generational change and society-wide trends from one era to the next.

The idea that personality is tightly linked to ingrained life-cycle rhythms of personal growth and maturation is not one that can be simply dismissed or ignored. It feels intuitively right to anyone over a certain age who can find themselves wondering "who *was* that person?" when they reflect back on their younger self. It definitely feels right to politicians on the campaign trail when faced with allegations about questionable actions dating back to when they were teenagers or young adults—whether it's the hazards of inhaling (Bill Clinton), the shirking of military duty (George W. Bush), or the bullying behavior of a dominating extrovert (Mitt Romney). The politicians would like to believe, and have us believe, that that was a *totally* different person back then. Luckily for them, the scientific evidence does back up their claims about the eventual mitigation of wayward adolescent tendencies. Studies that track the same individuals over many years consistently find evidence of significant changes in basic personality traits as we grow older, ones consistent with the gradual shedding of adolescent qualities.

The two perspectives on personality development lead to very different interpretations of the same empirical data. If a study carried out in the year 2010, for example, found that young adults in their twenties were less conscientious than those in their fifties, the generational interpretation would be that those born in the 1980s are less conscientious than those born in the 1950s—a generational shift with important implications for where we are headed as a society. The maturational interpretation, on the other hand, would argue that people simply become more conscientious as they move from young adulthood to middle age and that there is nothing remarkable or unusual in the current pattern.

What neither camp seems to acknowledge is that it's possible, in fact plausible, for both sides to be correct. Twenge contends—and her research findings are very persuasive on this point—that today's young adults are different, in the aggregate, from earlier generations of young adults on a number of key personality traits and related social values. This doesn't mean, however, that they won't experience significant personality and value change as they age.[44] As advocates of the maturational viewpoint insist, their basic temperament and outlook will not remain frozen in place, but will instead be subject to ongoing modification as part of the aging process.

What it does mean, however—and this is still a very important point—is that this maturation process is unlikely to deliver them to the same endpoint as earlier generations. If Generation Me are currently more extroverted, narcissistic, disagreeable, and skeptical of social rules and norms than previous generations were *at the same age*, they are likely to *remain so* at each point along the road from early adulthood to their golden years. By the time they reach age sixty, Generation Me certainly will be different from how they were at age twenty—but they will also be very different from the sixty-year olds of earlier periods.

This modified version of the generational change perspective, essentially a blending of the aging and generational perspectives, lies at the heart of the adolescent society argument. The first of these perspectives, differences in personality linked to age and life stage, formed our point of departure back in chapter 1. There we saw evidence of the distinctive personality traits of adolescents, drawing on studies that have measured the Big Five in representative samples of people of different age groups, along with other salient features of the adolescent character. Subsequent chapters, however, have added a generational change perspective, arguing that qualities natural to adolescents have slowly migrated upward into adult society as a result of peer immersion and heightened influence during the teenage years. In the early part of the twentieth century, we started to linger longer in adolescence, absorbing adolescent ways more deeply and bringing them forward with us to adulthood. Even as we moved on in life and experienced personality changes tied to the aging process, we followed a slightly different trajectory from those who came before and arrived at a different destination. Each new generation has taken the process one step further, leading to the slow but steady infusion of adolescent qualities into adult society.

Any theory proposing generational change in basic personality traits must acknowledge that personality is also a function of the aging and maturation process—there is simply too much hard evidence that this is the case. The adolescent society thesis does more than just acknowledge the two processes at work. It explicitly links them, highlighting how the salient traits of a particular stage of life, one that has assumed greater prominence and significance in modern times, have served as the wellspring of gradual generational change.

Up Close and Personal

There is another way in which the adolescent society argument diverges from prevailing interpretations. A core premise is that environmental influences on character development are important, especially environmental influences in the formative years of adolescence. The establishment of the adolescent stage of life altered the social environment of the teenage years, and it is this mechanism that has led to steady changes in personality traits and deeply held values over the long haul.

The distinctiveness of this idea can better be appreciated by drawing a clear distinction between two different ways of thinking about the environmental influences that can potentially shape people's basic character. One type of environmental influence consists of the people we know personally and interact with on a regular basis—our personal social network. When Judith Harris makes the case that same-age peers are very important to our development during childhood, and when I echo her views by underlining the impact of teenage peers in the adolescent years, it is this form of environmental influence—up close and personal—that is being emphasized.

The idea that social networks have powerful effects on the individuals embedded within them has gained many adherents in different branches of the social sciences in recent years. Research has been steadily accumulating showing that all sorts of behaviors, attitudes, and norms have a contagious quality, spreading virally through personal social networks from one person to another—and then, in many cases, to another and yet another. (Three "degrees of separation" seem to be about the limit of these effects.)

An excellent summary of these intriguing patterns can be found in the 2009 book *Connected: The Surprising Power of Our Social Networks and How They Shape Our Lives*. Authors Nicholas Christakis and James Fowler—one a medical researcher *cum* sociologist, the other a political scientist—document some striking examples that give us a sense of how pervasive social contagion really is. Did you know, for example, that when one person gains weight, others in that person's social network are more likely to put on a few extra pounds as well? Or when someone votes in an election, people around that individual are more apt to cast a ballot as well? Or when our friends, associates, and acquaintances experience periods of happiness or bouts of sadness—even those at two or three degrees of separation—we are more likely to experience those same emotions as well?

These findings partly reflect the fact that most of us choose to hang out with people who are similar to us to begin with—as the old cliché goes, that birds of a feather flock together. People who vote, for example, are more likely, for one reason or another, to move in social circles with other people who vote. But researchers are aware of this and have designed their studies to find out how much influence people have on one another *once* they are connected in social networks. The consistent answer is a great deal. The effects of those around us are far from trivial, often outweighing the impact of many traditional factors known to influence happiness, obesity, voting, and so on. Through this accumulating body of research, we are coming to recognize the powerful impact of personal social networks, an environmental influence not always properly acknowledged in the past.

There is, however, another way of thinking about environmental effects on our actions and character, and this is to focus on the larger cultural environment in which we are embedded—in other words, the prevailing norms and customs of the particular society and times in which we live. This is the more common way of thinking, and it lies at the heart of Jean Twenge's analysis of generational personality change. Instead of concentrating on personal social networks, she analyzes how character is shaped by the larger cultural environment surrounding us all.

In their book about the worrying rise in narcissism, for example, she and coauthor Campbell argue that "three social trends seem to be the main culprit" for the epidemic that began in the 1970s. One was the "movement toward self-esteem"; the second was the emphasis on "self-expression"; and the third was a trend in which "the culture began to move away from community-oriented thinking."[45] These movements, in turn, grew out of the more general culture shift in favor of individualism that the baby boomers initiated as young adults in the 1960s. While pointing to teachers and parents as key promoters of messages such as self-esteem that helped steer young people in the direction of excessive individualism, these actors were not the instigators of change, just the messengers. Parents and teachers chose to emphasize doctrines of the self because they too were caught up in the general social trends that were ultimately responsible for the changes we have seen. The bottom line is that we have all been swept along in an overwhelming cultural tsunami. "Personality does not exist in isolation," Twenge and Campbell write. "This increase in narcissism among individuals is, we believe, just an outcome of a massive shift in culture towards a greater focus on self-admiration."[46]

On the face of it, the approach taken by Twenge and Campbell seems like the more sensible way of thinking about how environmental changes have influenced individual character. Rather than focusing on personal social networks, which sounds as though it could be a cumbersome and complex way to proceed, we instead should look at the general social trends and the larger cultural setting that have influenced one and all. Yet on closer reflection, something is lacking in this approach. What does it really mean to say that a general social trend has affected how people think and act? A social trend, after all, is itself nothing more than a noteworthy pattern or change in how people think and act—by placing greater emphasis on self-esteem and self-admiration, for example. Yet these are precisely the changes in individual character that the social trend is supposed to explain.

Put this way, the culture change explanation that Twenge and Campbell (and many others) favor starts to sound like circular reasoning. Culture change—consisting of lots of people thinking and acting differently from before—has led to character change evident in lots of people thinking and acting differently from before. It amounts to saying we changed because we changed. Or we changed us.[47]

The adolescent society idea offers both a way out of this causal loop and more explanatory punch. Building on the premise that *personal social networks* are a crucial environmental influence on character development, it proposes that extending the period of peer immersion to include the adolescent years represented a fundamental change in the *general architecture of social networks* in society. Though each teenager's personal web of friends and acquaintances was unique and idiosyncratic, the common denominator was that they were now more dominated by adolescent peers than in the past—which is to say, like-minded individuals who helped reinforce the adolescence mind-set. In this way, adolescent qualities became more deeply etched and were carried forward to the adult years.

This offers a more satisfying response to the question of where the important sea changes in character that have marked the past century originated. The answer is that they came from within, in the form of a bundle of tendencies and dispositions that were always present in the teenage years and which have now been given freer rein and more permanent expression. So it is correct to say that we changed us—in the sense that we, our adolescent selves, changed us, our adult selves. Or perhaps it might be simpler just to say that a certain side of us, always present but somewhat obscured historically, has now come to the fore.

This opens up new ways of thinking about the long-term trends that have been at work over past decades reshaping our society for better and for worse. Twenge's culture-shift account reflects the common wisdom on these matters. Broadly speaking, this perspective sees individualism—the cluster of norms, dispositions, and traits that involve freer individual expression and greater focus on the self—as originating in the *conscious and deliberate adoption of a new constellation of values* at a fairly precise moment in time. The critical period, in this view, was the 1960s, a decade of great tumult and agitation in the United States and other industrialized nations in North America and Europe. The baby boomers, coming of age in the 1960s, are credited with creating a new cultural ethos during those years, one that emphasized the self under various labels: self-esteem, self-expression, resistance to authority, and so on. They were pioneers breaking new ground. As Twenge puts it in *Generation Me*, the boomers were "making their way in the uncharted world of the self" and had to "reinvent their way of thinking." The boomers were highly successful in this, and the new ethos soon became so dominant that it was accepted unquestioningly by those who followed. "The self-focus that blossomed in the 1970s became mundane and commonplace over the next two decades, and Gen Me accepts it like a fish accepts water."[48] On this interpretation, the critical starting point for the profound social changes of the past half century was the decisive move by the baby boomers to embrace and propagate a new set of individualistic values in the 1960s.

Others adopt this same line of thinking, emphasizing critical choices and turning points that have brought us to where we are now. Conservatives, for example, see the 1960s as the decade when we took a decisive wrong turn, abandoning traditional virtues in favor of social rebellion and loose morals. They've been trying to get us back on track ever since, calling for the reestablishment of venerable norms of personal righteousness and responsibility. The phrase "culture wars," used to describe the differences between liberals and conservatives on social and moral issues, is predicated on the idea of conscious choices between competing value systems—bad choices made in the past, in the eyes of conservatives, along with better choices to be made in the present.

The adolescent society account, with its emphasis on the peer environment and social network influences, is very different. Rather than the conscious adoption of a new set of values, it suggests a subtle, inadvertent process of social change grounded in slow but steady shifts in personal character. It also looks to earlier developments that set the stage for postwar social evolution; the first half of the twentieth century was when the ground was being softened for later developments. The establishment of universal secondary schooling created a more defined adolescent stage of life and encouraged the expression and retention of adolescent character traits. Signs of change appeared early on, including an emphasis on extroversion as a desirable personality trait, an emergent youth culture emphasizing fun and new experiences, as well as the weakening of traditional social norms and taboos linked to conscientiousness and agreeableness. The adolescent stage of life became more entrenched, teenagers more clearly identified as a distinct social grouping. Even as external events shook the adult world, wreaking havoc and hardship, these developments in the teenage realm moved steadily forward through the 1930s and into the postwar years.

The 1960s was the period when this trajectory of change became more transparent and undeniable. The youth of those years expressed their adolescent ways more fully and freely than any had before, but with the tacit encouragement of a society that had been moving in this general direction for a great many years.

There was also much greater public consciousness of the changes that had been occurring, and subtle changes in character started to be articulated as ideologies of the self—self-expression, self-fulfillment, self-esteem. This was also the period that saw the greatest changes taking place in the realm of social norms and behaviors, everything from sexual liberation to political rebellion to outlandish fashion and raucous music. So the 1960s do stand out as an important chapter in this alternative story of social change. But in this reading, the decade was more of a tipping point than a starting point, the period when changes that had been quietly simmering for a number of decades finally boiled over.

At the risk of being glib, what I'm suggesting is that the 1960s, and all that flowed from that decisive decade of social upheaval and transparent value change, really began in the 1920s. It was after the First World War, when universal secondary education started to become a reality, and enclaves of adolescents were formed in communities and high schools across the land, that the seeds of social change started to germinate. Rather than dramatic cultural change leading to widespread changes in individual character, it was widespread changes in individual character, quietly forged in the adolescent crucibles of high schools everywhere, that eventually sparked dramatic cultural change.

This is not to entirely discount the Twenge-Campbell way of thinking about these matters. A process that originated in the social circles of adolescence a century ago has diffused widely over the course of time to the point that we can today speak sensibly of a culture infused with adolescent values and sensibilities that does, in a meaningful sense, reinforce and reproduce itself. The adolescent ethos comes at us from all directions—from the media and popular culture, in the workplace and other venues of daily life, in the cues and actions of adults and teenagers alike—and it affects us all. High-school dropouts, for example, who do not experience the full peer immersion effects of secondary schooling, are as much the product and embodiment of today's adolescent society as anyone else; no one is fully immune. But describing where matters stand today is quite different from determining how they came to be. Developments in the adolescent social realm were the catalyst that served to initiate a process of social change that eventually became an all-encompassing transformation and thereby acquired a certain self-reinforcing momentum.

Adolescence to the Fore

The new ground being broken here rests on combining a number of existing ideas and theories in a novel way. This hybrid account offers an alternative way of thinking about the evolution of our society over the past century by focusing on subtle yet pervasive forces influencing the process of character development among rising generations. Early authors, like the Lynds with their studies of teenage life in Middletown in the 1920s and 1930s, and James Coleman with his work on the adolescent society in the American high school system of the late 1950s, highlighted the significance of secondary education—not just in producing a more educated population, but also in creating something that had not previously existed in quite the same way before: the adolescent social realm. The analysis of research psychologist Judith Harris clears up some of the confusion about the role of parents in molding our basic personality and temperament, emphasizing that their contribution is mainly genetic and that it is others directly around us who provide most of the environmental influence on our character development at different stages of life. This explains why the establishment of adolescent enclaves was such an auspicious development: now, at the very point when we were establishing our provisional sense of adult self, we remained in the company of like-minded peers more apt to reinforce than to challenge our adolescent mind-set.

Inevitably, this led to changes in both our adolescent and adult selves, as we carried some of our entrenched adolescent dispositions forward to adulthood. The work of Susan Cain and Jean Twenge can fruitfully be interpreted in this light. Both describe changes in key personality traits that have taken place over the long haul, Cain using works of social history to trace the rise in extroversion (and allied qualities) over the course of a century, Twenge providing a more scientifically grounded account of generational change in the Big Five traits in the postwar period. In describing these trends, they also highlight some of the problems (as well as a few benefits) associated with a society where adolescent-infused character traits have become so prevalent.

I come at these ideas, mainly pilfered from researchers in the fields of psychology and sociology, as something of an outsider—a political scientist originally interested in understanding changing patterns of citizen engagement in politics. The kinds of questions I was looking at were seemingly far removed from the ideas addressed in this book. But the connections gradually became apparent. In seeking to understand citizen engagement and disengagement, I was drawn to theories from my own field that emphasized changes in the value orientations of citizens with implications for politics. They suggested a general perspective that seemed right to me—that it wasn't just the political system causing people to turn away from politics or to gravitate toward a different kind of politics, it was something about society and citizens themselves.

Reading more widely, I was persuaded by ideas from other fields that drew important linkages between values and basic personality traits; yet I didn't find fully satisfying answers as to why these foundational qualities would have been subject to major evolution over the course of time. There was some general agreement that the changes we have seen were generationally driven, but exactly why younger generations were turning out differently from previous ones wasn't well explained. Notions of cultural change sweeping over us didn't seem up to the task, as they failed to explain where cultural change comes from, what culture change is, if not simply changes in us.

The adolescent society concept offered a more precise and forceful explanation, resting on a simple idea. A youth-oriented society with a clearly defined adolescent stage doesn't just alter the texture of teenage life. It also has more general effects on society as a whole, lending an adolescent coloration to society at large as people move forward to adulthood with their youthful ways more fully intact.

Stated this way, the theory clearly lends itself to a wider consideration of the effects of adolescent traits and values on modern society; for we are affected not only in our capacity as democratic citizens (though that is one interesting area to consider) but also in our roles as workers, consumers, friends, spouses, and more. In the next few chapters, we'll take stock of some of these facets of our lives and see how critical changes in the way we commonly think and act nowadays reflect the adolescent nature of today's society. We'll also stop to think about the good and the bad in these developments, asking whether we should be happy with the way our adolescent society is evolving, or whether—in some areas at least—we should be striving to temper our adolescent spirit and coaxing our inner adult to reemerge.

4

PROBLEMS OF THE PRESENT

To explore the many ways in which adolescent attributes have reshaped society over time, a natural place to turn is the research literature on adolescence. Spread across numerous disciplines, this is a sprawling field of study tackling the subject from many different angles. To try to get an initial handle on this, I enter "adolescent" or "adolescence" as search terms in *Psycinfo*, a comprehensive database of scholarly articles in the field of psychology. This produces a list of roughly 233,000 articles. Not having decades at my disposal to read through all this material, I scroll through the titles looking for general trends.

As I scan the first several hundred, two patterns emerge. One is that much of the focus is on the psychological dimension of problems faced by troubled adolescents—whether it's juvenile delinquency, depression, unplanned pregnancies, or the reckless use of drugs and alcohol. Considerably less research is conducted on the behavior or psychology of the average teenager. The second is that the research concentrates on the way adolescence impacts adolescents, rather than the way adolescence influences who we are as adults. Sometimes research on the troubled teen does adopt a longer perspective, recognizing that problems in the younger years can persist into adulthood. But when it comes to propensities of the "normal" adolescent, there is little effort to trace them forward. The assumption would seem to be that normal adolescents simply mature into normal adults, and there isn't much of a story in that.

It only becomes interesting when we consider that what it means to be a normal adult has changed down the years as a result of normal adolescent qualities slowly migrating upward into adulthood—a perspective that isn't well represented in the many volumes of research in the field and which underlies the analysis in the chapters that follow. Stated in terms of Big Five traits, the key changes include rising extroversion levels and openness to experience over time, along with the gradual ebbing of conscientiousness and agreeableness. These changes in personality traits are interwoven with notable trends in social values and lifestyle choices; we've grown more individualistic over time, putting less stock in established norms and greater emphasis on our own priorities and desires. We have become more disinhibited, impulsive, free-spirited, and adventurous.

These changes in basic character traits and their diverse consequences certainly haven't gone unnoticed—they just haven't typically been identified as reflections of the adolescent nature of today's society. There is no shortage of references in current social commentary to problems that have crept up on us over time and which appear to stem from the gradual erosion of traditional norms and practices of adulthood. Among the most commonly cited trends: we don't participate in politics or civic affairs the way we used to; we've become overly materialistic, hedonistic, and detached from the more meaningful aspects of our lives; our shared cultural life has been hollowed out and dumbed down; civility in personal relations and the public sphere has fallen by the wayside. Such laments are sometimes countered, rightly so, by noting that we have also left behind much of the rigidity and dogmatic thinking that characterized the adult world of the past. The adolescent society perspective casts these diverse trends in a new light by linking them to a common source of social change. In the next few chapters, we'll look at them one by one to gain a better appreciation of the wide-ranging impact of adolescent character and culture on today's society.[1]

The Brash and the Bold

While it may sound like the title of a melodramatic soap opera, "the brash and the bold" is instead meant as a pithy summation of the manner in which many people conduct themselves nowadays. Quintessentially adolescent traits connected to disinhibition and disregard for conventional norms have become endemic in the adult population.

Television does offer us a window into the phenomenon in the guise of those twenty-first-century soap operas known as reality TV. Programs like *Jersey Shore*, *Big Brother*, *The Apprentice*, and *The Real Housewives of Orange County* provide a window into the behavior of people from different walks of life in a variety of social settings. The principal talent of most of the participants in these shows is their willingness, in fact eagerness, to expose themselves publicly without restraint or embarrassment. They are people happy to bare all, emotionally or otherwise, for anonymous viewers at home to observe and enjoy. They are also, for the most part, happy to tangle with one another. The lack of inhibition that guides their personal conduct makes them all too willing to push their own agenda and speak their minds without concern for the social consequences. Insults and abuse fly freely between the participants, to the delight of the shows' producers and audiences everywhere.

Of course, all this usually takes place in an artificial environment, with the structure of the programs deliberately designed to promote friction by pitting people against one another in the pursuit of fame and fortune. Nevertheless, the basic tensions they pick up seem real enough. Rather than complete artifice, I tend to think of them as offering a concentrated distillation of a genuine problem: uncivil behavior and fractious relations in today's brash and bold society.

One person keenly aware of the broader problem was Pier Forni, professor of Italian literature at Johns Hopkins University until his passing in 2018. In 1997, Forni cofounded the Civility Initiative out of concern over the growing "coarseness" of American society. His writing and speeches on the topic earned him attention and accolades, as he put his finger on something about today's society that many of us find both grating and disturbing. Among Forni's examples of people failing to observe basic norms of civility are tailgating, hogging the armrest on airplanes, rudeness on internet chat rooms, and cell phone conversations at top volume in public spaces.[2] Near the top of my own list of minor yet maddening incivilities is when the person standing last in line at the grocery store quickly hops over as a new cash register opens up, seemingly unacquainted with the concept "next in line."

To address this situation, Forni believed we need to learn, or relearn, how to conduct ourselves with decorum and dignity in social situations. Proper manners are part of his prescription, and on Amazon.com his books on the topic can be found in the etiquette section of the site, alongside works on genteel behavior by Emily Post and Miss Manners. But it runs deeper than this. "Good manners and civility are not about which fork to choose for the salad," Forni observes. "They're how we treat one another in everyday life. And what's more important than that?"[3] The fundamental challenge, he believes, is to restore adherence to the core principles that underwrite civility in social relations: respect, restraint, and responsibility.[4]

The most obvious symptom of the problems Forni identifies is the multitude of inconsiderate acts that we encounter (and commit?) as we go about our daily lives. But it also is apparent in various trends that reveal a general fraying of social relations over the past number of decades. Our connections with friends, family, and acquaintances have been strained by the brash and cavalier manner that characterizes so many relationships nowadays.

One barometer of the changing tenor of personal connections is divorce rates. In the early 1900s, roughly one in nine marriages eventually ended in divorce; by the 1970s, this had climbed to nearly one in two.[5] The normal explanation for this dramatic rise in the rate of marital breakdown is a profound shift in cultural norms around divorce, coupled with the removal of legal restrictions on the practice. Once a social taboo, divorce is now a widely accepted and available option and therefore more readily contemplated by those suffering in unhappy marriages. But we also have to consider factors influencing the dynamics of martial relations for a fuller understanding of why people have trouble forming a stable lifelong bond nowadays. The connection between marriage partners suffers when civility in intimate relationships is lacking.

One columnist who writes frequently about personal relationships asks why "the last few generations found it so tough to maintain stable couplehood? Part of what happens, I think, is people forget their manners. Someday, I'd like to write a book called *Manners for Marriages*, in which I'd say we should treat our spouses better, not worse, than everyone else."[6] How we treat our significant others, in turn, is influenced by key personality traits. Researchers have found agreeableness and conscientiousness to be the most important personal qualities that ensure partners treat one another civilly and are able to prevent the conflicts that inevitably arise in close relationships from spiraling out of control.[7]

When marital problems do surface, they are often evident right from the start. This testimony comes from an anonymous poster at tackyweddings.com under the discussion topic "Wedding Cake Face Smashers": "On my wedding day, I fed my husband first . . . no cake face smashing. Then, my husband's turn . . . an entire piece violently smashed into my face, so much so that it actually hurt. I was embarrassed in front of my entire family and the money spent on my make-up for the day was a loss. Needless to say three years later we were divorced. I do think it is a sign of resentment. Why would you do something so hostile to someone you love? Be kind to each other."[8] A larger study comparing divorce rates among those who cake-smash on their wedding day and those who refrain from this novel practice has yet to be conducted, but I would be surprised if it didn't reveal a significant connection. The character traits that would lead people to act in this manner on the first day of their marriage don't seem particularly conducive to a harmonious, lasting partnership.

Other intimate relationships also appear to be suffering in our brash and bold society. A headline-making study from 2006 looked at the close personal connections of Americans by asking them to list the people with whom they had discussed matters important to them in the past six months.[9] The same question was asked on surveys conducted in 1985 and 2004, so the researchers were particularly interested in any changes taking place over the twenty-year period. The scale of the change took them by surprise: the average number of close confidants fell from just under three in 1985 (2.94) to just over two by 2004 (2.08). In 1985, 25 percent mentioned either no one or just one person in their network of close confidants; by 2004, this had jumped to 43 percent. As close ties have diminished, they also have become concentrated closer to home: more than half (53 percent) of those in the later survey had no one outside family with whom they discussed important matters.[10] We may interact with many people as we move about in our busy, interconnected world, but true intimacy, it would appear, is becoming less common.

Relationships at a greater remove, outside the circle of significant others and closest friends, have also been suffering. The most thorough documentation of these changes comes from Robert Putnam's extensive research in his much discussed book, *Bowling Alone*, published in the year 2000. A political scientist at Harvard University, Putnam believed that we can't really get a handle on how the political system is working (or not working) without examining the social setting in which politics is rooted. He set about assessing the condition of the American social terrain, looking at various ways in which Americans were socially connected, everything from volunteering to community clubs to participation in bowling leagues. On virtually every score, he found evidence of diminished social involvement over time, especially since the mid-1960s. This partly reflected people not joining organizations or taking on formal commitments the way they used to. But everyday, informal connections were also on the decline. Americans by the mid-1990s were spending substantially less time socializing with friends and neighbors—be it chatting over the fence or spending a casual evening together—than they had thirty or forty years earlier.[11] The changes were primarily rooted in generational change, as younger Americans scored lower on most of Putnam's measures of social engagement—a worrying trend, since it suggested the downward slide was likely to continue.

Not everyone was impressed or distressed by Putnam's findings, however, believing his analysis of social connections was mired in the past, focusing on older styles of interacting from a bygone era. Our grandparents might have belonged to a bowling league and had the neighbors over for meatloaf every fortnight, but people nowadays connect in different ways.

There is truth in this observation, but the changing ways in which we interact may also signal some decline in the quality of our connections. The ties we have now are often weaker, representing shallower and more fleeting relationships. The current hub, and perfect vehicle, for this new style of interaction is social media. The average Facebook user has 155 friends,[12] substantially more than the two people with whom the average person has discussed important matters in the past six months. With their other 153 "friends," the exchanges are presumably more lightweight. This would seem to capture Facebook fairly well—a virtual meeting place where people broadcast snippets they find interesting or amusing, alongside news of their daily activities. We might announce to our 153 Facebook-only friends where we're going for dinner or what we're having for dinner, but we don't actually invite them over for dinner. It is a form of indiscriminate sharing that is at one with the extroverted character of the adolescent society. It is also, in many cases, highly self-oriented sharing. Studies have found that the most avid Facebook users display narcissistic tendencies, seeking to place themselves at the center of a vast network of followers eager (in theory) to hear of their every move and thought. For these individuals, one researcher suggests, Facebook "offers a gateway for hundreds of shallow relationships and emotionally detached communication."[13]

It is a commonly observed paradox of the modern world: even as we grow more connected, we often feel more disconnected.[14] Another marker of this shift lies in our abstract feelings toward people in general. One finding from Putnam's work that caught particular attention was based on a question about general social trust asked on numerous surveys over the years: "Generally speaking would you say most people can be trusted, or that you cannot be too careful in dealing with people?" The numbers who think "most people" can be trusted have been steadily dropping since the early 1960s, falling from the mid–50 percent range to about the mid-30s. As with many of the changes that mark the rise of the adolescent society, dwindling trust is largely a result of the steady churn of generational change: younger cohorts are more likely to express distrusting attitudes, and as these cohorts have come to count for more of the population, overall trust levels have declined. The drop is all the more striking, given that those with more years of education under their belt tend to be more trusting.[15] Despite the higher education levels of younger generations, their trust levels are substantially lower.[16]

Putnam has a distinctive phrase to describe the tangible connections and abstract norms that knit people together: social capital. He likens social capital to sociological WD-40—an all-purpose lubricant that makes social mechanisms work more smoothly and efficiently—and laments its steady decline. His critics have mainly focused on the idea that new forms of social capital have taken the place of older ways of connecting, a viewpoint with which I would largely agree. People do still interact in myriad ways; it's not as if we've become social hermits. The main concern nowadays is with the quality rather than quantity of our social interactions. Connections with others have become more superficial and fractious, reflecting the brash and bold character that has become so common in our adolescent society.

Lyin' and Cheatin': The Rise of Antisocial Behavior

A lack of social trust does not, of course, simply signal disconnection from others. It also implies wariness about their motives and intentions. The question arises as to whether this sentiment is justified. Have there been widespread changes in behavior and attitudes that could support the view that people nowadays cannot generally be trusted?

Certainly, there are signs pointing in that direction. I was struck a few years back when I came across some results from a large national survey conducted in Canada in 2003. Respondents were asked if they felt it was ever justified to "lie in your own self-interest" and prompted to respond using a 1 to 5 scale, where 1 meant "it can never be justified" and 5 meant "it can always be justified." The wording was simple and transparent, offering no suggestion of lying for altruistic reasons or any kind of higher social purpose. This was a question about self-serving dishonesty, plain and simple.

It was the stark differences across age groups in response to this question that caught my attention. As figure 4.1 shows, the percentage who felt that self-serving lying can sometimes be justified—in other words, those who gave a response greater than 1—differed sharply across age categories, from a high of 65 percent among the youngest respondents to a low of 31 percent among the oldest. What

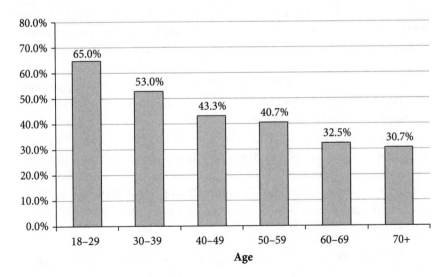

FIGURE 4.1 Is it OK to lie in your own self-interest? (Canada)
Source: General Social Survey, Cycle 17, 2003. N = 22,466.

is equally interesting is that the graph doesn't just show young adults and seniors taking strongly divergent positions. Adults across the full gamut of age groups vary substantially in their responses. Those in their sixties are a shade more likely than those in their seventies to allow that self-interested lying can sometimes be justified; those in their fifties and forties more likely still. The trend continues this way down the full range of ages until we reach the under-thirty category.

Are these differences a reflection of the aging process, or what are sometimes called life-cycle effects? That is, do people gradually become more scrupulous, more respectful of social norms with each passing decade of life? Perhaps. Yet at the same time, we normally tend to think that there comes a point in our adult lives when we develop strong convictions about such matters and hold firm in our views thereafter. If this is correct, at least part of the explanation for the variation across age groups must be generational change—that is, those born at later points in time developing laxer views on the importance of honesty in personal behavior and maintaining those attitudes as they grow older.

It later came to my attention that this same question about self-interested lying has been asked in other countries as part of the World Values Survey (WVS) and European Values Study (EVS). In both cases, the pattern of responses mirrors the Canadian result. In the 2008–2009 wave of the EVS, for example, 70 percent of European respondents under age thirty saw some justification for self-interested lying, compared to just 40 percent of those seventy-plus. In the United States back in 1990 (the last time the question appeared on the US World Values Survey) the respective figures for young and old on this same question were 59 percent and 31 percent. In both cases, age groups between the two endpoints were separated by small but steady gaps suggestive of steady generational slippage in adherence to this important social norm.[17]

The persistent response pattern across these surveys struck me as a possible canary in a coal mine—a signal of something potentially amiss that needed to be investigated further. The fact that the lying question, along with others in a similar vein, have appeared on different waves of the WVS and EVS allows for closer examination of these attitudes and how they have evolved over time within age groups and across generations. Four further questions tapping into what might be deemed antisocial dispositions have appeared on all waves of the studies. They ask respondents whether the following actions are ever justifiable:

- Cheating on taxes if you have a chance
- Someone accepting a bribe in the course of their duties
- Claiming government benefits to which you are not entitled
- Avoiding a fare on public transport

Like the question about self-serving lying, the principled response in each instance would be that the action is never justifiable—a response offered by a solid majority of respondents in most cases.[18] To say otherwise is to allow that people can sometimes skirt the rules, or even break the law, to suit their own purposes. Using these four questions, along with the original lying question, a simple additive index was created based on the number of actions that respondents felt were at least somewhat justifiable—a scale running from 0 to 5.[19] Those scoring 0 took the principled position in every instance that the action in question was never justifiable. Those scoring 5 saw at least some justification for lying, cheating on taxes, accepting bribes, wrongfully claiming government benefits, *and* skipping out on public transit fares—a fairly significant litany of crimes and misdemeanors.

Figure 4.2 shows the average scores on this 0–5 scale for respondents of different ages in the earliest (1981–1982) and most recently available (2008–2009) EVS studies for the European countries.[20] The arrows on the graph give us a sense of how much life-cycle change is contributing to the sharp differences across age

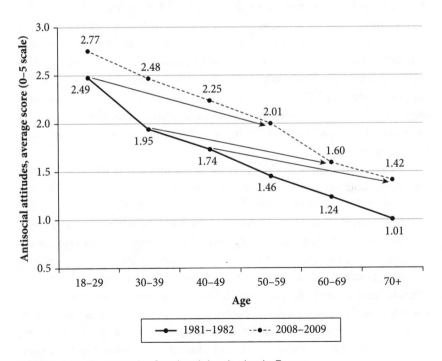

FIGURE 4.2 The growth of antisocial attitudes in Europe
Source: European Values Study, waves 1 and 4. N (wave 1) = 13,502. N (wave 4) = 15,791.

groups. These arrows trace particular age groups as they moved up the age ladder from 1981–1982 to 2008–2009. For example, the under-thirty group in the earlier survey would have formed the fifty to fifty-nine age category (roughly speaking) in the later survey.[21] For this group specifically, the aging process appeared to have a mitigating effect on antisocial attitudes: the 2.49 score from the early 1980s fell to 2.01 as the respondents reached their fifties in 2008–2009. But if antisocial attitudes were solely a function of the life-cycle—the process of getting older and, as a consequence, more mature, responsible, and mindful of social norms— we would have expected this number to fall further still, down to the level of the fifty to fifty-nine group from the early 1980s (1.46). The fact that the score fell only about half that much suggests there is also a generational dynamic at work; this explains why the young adults of the early 1980s showed stronger antisocial attitudes at later stages of life than those who came before them. A similar result is apparent for the other age categories traced over time by the arrows in figure 4.2. Their average scores on the antisocial attitudes scale certainly dropped over the thirty-year period, yet their scores from 2008–2009 remained substantially higher than those of their same-age counterparts from the early 1980s—again suggesting that both age and generation have some impact on these attitudes.

The same general result can be seen in the American data from the WVS shown in figure 4.3. (In this case, the five-item index of antisocial attitudes becomes a four-item index because the lying question has not been asked with the same regularity on the American WVS.) There is some decrease in average scores as the groups age from 1982 to 2011 but not as much as we would expect to see if life-cycle effects were the sole driver of these attitudes. (In fact, the forty to forty-nine group from 1982 shows no change as the respondents reach their seventies three decades later.)

All these results point toward the conclusion that antisocial attitudes are a function of both age and generation—in other words, tending to diminish with increasing age, yet growing more common among rising birth cohorts. To test this more closely, we can turn to more formal statistical methods, and in doing so draw upon all available waves of the WVS/EVS studies. Table 4.1 presents the key results of this analysis.[22] For the European countries (column 1), the results suggest a sizable life-cycle effect: average scores on the 0–5 antisocial index are estimated to decrease by 0.79 between the ages of eighteen and seventy, or nearly one full item. So young adults do become more mindful of social norms over the course of their adult lives. At the same time, however, rising cohorts exhibit increasing tolerance of antisocial behaviors, the effects growing stronger among more recent generations. Those born in the 1920s score 0.25 higher on the antisocial index than those born prior to 1920, for example, while those born in the 1970s through early 1990s score just over one full item higher.

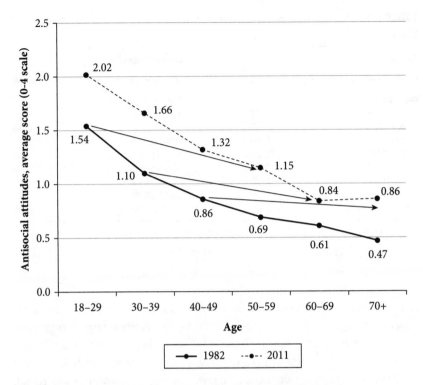

FIGURE 4.3 The growth of antisocial attitudes in the United States
Source: US World Values Survey, waves 1 and 6. N (wave 1) = 2,242. N (wave 6) = 2,165.

The same general pattern can be seen in the American results (column 2). Antisocial attitudes in the US follow a clear life-cycle trajectory, as average scores on the four-item index are estimated to decrease by 0.53 (half an item) between ages eighteen and seventy. But cohort effects are also substantial and date far back in time, ranging in size from 0.18 to 1.07.[23] These are comparable to the European results and confirm that there has been a steady growth in antisocial dispositions that began long ago, among cohorts born as early as the 1920s.

Using the WVS/EVS data sets to track attitudes over time reinforces what the initial Canadian finding had hinted at: that there has been a gradual rise in antisocial dispositions over the long haul due to changing mores and attitudes of successive birth cohorts. That this can be traced as far back as the 1920s lends credence to the idea that these changes can be connected to the impact of the adolescent experience on the character of rising generations. While it is impossible to provide definitive evidence of a cause-effect relationship for a social process that has unfolded over the better part of a century, there is a strong circumstantial

TABLE 4.1   Age, generation, and antisocial attitudes in Europe and the United States

Europe		United States	
Life-cycle effect (18 to 70):	−0.79	Life-cycle effect (18 to 70):	−0.53
Cohort effects		Cohort effects	
1920–1929	0.25	1920–1929	0.18
1930–1939	0.39	1930–1939	0.34
1940–1949	0.49	1940–1949	0.39
1950–1959	0.70	1950–1959	0.50
1960–1969	0.89	1960–1969	0.68
1970–1979	1.03	1970–1979	0.86
1980–1989	1.04	1980–1989	1.07
1990 and later	1.09	1990 and later	0.87

Sources: European Values Study, waves 1–4; US World Values Survey, waves 1–6.

N (Europe) = 58,877. N (US) = 10,045. Comparison cohort: pre-1920.

case to be made: core character traits and related social attitudes that are clearly elevated among adolescents have come to the fore in society at large over the time frame in which young people have started to spend key formative years subject to the powerful influence of peer socialization.[24] The brash and bold manner of adolescents, these results would suggest, has filtered upward to adulthood, contributing to a marked erosion in respect for basic social norms and, more generally, the intemperate quality of the current age.

The Erosion of Inner Restraint

If this is a sobering conclusion, one comforting caveat is that among the various antisocial actions queried on the EVS and WVS, it is the more minor transgressions that show the greatest increase in perceived justifiability over the thirty-year period from the early 1980s to around 2010. The number who considered it sometimes justifiable to avoid a fare on public transit, for example, jumped by 13 percentage points in Europe (from 34 percent to 47 percent) and 18 points in the United States (from 29 percent to 47 percent), while tolerance for wrongfully claiming a government benefit climbed by roughly 10 percentage points in both places, as did tolerance of self-interested lying in the European countries. The perceived justifiability of accepting a bribe and tax evasion, on the other hand, moved up by at most a few percentage points.[25]

The latter are, of course, more serious offenses, and as such are more likely to be held in check, both in the real world and in respondents' minds, by fear of detection and punishment. Tax evasion and bribery are felony offenses in most jurisdictions that can result in significant prison time. Avoiding a fare on public transit and wrongfully claiming a government benefit, on the other hand, are more likely to be treated as misdemeanors, punishable by a fine or perhaps just a stern warning for first-time offenders. And lying, of course, is only an unethical, not an unlawful, act.

Since fear of legal repercussions is weaker or nonexistent for the more minor transgressions, it follows that they are more prone to be influenced by the force of inner restraint. Inner restraint is partly a function of the social rules that we acknowledge as legitimate and important; respect for these principles, as we have seen, has been eroding among rising generations for some time now. Inner restraint is also, however, a function of personal traits that influence whether we actually adhere to the moral and social code we might recognize as valid in the abstract. The most important of those traits are those that influence the propensity to feel *guilt*, an emotional response researchers have been looking at more closely in the past few years. Feeling guilty is an unpleasant emotion that many of us would rather not experience; it was a key target of personal liberation movements of the 1960s that held that guilt was a largely pointless sentiment produced by restrictive ideas about right and wrong and oppressive authority structures. I would be among the first to admit it can be taken too far: for reasons I can't quite fathom, I always feel deeply guilt-ridden as I'm being interrogated at the Canada-US border crossing by an unsmiling agent behind mirrored sunglasses, even though I have nothing to declare or hide. But clearly if I were smuggling something, these feelings would not be out of place: in the right circumstances, guilt serves the valuable purpose of holding antisocial behavior in check. (Not coincidentally, the clinical version of the social phenomenon I am describing—antisocial personality disorder—includes "lack of remorse, as indicated by being indifferent to or rationalizing having hurt, mistreated, or stolen from another" among its official diagnostic criteria.)[26]

Guilt proneness, it turns out, is strongly linked to the personality traits of conscientiousness and agreeableness.[27] When these personality traits are in short supply, people are less apt to feel guilty and therefore less likely to adhere to established norms of social conduct.[28] As these traits have diminished among rising generations, the tendency to feel guilty has likewise eroded. Surveys that have directly probed the propensity to feel guilt in various social scenarios have indeed discovered that those in younger age categories are less inclined to express feelings of remorse or to indicate behavioral responses guided by guilt.[29]

The erosion of guilt mechanisms almost certainly plays a key role in one important example of unethical behavior: cheating. A number of investigations have suggested that we have been suffering from an epidemic of cheating in recent times. One place where this is an obvious concern is schools and universities. In the late 1960s, the proportion of American high school students who admitted to cheating on a test was 34 percent; twenty years later, this had doubled to 68 percent.[30] Similar results have been found at the postsecondary level: in the first large-scale study of the subject in 1963, 39 percent of university students sampled admitted to "serious test cheating." In a follow-up study in 1993, this had climbed to 64 percent.[31]

In seeking to understand the trend, researchers have sifted through various personality traits, with weak levels of conscientiousness and agreeableness, predictably enough, cropping up as consistent correlates of cheating behavior. But another trait that has been identified as highly relevant is narcissism, which has the perverse effect of making people feel *good* about themselves by cheating.[32] One group of researchers report, "We find that those who exploit opportunities to cheat on tests are likely to engage in self-deception, inferring that their elevated performance is a sign of intelligence. . . . Our findings show that people not only fail to judge themselves harshly for unethical behavior, but can even use the positive results of such behavior to see themselves as better than ever."[33]

A documentary program called *Faking the Grade* corroborates these findings. Exploring the cheating phenomenon from various angles, it includes testimony from individuals who are proud of themselves for designing clever ways to cheat on exams without being caught—changing the label on a soda bottle to include exam answers, for example, or writing cheat notes on a fully stretched elastic band that become indecipherable ink blobs when the band is slackened. The inventor of the second method posted a video to YouTube, sharing both his technique and philosophy of life with interested viewers. "Igor," who looks to be in his mid-twenties, has a smirk on his face as he smugly advises, "I did it for years, and no one ever caught me or came close to catching me. I would recommend you using it whenever possible to trick as many people as possible. . . . [Use] it for anything you want, cheat as much as you want. It'll only make you a better person." Wise words, apparently. When I last checked, the clip had more than 700,000 views, which no doubt has only added to Igor's plentiful self-esteem.[34]

If the education system is one place where the issue of cheating crops up, it is wrong to think that the problem is restricted to young people or that it magically disappears once they mature and absorb the social codes of the adult world. The adult world is itself rife with cheating, as the character traits that ensure people adhere to ethical standards have been steadily weakening. David Callahan, a senior fellow at the New York think tank Demos, and author of *The Cheating Culture*, says that "many young people feel that the way you get ahead is by cheating. Where do they get that idea from? They get that idea from watching the news. Seeing what's going on Wall Street, seeing what's going on in major league baseball and sports. In any sector of society where the adults are in charge,

PROBLEMS OF THE PRESENT   87

there seems to be a lot of cheating. So I think that a lot of young people believe that's the way the world works."[35] In recent times, the most famous example from the world of sports, Lance Armstrong, confessed his sins to Oprah on national television; but after years of his denials and attacks on those who knew the true story of his doping history, this act of contrition rang hollow. Experts in the field of psychology suggest that Armstrong showed all the signs of aggressive narcissism in both his initial cheating in cycling competition and his later efforts to cover his tracks with a tangled web of lies and counteraccusations.[36] Similarly, in the business world, the prevalence of cheating has come to our attention through high-profile scandals involving fraud and deception that have brought down major corporations and entire economies. The 2008 economic crisis was largely precipitated by Igor-esque bond traders engaging in the shady practice of bundling risky sub-prime mortgages and selling them to unwitting investors through opaque investment vehicles—lining their own pockets nicely and feeling quite pleased with themselves no doubt, even as millions lost their homes and life savings.

These various examples of antisocial behavior, both criminal and merely unethical, suggest a willingness to transgress social norms and boundaries for the sake of personal advantage and a capacity to do so without compunction or guilt—in certain cases to feel quite proud about doing so and successfully gaming the system. These kinds of attitudes and behaviors are clearly damaging to the social fabric and represent one of the more pernicious consequences of the ascension and diffusion of adolescent character traits over the course of time.

Connected Concerns

Most of us are not oblivious to all of this wrongdoing. We decry these trends and continue to punish the most egregious offenders (at least those who get caught). But we often fail to see how a series of problems—the decline in civility and the fraying of personal relationships, the waning of social trust, the rise of cheating and other antisocial behaviors—are of a piece, tied together by their common linkage to important character traits on the decline. Ethical behavior has its roots in traditional adult traits of conscientiousness and agreeableness and in the allied virtues of interpersonal conduct that Pier Forni believes underwrite a civil society: respect, restraint, and responsibility. These are in shorter supply nowadays, and we have witnessed the unfortunate consequences cropping up across many different spheres of our lives.

I'm hardly the first to lament this state of affairs. Others have arrived at similar disheartening conclusions. Nearly twenty years ago, psychologist Urie

Bronfenbrenner led a team of researchers from across the social science disciplines in taking stock of generational changes that were reshaping American society. Finding evidence of a "seismic shift . . . in the beliefs and values in this country," they concluded that there had been an "unravelling of the moral fabric" and a palpable sense that something was "terribly wrong."[37] More recently, journalist Dick Meyer offers a more impressionistic and personal exploration of similar territory in his bluntly titled book, *Why We Hate Us*. We hate us, Meyer believes, because we've become unbearably belligerent, boorish, and self-absorbed.[38]

Meyer paints a picture of a society that has gone astray, but his book's title implies we haven't completely lost our bearings. If "we hate us," we're clearly not oblivious to the problems we've created and realize that something is seriously amiss. But presumably this also means there should be a great deal of pressure and momentum for change. If we recognize the problems created by our brash and bold adolescent selves, why don't we try harder to curb these shortcomings for the sake of both individual betterment and collective renewal? The answer to this question involves taking wider stock of the diverse changes connected to the emergence of the adolescent society—chief among them the effects on personal choice and freedom that are the focus of the following chapter.

LIBERATING EFFECTS

Despite the evident frustrations that come with living in a brash and bold society, we soldier on—complaining about various irritants, wishing they would go away, but apparently not distressed enough to mount a powerful collective response. Why is this the case?

Part of the reason is that these features of the contemporary social landscape are so firmly rooted. The irksome patterns of behavior that have emerged in our adolescent-inspired era are not mere cultural or social "trends" that can be altered by promoting a new and improved trend. They are entrenched reflexes deriving from adolescent character traits and values deeply ingrained in us as individuals and as a society. Simply put, it's hard to change our stripes.

But there is another important barrier to change as well. The brash and bold manner of the current age reflects a more general loosening of social rules that has come with substantial benefits as well as costs. If some constraints of the past served a useful purpose, others were unduly restrictive. People in the past were needlessly stifled by arbitrary ideas about proper and appropriate conduct. The prevailing philosophy these days is that we should be free to do just as we please if it does no direct and evident harm to others.

In short, there are considerable liberating effects associated with the rise of adolescent traits and values. These must be acknowledged as one of the principal benefits of living in today's adolescent society. At the same time, there are areas of modern life where we can reasonably ask if these liberating effects have gone too far and whether our newfound freedoms might be put to better use if more closely harnessed to adult goals and sensibilities. In the analysis that follows, we

consider both the upside and the downside of the expansion of personal freedoms that is one of the hallmark features of the adolescent society.

Expanding Freedoms for All

The wide-ranging freedom of the current age has meant both liberation for ourselves and liberation for others. Freedom for ourselves means being permitted to
follow our own course in life, without the burden of social expectation and pressure. We can live our lives the way we wish, not in accordance with someone else's
plans, exploring options that would have been foreclosed to earlier generations.
The adolescent in us, with an open spirit and a thirst for all of life's potential
experiences and pleasures, revels in this state of affairs.

Freedom for others means they too can be true to themselves without fear of cen-
sure or abuse. Groups that have historically suffered discrimination and hostility—
racial and cultural minorities, the LGBTQ community—are accorded greater recognition and respect, given the opportunity to either follow their own path or to
integrate and participate in "mainstream" society on an equal footing with everyone else. Sociologist Michael Schudson is one observer who takes the position that
we shouldn't be too quick to yearn for a golden age of the past or to discount the
advances that have been achieved through ample doses of freedom and freethinking. The shift from a disciplined and orderly society to one that is more open and
liberated is, in his view, essentially "a trade-off between hierarchy and egalitarian-
ism, between authoritarian codes and democratic ones, between unitary, rigid ways
of living and pluralistic ones, between imposition and individual choice."[1]

As one of the more prominent social changes of the past number of decades,
the movement toward a more open, tolerant, and egalitarian society has been
analyzed from various angles and theoretical perspectives. One influential theory
within the social sciences connects increased tolerance to a growing preponder-
ance of "post-materialist" values among rising generations in the postwar era.
Pioneered by political scientist Ronald Inglehart in the early 1970s, the theory
maintains that core value orientations are shaped by the economic and political conditions prevailing during one's formative (pre-adult) years. Those who
grow up in times of economic hardship and/or warfare tend to place the greatest emphasis on material values of economic well-being and physical security.
For those who come of age in more propitious times—periods marked by economic prosperity and peace between nations—material and security concerns
recede in significance, and post-material values become more prominent. The
latter include such higher-order values as self-esteem, belonging, autonomy, and
self-actualization; recent work by Inglehart and his collaborators sometimes

summarize these as "self-expression" or "emancipative" values.[2] Post-materialists seek autonomy for themselves, but they are also sympathetic toward marginalized others pressing for enhanced recognition and acceptance. Hence post-material values are associated with tolerant dispositions and favorable attitudes toward groups that have suffered past discrimination and unequal treatment.

Throughout Inglehart's research, emphasis is placed on the leading role of postwar generations in ushering in a more tolerant society. As he notes in a recent summation of his work, "Although the older cohorts had experienced the slaughter and starvation of two World Wars and the Great Depression, the postwar birth cohorts in Western democracies grew up in prosperity, with welfare states reinforcing the feeling that survival was secure, during the longest period in history without war between the major powers. These differences between the formative experiences of the postwar birth cohorts and all older cohorts, produced major differences in their value priorities."[3] The change was not apparent immediately, however, as it took time for this value shift in the population to make its mark on events on the ground. Value differences "started to become evident only when the first post-war birth cohort became politically-relevant young adults two decades after World War II, contributing to the era of Student Protest in the late 1960s and 1970s."[4] Whereas earlier political movements had often focused on achieving economic equality and working conditions for the working class—that is to say, on material concerns—the 1960s and subsequent decades witnessed a proliferation of movements with the primary aim of achieving liberation, recognition, and equality for various marginalized groups: African Americans and other minorities, women, the LGBTQ community.

The 1960s were clearly a notable turning point in our social history, as movements pressing for greater acceptance and tolerance emerged with force, and postwar generations, especially the youth of the 1960s, stood on the front lines pressing for change. This should not, however, be taken as evidence that the underlying value change lending support to these movements only began with generations coming of age in the prosperous and peaceful postwar years. The survey record suggests instead that there was—that there had been—more gradual movement in favor of tolerant and accepting values since the early years of the twentieth century.

Evidence to this effect can be seen in figure 5.1 (a, b, and c), which draws on combined data from various waves of the US General Social Survey from the 1970s and 1980s. Over this period, the surveys posed a series of questions that spoke to attitudes of tolerance and equal acceptance of homosexuals (the survey's terminology), blacks, and women. The three figure 5.1 graphs respectively show the percentage in each birth cohort who consistently gave the tolerant or egalitarian response to each of the following sets of (paraphrased) questions:

- Gay rights: Should a man who admits to being a homosexual be allowed to make a speech in your community? To teach in a college or university? Should a book he wrote in favor of homosexuality be taken out of your public library?
- Racial equality: Do you think there should be laws against marriages between blacks and whites? Would you vote for a black man for president?
- Gender equality: Do you approve of a married woman earning money if she has a husband capable of supporting her? Do you agree that most men are better suited emotionally for politics than are most women? Do you agree that women should take care of running their homes and leave running the country up to men?

Results are consistent across the three graphs. While there is, on the one hand, support for the point that Inglehart and others emphasize—that those born after World War II tend, on the whole, to be more sympathetic than prewar generations in their attitudes toward marginalized groups in society—the graphs also clearly demonstrate that the shift toward greater tolerance and acceptance did not begin with those born after the war. The differences *between* prewar cohorts

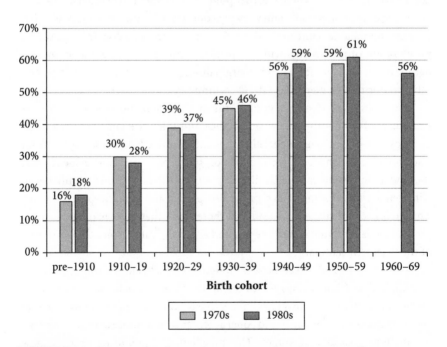

FIGURE 5.1A Tolerance and acceptance across American generations—gay rights
Source: General Social Survey. N (1970s) = 5,559. N (1980s) = 9,365.

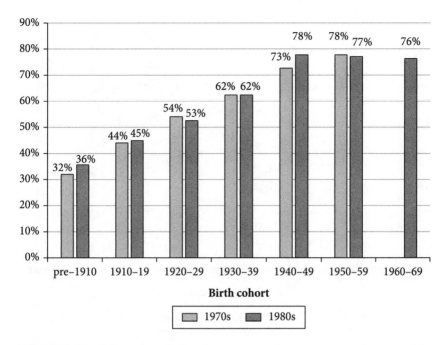

FIGURE 5.1B Tolerance and acceptance across American generations—racial equality

Source: General Social Survey. N (1970s) = 4,931. N (1980s) = 3,199.

are just as striking as the prewar/postwar gap. Focusing first on the 1970s data—the lighter bars on the left—we see that the cohort born prior to 1910 were the least accepting of gay rights and that those following immediately in their footsteps were increasingly willing to extend basic civil liberties regardless of sexual orientation. The percentage offering the tolerant response to all three questions climbs steadily from 16 percent to 30 percent to 39 percent to 45 percent across the pre–World War II birth cohorts. The same pattern holds true in the second graph, looking at attitudes toward African Americans.[5] Focusing again on the light-bar 1970s data, only a third (32 percent) of those born prior to 1910 were willing to vote for a black man for president and felt there should be no laws against marriages between blacks and whites; that percentage climbs steadily, reaching nearly two-thirds (62 percent) among those born in the 1930s. Finally, the 1970s data in the third graph show support for gender equality steadily increasing across these same prewar cohorts (from 17 percent to 41 percent).

The 1980s data—the darker bars on the right in each graph—offer evidence of another important point: that the differences across birth cohorts evident in the 1970s data did *not* reflect life-course effects. As each cohort aged by ten years

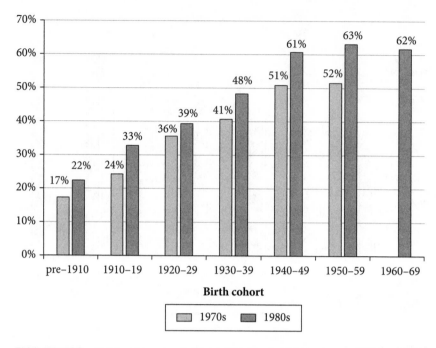

FIGURE 5.1C   Tolerance and acceptance across American generations—gender equality
Source: General Social Survey. N (1970s) = 4,838. N (1980s) = 6,828.

from the 1970s to 1980s, none exhibited a significant decline in tolerance in any of these three areas (as would be expected if tolerance were primarily a function of age). Instead, they more or less held steady at the same level of support from the prior decade, or, in the case of women's rights, showed modest increases. The stability in attitudes within birth cohorts from one decade to the next is consistent with a model of value formation—the same posited by post-materialist theory—in which these kinds of value orientations crystallize early in life and remain highly stable thereafter. If this is correct, we can use the GSS data from the 1970s and 1980s to look back in time and infer that generations who came of age just after World War I, during the 1920s and into the Great Depression of the 1930s, were substantially more tolerant than those born earlier. Their formative years were far from comfortable and secure, marked as they were by economic turbulence and the unsettled environment engendered by two world wars, yet they were slowly embracing a more open and tolerant outlook nonetheless.

If the post-materialist perspective misses something important by focusing attention too much on the postwar period, the same is true of other prominent theories seeking to explain rising tolerance over time, including those that emphasize the decisive influence of education.[6] The reasoning behind such theories is straightforward: education, which opens our eyes and expands our minds in many ways, is one of the strongest correlates of tolerant attitudes; this is why the populations of Western democracies have grown ever more tolerant as average education levels have increased steadily over time. There were, of course, two distinct waves of educational change in the twentieth century. The first involved the rapidly rising enrollments in secondary education after World War I that saw a large majority of teenagers attending high school by the eve of World War II. The second wave involved massive increases in postsecondary education after the war, for while university enrollments also grew in the earlier decades of the century—from 2 percent college enrollment among eighteen- to twenty-four-year-olds at the turn of the century to 9 percent by 1939—it was not until the 1950s and 1960s that they truly exploded. By 1969, the college enrollment rate in the United States had reached 35 percent, representing about eight million young people.[7]

It is this latter educational transformation, the postwar college boom, that tends to receive the greatest emphasis in studies of rising tolerance. This is partly because university education is thought to be especially enlightening, the curriculum focused less on rote learning and more on the type of open and critical thinking that causes people to challenge their entrenched preconceptions and biases. Notes one study on the topic: "College education in particular is thought to influence cognitive processes and introduce students to the importance of diversity, and thus encourage greater tolerance of out-groups. . . . College or university education fosters less dogmatic forms of cognition . . . and produces a shift in values that elevates the importance of diversity and tolerance."[8] But the emphasis on postsecondary education, as with post-materialist theory, is likely also influenced by timing. The surge in postsecondary enrollments came just as various social movements gathered steam in the 1960s, mobilizing politically and in the streets to demand legal and policy changes on behalf of various marginalized groups. As these movements won considerable success and social acceptance, it started to become clear that broader public attitudes had shifted markedly in favor of greater tolerance and equality for all.

Yet if the pattern of cohort effects from figure 5.1 suggests we should look further back in time to see when and why more tolerant social attitudes emerged, then greater attention really should be given to the first great wave of educational reform, the mass expansion in secondary education in the first half of the twentieth century. And in doing so, it is good to keep an open mind about the possible mechanisms whereby high school engenders attitudes of tolerance and acceptance. No doubt, the standard understanding of the effects of education is part of the story: a high school education broadens people's horizons (more so than primary schooling) and teaches students, in ways both direct and indirect, the value of diversity and the importance of tolerance and equality in a free and democratic society. The growing number of young citizens with high school diplomas who had absorbed tolerant values through their classroom learning was helping to produce significant changes in social attitudes among those coming of age in the 1920s and 1930s. But the social dimension of secondary schooling represents another important mechanism of change. Young people in the high school setting were subjected to unprecedented peer influence during their formative years, leading to the etching of adolescent dispositions conducive to greater tolerance and acceptance—in particular, openness to experience and an associated emphasis on respect for individual and group differences.

This perspective gains support from studies that have found a powerful connection between tolerance and core personality traits. In the early 1980s, a handful of political scientists started to incorporate measures of personality into their studies of political tolerance.[9] As this research continued, they started to draw upon the nascent Big Five framework to determine which personality traits had the strongest influence; their principal finding was that openness to experience is the most powerful personality correlate of attitudes reflecting social and political tolerance.[10] That same conclusion has come from leading researchers in the field of personality psychology. In a wide-ranging review of the social consequences of openness to experience, Robert McCrae writes, "If Openness is seen in the need for novelty, variety, and complexity and an intrinsic appreciation for experience, then Closedness to Experience (Closedness) is manifested in a preference for familiarity, simplicity, and closure. . . . Given these basic features of experiential style, it is clear that closed individuals will tend to draw sharp lines between in-group and out-group and prefer the former to the latter,"[11] whereas open individuals will resist such distinctions. As McCrae points out, such conclusions are consistent with the theoretical framework and empirical results of earlier studies that had focused on the origins of authoritarian attitudes. In the aftermath of World War II and the fascist experience, researchers developed models of what they called "the authoritarian personality" (the title of a seminal study from 1950) to help explain why some individuals exhibited high levels of dogmatism, conventionality, and hostility toward minority groups. While the older method of measuring the "authoritarian personality" (the F-scale, where F stood for fascist) has fallen by the wayside, the original idea that personality is a critical determinant of tolerant attitudes remains influential and persuasive.

Given this body of evidence, it follows that the social atmosphere of adolescence, where teenagers scoring relatively high on the trait of openness are freely exchanging ideas, feelings, and values with one another, would be conducive to the development—and reinforcement—of tolerant and open-minded disposi-tions. Young people influenced more by one another rather than by the prevail-ing rigidities of the adult world naturally come to acquire a different outlook on matters pertaining to social difference and diversity. As with many changes I am attributing to the social impact of adolescence, this trend appears to have started without much fanfare in the earlier years of the twentieth century, quietly incu-bating among rising birth cohorts first experiencing the powerful conditioning effects of peer socialization during adolescence. Consistent with this conclusion, one in-depth study of American youth in the interwar period notes that while they were on the whole "politically apathetic," their conversation "barren of social and political topics," they were nonetheless staunch cultural liberals who consis-tently "registered their strong opposition to attempts to control and repress . . . self-determination in behavior" owing to a "socialization process [that] stressed self-expression and personality."[12] The shift in personal and cultural preferences that quietly took hold among this generation set the stage for what would eventu-ally become a major social and political transformation in the postwar period.

For many, of course, this sea change in social attitudes is all to the good. It is one of the major achievements of the past century that we have become more accepting of people and practices once treated as anathema; great progress has been made, and we can now see a day in sight when all are treated equally without reference to any superficial differences of skin pigmentation, cultural background, or sexual orientation. We can also therefore appreciate why we are conflicted about the state of modern society and what I have characterized as the liberating influence of our adolescent character. If the ascent of adolescent qualities is largely responsible for the emergence of a brash and bold society marked by rising antisocial attitudes and attendant social problems, as argued in the previous chapter, it also is closely connected to the expansion of open-ness and greater acceptance of human difference and diversity. We may lament some of the consequences that have come from the loosening of social rules and the expansion of personal freedoms, but we have to recognize very important benefits as well. The adolescent society involves a mixed bag of gains and losses, which helps explain our willingness to accept the consequences of living in an era where brash and bold behavior often tests our patience.

Living for Today: Impulsive Behavior

Even as we acknowledge these important benefits, however, it's fair to ask further questions about the downside of opening the floodgates on personal freedom—not just for those sometimes affected by the kind of social unruliness described in the previous chapter, but also for those taking full advantage of the personal license we've come to enjoy. Without suggesting we need to roll back the clock and give back some of our cherished freedoms, we can reasonably ask whether they might be put to better use if guided by more adult sensibilities.

One concern is that the choices we make sometimes involve an element of recklessness and potential self-harm. As with other features of the adolescent society, there were earlier antecedents of this trend in some of the behaviors that became common among youth in the 1920s and 1930s: drinking, premarital sexual experimentation, and smoking (a long-standing habit among men, but a new vice for young women). Some of these "risky" behaviors seem fairly tame by today's standards, but it is important to remember that they were seen by many at the time as manifestations of rampant youth debauchery.[13] The 1960s is the decade when this kind of behavior ramped up to another level, as young people embraced the classical trio of sex, drugs, and rock 'n' roll. While partly a reflection of the rising penchant for personal exploration and alternative life-styles, this movement also reflected a continuing trend toward more impulsive and risky behavior. As the 1970s rolled around, souped-up versions of earlier vices were added to the mix, including more potent and addictive drugs (cocaine, heroin, crack cocaine), more promiscuous sexual practices, and more nihilistic and antisocial music (punk, grunge, and rap, or at least some variants thereof). Substantial risks came along with all this, among them sexual disease, unwanted pregnancies, and rising rates of substance addiction. The dangers of rock 'n' roll remain more uncertain, but certainly a high-octane lifestyle, if practiced too long and hard, can interfere with long-term goals of personal development and achievement.

This style of behaving has always manifested itself more conspicuously among youth, and some of the most blatant examples of impulsive and risky behavior remain more common to young people (for recent examples, have a look at YouTube videos on the cinnamon challenge, vodka eyeballing, and the Kylie Jenner lip challenge). But rising rates of subtler and more insidious forms of self-destructive behavior are apparent among older age groups. Public health officials were alarmed, for example, when a 2015 study by Princeton University research-ers revealed a significant jump in the mortality rate—more than 20 percent—among less-educated middle-aged white Americans between 1999 and 2013. No less alarming was the finding that this was primarily due to "increasing death rates from drug and alcohol poisonings, suicide, and chronic liver diseases and cirrhosis."[14]

Other examples also suggest an upward drift of impulsive and sometimes harmful adolescent proclivities that have come to influence decision making in the adult population. Part of what gives rise to impulsive behavior is an emphasis on immediate gratification: enjoy something now, pay the price later. This behavioral pattern crops up in various spheres of contemporary life. Some would suggest, for example, that a thirst for immediate gratification is the driving force behind today's rampant consumerism. In many cases, the products purchased are not needed or even much valued after a certain time; the main attraction is the "buzz" that comes from the purchase of a new TV, clothing item, or shiny home appliance. The downside, of course, is accumulated debt, which can be crippling for many. Immediate benefit from the exhilaration of consuming comes at the expense of long-term financial well-being.

The same emphasis on immediate gratification can be linked to other lifestyle choices common nowadays that are harmful to our personal welfare. Consider decisions we make about healthy living. It can seem sometimes that we are a health-obsessed society, considering the amount of attention given to the dangers of cholesterol, high fructose corn syrup, trans fats, and other unhealthful substances. But the reality on the ground suggests a lot of us are not giving much heed to these warnings. The most obvious indicator is our expanding waistlines. The obesity epidemic continues to spread, encompassing ever more of the population. A study published in the *American Journal of Preventive Medicine* in 2012 reported that as of 2007–2008, 33.8 percent of adult Americans were obese, a more than 100 percent increase since the late 1970s. The same study predicted that the obesity rate among American adults was on track to hit 42 percent by 2030.[15]

The causes of this problem are complex, including a food industry that hides all manner of unhealthy ingredients in its packaged products and a fast food industry with outlets on every corner tempting us with rock-bottom prices for a quick caloric infusion of dubious nutritional value. Problems with the modern food system are a major contributor to the obesity trend. But when researchers look at individual factors that contribute to weight problems, a consistent conclusion is that low levels of conscientiousness are an important influence. The less conscientious we are, the more impulsive we tend to be, placing reduced emphasis on order and self-discipline in our lives. We tend not to do the things conducive to maintaining a healthy weight, such as exhibiting dietary restraint, maintaining regular meal rhythms, or following exercise routines.[16] Lackadaisical attitudes toward personal health, coupled with an enabling food environment, have combined to produce an epidemic of inflating waistlines.

In addition to the desire for immediate gratification, the tendency to enjoy life's pleasures now and pay the potential price later is fueled by a willingness to accept risk—another attitudinal shift that can be linked to the influence of the adolescent mentality. Perhaps, people say to themselves, I won't be the one to suffer the consequences down the road from my current bad habits or overindulgence.[17] Survey results show a greater appetite for living on the edge among younger adults, the pattern again suggestive of a gradual generational trend. In the US World Values Survey in 2011, for example, Americans were asked whether they were the kind of person who "looks for adventure and likes to take risks." Precisely half of those under age forty concurred, compared to 33 percent of those forty to sixty, and 20 percent of those over age sixty.[18] Other studies indicate that this appetite for risk is closely connected to key personality traits; those who are conscientious and agreeable shy away from risk, while those extroverted and open are more prone to accept it.[19] Adolescent traits have made us more insensitive to risk and therefore willing to take a chance we can emerge unscathed from our current flirtation with harmful habits.

The general picture is of a society where more and more people put off thinking about the future in order to enjoy life to the fullest today. Caution and deferred gratification—forgoing pleasurable experiences now for the sake of later well-being—are hallmark behaviors of the conscientious individual. A desire for fulfillment in the present, coupled with a willingness to roll the dice on future consequences, is a quintessentially adolescent way of acting, one that has been gaining the upper hand as time wears on.

We All Just Wanna Have Fun

Another dubious feature of current ways of living, emerging from the fullest exercise of freedom by our untethered adolescent selves, is a tremendous emphasis on the lighter side of life. Just as the 2011 World Values Survey suggested an increasing appetite for risk among younger generations of Americans, it also pointed toward their growing attraction to the pleasure principle: 47 percent of those under age forty said they were the kind of person who likes to "have a good time" and "spoil oneself," compared to 29 percent of those forty to sixty, and 20 percent of those over age sixty. The widespread desire for simple, unadulterated fun—novelty, stimulation, excitement, and pleasure—is one of the more prominent and consequential features of today's adolescent society.

Popular culture, which occupies so much of people's time and attention these days, is very much geared toward these adolescent sensibilities. Hollywood movies, for example, have gradually come to be dominated by thrills, action, fantasy, and laughs—lightweight fare designed to divert and delight audiences. Writing some years back, Benjamin Barber pointed out that four of the five top-grossing films of 2004 fit this description: *Shrek 2*, *Spider-Man 2*, *Harry Potter and the Prisoner of Azkaban*, and *The Incredibles*.[20] Notionally geared toward the youth market, these Hollywood offerings were lapped up by fun-loving moviegoers of all ages in our adolescent society. When I checked the figures for 2017, the same was true. Four of the five top-grossing movies were kids' movies enjoyed by young and old alike: *Star Wars: The Last Jedi*, *Guardians of the Galaxy Vol. 2*, *Beauty and the Beast*, and *Despicable Me 3*. Films that make us think—involving deeper character development, more complex narratives, or serious real-world themes—do still get made, but they generally attract a smaller audience and struggle to compete.

In light of these trends and similar developments in other branches of the entertainment industry, concerns are often heard about the dumbing down of modern culture—not only do we want to have fun, we want to have mindless fun. The critics on this count are many and varied, as are their targets of scorn. Barber describes the changes he sees in Hollywood and elsewhere as representing the "infantilization" of our culture. Mark Bauerlein, professor at Emory University, believes that screen time is the chief culprit, blaming video games and the trivialities of social media for helping to create the "dumbest generation" ever.[21] Pulitzer prize–winning author Chris Hedges denounces the modern-day triumph of mindless spectacle, offering diverse examples, from professional wrestling to personal makeover shows, to Jerry Springer and his rambunctious guests. "We have transformed our culture into a vast replica of Pinocchio's Pleasure Island," Hedges writes, "where boys were lured with the promise of no school and endless fun. They were all, however, turned into donkeys—a symbol, in Italian culture, of ignorance and stupidity."[22]

There is no denying the vacuity of some of these examples of popular culture and their widespread popularity. However, modern popular culture is equally notable for its variety and diversity. For every TV show or video game that might be seen as simple-minded pap, there is another that is smart and original. Nor should it really surprise us that clever cultural fare continues to thrive in the adolescent society. While it might be tempting to draw a connection between the rising influence of adolescent qualities and the dumbing down of popular culture, the connection is tenuous—simply because deficient intellect is not among the characteristic qualities of adolescents. They are, as a group, as quick-witted and clever as the rest of us. The notion that adolescent qualities have infiltrated modern life refers more to sensibilities than smarts. Many of today's blockbuster films are juvenile in their broad strokes, yet filled with witty banter, subtle pop-cult allusions, and double-entendres that keep adults on their toes. A TV show like *Seinfeld* is another case in point—an undeniably clever show in its composition and writing, widely appreciated by many, yet quintessentially adolescent in its tone and attitude.

Rather than dumbing down, it is another issue relating to our adolescent desire to be endlessly entertained that is of greater concern and consequence. The more troubling transformation is the way in which entertainment values have invaded sectors of our life where they have no rightful place.

This issue was most eloquently addressed three decades ago by one of the leading sociologists of the past half century, Neil Postman, in his classic book, *Amusing Ourselves to Death*. Postman didn't have a problem with schlocky entertainment, of which there was plenty to enjoy at the time he was writing in the early 1980s. TV shows like *The A-Team* were as schlocky as they get, but they were, Postman assured us, "no threat to our public health."[23] The real concern, he suggested, was the way in which the entertainment expectation had come to be the norm in other important areas of our lives: politics, religion, education. The most successful churches, he noted, had learned to bring out the religious bells and whistles to pull in the crowds; those sticking closely to chapter and verse were the ones suffering from empty pews. The serious business of politics had been gradually transformed into a contest of charisma and showmanship. Educators had come to believe that learning must be fun, turning to technology and humor to liven up the classroom. In one of my classes a few years back, I described to my students an innovative political project where a group of randomly chosen citizens in one Canadian province were given the task of coming up with a new voting system through extensive deliberation and debate over a nine-month period. I showed them a video of this Citizens Assembly at work, thinking they might find it intriguing to see grassroots democracy in action. The immediate reaction of one student (more honest than most, I suppose) was that it all just looked "incredibly boring." It is difficult to penetrate to a more meaningful level of analysis when entertainment value is the immediate, and sometimes only, consideration in people's minds.

Postman had his own ideas about why this was happening, fingering television as the principal culprit. TV favors images over words and for that reason is better suited to the rapid-fire display of colorful pictures than to the presentation of complex thought. As the dominant medium of the past half century, TV has reshaped our tastes and sensibilities; we've come to expect all we encounter to be provided in the same kind of animated and colorful packaging that television offers. For my part, I don't see television reshaping so much as reinforcing prevailing sensibilities. At a point in time when people imbued with the adolescent spirit were increasingly on the lookout for fun and diversion, along came a medium extremely well suited to delivering it into their homes on a nightly basis. The allure of entertainment for younger generations had already been clearly revealed through their attraction to the big screen; they were far and away the most avid moviegoers throughout the 1920s and 1930s.[24] With the postwar introduction of the small screen, television became an important new entertainment vehicle, lending further momentum to currents of change already under way within the adolescent society.

The consequences, as Postman points out, have been significant. When the urge to be entertained crowds out the desire to be enlightened, our powers of reflection and discernment suffer. What is valuable and worthwhile comes to depend more on feeling than thought, even in domains where reason should prevail. The simplest of these emotional responses is pleasure: if it pleases me, it gets a thumbs up, if not, a thumbs down. This is fine as a metric for the entertainment world but is not a sensible gauge in other domains of adult life.

The comedian Stephen Colbert famously coined the term "truthiness" to describe this approach to judging arguments in the realm of public debate. Unlike the stodgy old idea of truth, truthiness is based less on factual accuracy or compelling reasoning, and more on how we feel about the presenter and the style of presentation. Veracity, logic, and evidence don't matter as much as whether an idea or proposal just feels right. It was, ironically enough, Colbert's entertaining way of making a serious point about the shallowness of public discourse—the only way, it sometimes seems, that ideas of any weight can be successfully conveyed in the current age.

As this way of thinking envelops more areas of public life, we become a society lacking in deliberative capacity—smart in many ways, but not particularly wise. Increasingly, we all just "wanna have fun" and not be weighed down by mundane matters of the adult world; our individual freedom to do as we please undermines our collective capacity to deliberate together. The degradation of serious discourse in places where it ought to prevail ranks high among the more harmful consequences of the rise of the adolescent society.

Generational Change: Adventure, Risk, Good Times, and Fun

In reviewing various features of today's society that reflect a blend of carefree attitudes and hedonistic values, it is apparent that there may be both generational changes and life-cycle effects at play—a pattern we have seen before and which represents the basic engine of change at the heart of the adolescent society. While it is true, for example, that risky behaviors seem to have become more prevalent among rising generations, it is also apparent that young people remain considerably more likely than older adults to engage in truly foolhardy conduct of the sort displayed in sundry YouTube videos. Likewise, if adults of all ages might consider going to see *The Avengers* at the local cineplex for a bit of lightweight entertainment, only those under a certain age are lining up to see it five times. The 2011 US World Values Survey data cited above cannot help us determine the relative significance of these two demographic influences, for while they reveal large age gaps at a particular moment in time—on questions connected to adventure, risk taking, and having a good time—we need to trace groups over time, as they grow older, to see if they become more subdued and restrained with the passing years or instead retain their exuberant, youthful dispositions. From there, we can then better determine the degree of generational change that has been taking place.[25]

Another large, international data set allows for this kind of analysis. The European Social Survey (ESS), carried out at two-year intervals in a wide range of countries since 2002, has consistently included the same two questions that have recently appeared on the World Values Survey—asking respondents whether they are the kind of person who seeks adventure and risk, and whether they are the type who likes to have a good time and spoil oneself—along with a third, asking respondents whether they are the kind of person who "seeks every chance to have fun" and to do pleasurable things.[26]

Figure 5.2 shows the average levels of concurrence with the three items in question for various age groups, using only the surveys from the beginning (2002) and end (2016) of the time series.[27] The arrows on the graph give a sense of how responses to the questions change as groups grow older; fourteen-year age bands are used so that each group from 2002 moves up to the next age category by 2016. As the graph clearly demonstrates, the youngest group from 2002, those eighteen to thirty-one,

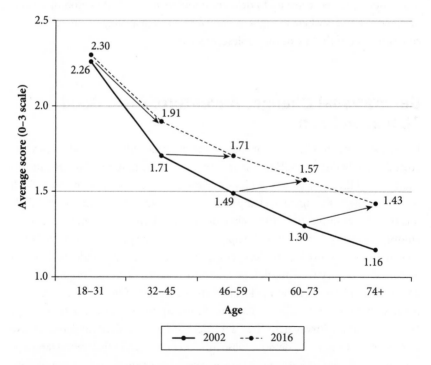

FIGURE 5.2   Fun and adventure on the rise among Europeans
Source: European Social Survey 2002 and 2016. N (2002) = 18,453. N (2016) = 18,781.

are less inclined as thirty-two- to forty-five-year-olds in 2016 to hanker after adventure, risk, fun, and good times; their average score on the three-point scale drops over the fourteen-year period from 2.26 to 1.91. This, however, still places them substantially higher on these measures than the thirty-two- to forty-five-year-olds of 2002 (1.71). Meanwhile, none of the older age groups from 2002 shows any signs of decreased scores as they move up an age category through to 2016. (In fact, the two oldest groups actually show slightly increased scores.) The simple summary, then, is that there appears to be a blend of life-cycle and cohort effects at work, with the life-cycle effect strongly concentrated at the younger end of the adult age spectrum.

As before, we need to use further statistical methods, based on all the survey data from 2002 to 2016, to put a finer point on these results (table 5.1). Using these techniques, the magnitude of the life-cycle effect from age eighteen to age seventy is estimated at −0.51—a decrease in average score across the three items of about half an item, reflecting a moderate diminishment in people's thirst for adventure, good times, and fun as they progress from youth to senior citizen. Meanwhile, cohort effects are also considerable and extend far back in time. Those born from 1930 to 1934 score 0.19 higher on the three-item index than those born prior to 1930; this cohort effect grows steadily larger with each successive cohort, reaching a value of 0.92 for those born in the 1990s.[28] Rising cohorts, this result would suggest, have been putting substantially greater emphasis on fun, good times, and adventure in their personal lives for a great many years.

TABLE 5.1 Age, generation, and the appetite for fun and adventure in Europe

Life-cycle effect (18 to 70):	−0.51
Cohort effects	
1930–1934	0.19
1935–1939	0.31
1940–1944	0.39
1945–1949	0.48
1950–1954	0.55
1955–1959	0.60
1960–1964	0.63
1965–1969	0.68
1970–1974	0.72
1975–1979	0.76
1980–1984	0.83
1985–1989	0.88
1990–1994	0.92
1995–1999	0.92

Source: European Social Survey, waves 1–8.

N = 147,703. Comparison cohort: pre-1930.

These findings add empirical backing to the presumptions embedded in earlier discussions in this chapter. Yes, the fact that young people are more carefree, risk taking, and hedonistic than older adults is partly a function of their stage of life, and such behaviors will almost certainly subside as they grow older. But there is more to it than this. There has also been a steady drift toward heightened emphasis on fun, adventure, and risk taking that began long ago and has been steadily growing over the course of time, driven principally by the shifting priorities and dispositions of rising generations.

Becoming an Adult in the Adolescent Society

Implicit in much of the above is some questioning of the degree of gravitas and maturity displayed by people nowadays. If we are brash, bold, impulsive, and wanting to be endlessly entertained, and if this represents the triumph of adolescent instincts over adult sensibilities, then the implication seems clear: we need to grow up.

This judgment on the adults of today, meaning all of us (in varying degrees), might strike some as overly critical and narrow-minded. There are undoubtedly substantial changes in how we live our lives and interact with others nowadays, but to label these as less than "adult" is a more debatable assertion. People will question whether we can really set timeless standards of what it means to be a grown-up. We can't judge people today against the norms and values of the past.

Yet certainly there is evidence of a different way in which people are not maturing at quite the same pace they used to. Young people moving out of their teenage years and into their twenties take significantly longer to reach milestones that have typically been seen as concrete markers of adulthood. These include finding a life partner, deciding on a career path, having children, and putting down roots in a community. Becoming an adult has come to be seen as a conscious decision rather than an inevitable transition, a shift in thinking reflected in the newly popular concept of "adulting"—a term sometimes used seriously, but other times facetiously, to describe the actions people purposefully undertake if and when they decide it is time to grow up.

Part of this delay and hesitation in assuming adult roles can be explained by the greater time now needed for life preparation. Staying in school longer is the most important factor and would have seemed the obvious explanation for delayed adulthood as university enrollments swelled in the 1960s and 1970s. But it has since become clear there is more to the story than this. Many young people now live at home with parents well beyond their graduation from university. Moving out for a period and then returning to the family nest has become a common pattern. And when young adults do leave for good, many choose to live alone for lengthy periods, avoiding other commitments of adult life apart from independent living.

Even when certain concrete milestones are attained, there is evidence nowadays of a reluctance to fully embrace adulthood. In one study, researchers Jennifer Lodi-Smith and Brent Roberts examined not just whether people had taken up certain adult roles but whether they felt psychologically committed to those roles—through workplace measures such as "supporting the beliefs and values of the organization, exerting effort for the organization, and wanting to continue to be a part of the organization," and through family measures such as "assessing knowledge of a child's friends, interests, and activities" or the amount of "energy and effort" put into their spousal relationship.[29] There was ample evidence that many who were parents or in the full-time workforce were not yet psychologically committed to these responsibilities. And this psychological dedication—feeling invested in work and family—was strongly linked to the personality traits of conscientiousness and agreeableness. With those traits on the decline in the adolescent society, young adults are increasingly resistant to fully embracing adult roles.

A different perspective on the trend of delayed adulthood comes from Jeffrey Arnett. Arnett is a psychologist who has found himself uncomfortable with disparaging assessments of young people taking their own sweet time to grow up. He sees the trend in a more positive light and gives this period of life a new label: "emerging adulthood." Rather than resistance to adult responsibilities, Arnett emphasizes the positive motivation of self-exploration as the reason for the delay. The search for a stable and secure sense of personal identity, which Erik Erikson told us was a fundamental feature of adolescence, now extends, Arnett suggests, beyond adolescence and into early adulthood. "Perhaps the most central feature of emerging adulthood," he explains, "is that it is the time when young people explore possibilities for their lives in a variety of areas, especially love and work. In the course of exploring . . . emerging adults clarify their identities, that is, they learn more about who they are and what they want out of life. Emerging adulthood offers the best opportunity for such self-exploration."[30]

Others remain much less sympathetic. The period Arnett calls emerging adulthood is given a more disparaging label by sociologist James Côté: arrested adulthood. In his examination of the lives of the young adults of today, Côté is struck by the many examples of antisocial behavior and narcissism that he feels point toward the "free-for-all, me-first undercurrent in the lives of . . . young adults."[31] Many, he believes, fail to develop any clear sense of life direction during these years, continuing to live only for the moment. Identity development takes shallow forms, focusing on "selecting the right wardrobe or developing slight affectations in speech, behavior, or appearance" rather than deeper forms of personal development involving "genuine intellectual and emotional growth."[32] Not everyone suffers from this failure to move toward what Côté sees as the essential psychological milestones of adulthood, but he does suggest it is a growing problem in today's society.

For their part, young adults aren't too concerned about these academic debates, and their actions and words suggest their resistance to the trappings of adulthood involves a blend of adolescent-inspired motivations. In a feature article on the trend of solo living among young adults in Canadian urban centers, for example, one thirty-seven-year-old single male in downtown Toronto describes his current life stage this way: "You can do what you want. You're on your own clock. It seems like a selfish thing to say, but it's indicative of our generation. Is it selfish, or on the road to self-actualization? What's the difference between the two?"[33]

While different authors put their own particular spin on things, Côté does offer one additional insight that many miss. He recognizes that this trend is not just a matter of young people pushing back the entry point to adulthood. It is a story involving all of us and the present-day murkiness of adulthood. He moves back and forth in his observations between young people failing to come of age in current times and adults at large failing to serve as effective role models. Many of the latter remain in what he calls a "half-adult" condition, retaining adolescent instincts and manners even as they grapple with adult roles and responsibilities.[34] If these are the people meant to guide the next generation, it is akin to the half-blind leading the blind. It's no surprise that young adults are having trouble navigating toward adulthood, or are indifferent to the very idea, when the route—and final destination—are so poorly marked by those who have gone before. We've reached a stage in the development of the adolescent society where adulthood itself has become increasingly opaque and ill-defined—a liberating state of affairs to a point, but one that can potentially leave people feeling unsettled as the years roll by and, in some cases at least, ultimately unfulfilled in their adult lives.

Taking Stock

An important consequence of the infusion of teenage sensibilities and spirit into the adult world has been a great expansion in personal liberties in virtually every aspect of our lives. This has, on the one hand, brought undeniable benefits, both personal and collective. We have the freedom to make our own choices, to live our lives as we see fit. We are obliging toward others, giving them the space to live authentic lives true to their own inner selves. No doubt about it: much better to live in an accommodating and tolerant society than one that is intolerant and severe in its judgment and regulation. The world is a better place for the displacement of many of the rigidities of the adult world by the flexible, fluid, and open instincts of youth.

At the same time, there are some significant downsides to consider. An unfortunate number of the personal choices we make in this age of liberation are impulsive and shortsighted. This includes decisions that have the effect of delaying adulthood and its attendant responsibilities, even, some would say, the development of a meaningful sense of adult identity. We may enjoy some fun and laughs along the way but may not be well served in the long run. And while many of us are wrapped up in these self-focused diversions and pursuits, our ability to work together as a society of reasoning adults is thrown into question.

I mentioned before journalist Dick Meyer's blunt assessment of the current state of society: that "we hate us" for what we've become. I think it's more accurate to say we are deeply conflicted. There are features of contemporary life that many of us detest, but there are others that we embrace, or at least enjoy. And this is a key part of the challenge to be overcome. It means recognizing and respecting some of the very important gains of the adolescent society, even as we try to address some of the negative consequences—that is to say, sorting out how we can continue to respect individual freedoms and to enjoy exercising them ourselves, while encouraging some reengagement with traditional adult norms and roles.

Speaking of reengagement, this concern is particularly relevant in the contemporary political arena. As we will see in the following chapter, our shared political life is one key area of common endeavor that has been much diminished over the course of time by adolescent-inflected behavior and attitudes—and where some adult-inspired reinvestment is sorely needed to get us back on track.

GOVERNING TOGETHER
Politicians, Citizens, and Democracy

If we face challenges nowadays working together as a society of reasoning adults, the problem is nowhere more apparent than in the political arena. Politics matters—or should matter—a great deal. Elected officials make weighty decisions on a regular basis: how much tax to collect, where to spend public funds, what areas of our lives to regulate and control, all the while debating and determining the appropriate balance to be struck between overarching values such as freedom, equality, and security. One way or another, these decisions affect each and every one of us, making politics one of the few areas of modern life that can truly be considered a common societal undertaking.

In theory we should all be attuned to what's happening in the world of politics and seek to contribute to the process where we can. Yet there are numerous problems with how the system works in practice and a strong sense of detachment felt by many. The adolescent character of both politicians and citizens, I would argue, is largely to blame.

Puerile Politicians

Politicians themselves must shoulder a good share of the responsibility for the problems plaguing democracy in so many countries these days. In Canada, the shortcomings of elected representatives are on full display during Question Period in the House of Commons. Meant to be an opportunity for debate between opposition members and the government of the day on the most pressing issues facing the nation, it has gradually deteriorated into a daily dustup that is something of a national embarrassment. In one incident, questions about pet food safety following revelations of poisoned food imported from China prompted members of the opposition party to start barking from the back-benches. A favorite tactic of MPs on the governing side is to offer a quotation supportive of their government's position and then ask who might have said it—several times with colleagues cheering them along. The entirely predictable punch line is to gleefully reveal that the quotation actually comes from a member on the opposite side.[1] The "debate" during Question Period, televised for all to see, largely consists of these kinds of facile exchanges and juvenile antics, ramped up by party members egging one another on. It's no wonder that calls to make parliamentary debate more civil and constructive are heard on a regular basis, though never actually heeded.

Where political power is more divided and dispersed than in Canada, the dysfunction of the political system often extends to policy formulation itself. In the United States, for example, Democrats and Republicans have dug in their heels on issue after issue in recent years, refusing to give concessions to the other side and making the articulation of common ground incredibly challenging. The politics we see played out in Congress is a mix of showmanship and brinkman-ship that too often fails to produce sound policy and has pushed the United States to the edge on numerous occasions. On October 1, 2013, the country went over the brink, as disputes over the implementation of Obamacare led to fail-ure to pass a necessary appropriations bill, triggering a sixteen-day government shutdown. An even longer shutdown occurred in early 2019, precipitated by dis-agreements over President Donald Trump's plans to build a Mexico-US border wall. Instead of governing with a program and a plan, it often seems as if we lurch from crisis to crisis.

Conflict and differences of opinion are a normal and natural part of politics. We don't all see eye to eye on every issue. To make decisions and move ahead, we have to hash out these differences and accept some compromises. But the way conflict is handled in politics today falls far short of how we might expect sober and mature adults to act. The basic principles of civility—respect, restraint, and responsibility—are sorely lacking.

One former party leader in Canada, Michael Ignatieff, got it right when he observed in a speech delivered at Stanford University in 2012 that politicians used to see their political opposites as adversaries, but now view them as ene-mies.[2] Ignatieff should know. He and his Liberal Party were soundly thrashed in the 2011 Canadian election after being roundly trashed in a slew of TV ads spon-sored by the governing Conservative Party. These relentless attacks said nothing about the policies of either party; their sole purpose was to cast aspersions on

Ignatieff's personal integrity, which they apparently did quite effectively, judging by the election results. Battered and beaten, Ignatieff resigned from political life shortly thereafter.

In short: the character of our politics is very much affected by the character of our politicians, the character of politicians an unfortunate reflection of the times in which we live. To say this is to emphasize the personal dimension of the polarization in politics that has afflicted many countries in recent years. Ideological difference may be partly responsible, but current divisions on that front don't seem exceptional in the historical scheme of things. In many countries, those on the left have steadily yielded ground to the right on issues relating to government largesse and the welfare state, as a shift toward lower taxes and less generous social benefits has been the trend in most countries since the 1980s. In the years since 9/11, there has been considerable bipartisan agreement in many countries on core security issues and key measures to fight the "war on terror." Meanwhile, the right has conceded ground over the years on the left's agenda of equal rights for all and greater tolerance of diversity—resisting along the way, to be sure, but for the most part now acknowledging and accepting key gains made by women, minorities, and other traditionally disadvantaged groups.

This is not to deny important political differences on current issues, ranging from immigration policy to debt and deficit issues to greenhouse gas emissions; but it is to question whether these differences are really starker than at points past. The comportment of politicians, on the other hand, seems clearly to have deteriorated. Matters reached a new low in the United States during the 2016 election season when Republican candidates Trump and Marco Rubio exchanged juvenile barbs about small hands and excessive perspiration, while invoking the schoolyard-inspired "he did it first" defense—a clear example of what Alan Wolfe has recently described as the "politics of petulance."[3] When opponents belittle one another and are deeply abrasive, resentment and anger naturally build. Politicians are only human, after all. The polarized politics of today reflects this personal enmity as much as it does profound ideological difference.

Since Trump has taken office we have discovered that there were still further depths of bad behavior to plumb. The forty-fifth president could easily occupy a chapter all his own in a book about adolescent attitudes and conduct common among contemporary adults. Many commentators have picked up on this theme, seeing Trump's words and actions as more befitting of a petulant adolescent than a mature leader and statesperson. Writing in the *New York Times* in support of this idea, David Brooks cites several quintessentially adolescent predilections: Trump's impulsiveness and attendant inability to concentrate on serious matters (such as governing the country of which he is president); his deep-seated need for the approval of others and consequent tendency to wildly inflate his own abilities and accomplishments; his inability to put himself in the shoes or minds of others, leading to an acute lack of self-awareness about how he is perceived as he stumbles from one blunder to the next.[4] One could almost feel sorry for Trump, were it not for the other adolescent proclivities he displays in spades: the bullying, the attacking, the unchecked anger—the kind of storm-and-stress behavior that sometimes gives teenagers a bad name.

The intemperate behavior and incivility that mark contemporary political life, nowhere more so at present than in the highest office in the United States, are joined by another problematic trend reflecting wider developments in our adolescent society. Politicians, despite their role as chief overseers of the public good, all too often engage in various kinds of antisocial and unethical behavior. There are, of course, the sex scandals and financial breaches that come to the surface from time to time. Many will say this is as old as politics itself and that if these misdeeds seem more prevalent in current times, it is only because the media nowadays are so quick to pounce on any wrongdoing. A more pervasive problem, and the most basic form of antisocial behavior, is that elected representatives too often focus on their own self-interest at the expense of the public good. Again Donald Trump provides ample evidence of the problem, as he has spent much of his time in office occupied with his own interests—maintaining his business empire, keeping the Russia investigation at bay, burnishing his ego at every opportunity—at the expense of larger public concerns. For other elected officials, self-interest typically means that their actions are primarily guided by the overarching imperative of getting elected and then reelected, thereby retaining the power, prestige, and perks of elected office. In the United States, where money is critical to winning elections, this entails courting financial backers and catering to their interests in political decision making; for Republicans specifically, it means kowtowing to Donald Trump even when he says and does egregious things. In places like Canada, where party leaders exert ironclad control over the political careers of junior members, deciding who is allowed into the inner circle of power and who remains on the fringes, self-interest means accepting party discipline without a peep—voting as the party leader dictates even when conscience, constituent opinion, or common sense might suggest a different course of action.

Some of these are practices with a longer history, but the dominant sense is that self-interest has gradually become the primary motivation for politicians in our day, while the public interest is habitually pushed to the side. When the supposed stewards of our democracy treat one another uncivilly and are guided in their political pursuits by their own self-focused agenda, frustration naturally builds. The current state of politics falls squarely into the category of "why we hate us" problems: nobody seems to like how the political system—*our* political system—works these days, but we can't seem to come up with any viable solutions to fix it.

Disengaged Voters

How do citizens react to this state of affairs? Clearly, many are dismayed and dispirited. A connection is often drawn to the decline in voter turnout that has occurred in so many places, based on the reasonable assumption that people are less likely to participate in a process they find objectionable. Certainly it is true that elections in the United States, Canada, Britain, and other long-established democracies have seen a gradual decline in the number of people showing up at the polls at election time.

But there is more to the story of turnout decline than political discontent. In most places, distaste for politicians and politics is widespread, cutting across social and demographic categories. But declining turnout in those same places is more sharply defined—older generations are voting as much as ever, but younger generations are staying away from the voting booth in droves.[5] So it's not just the system, but citizens themselves, especially newer generations, who are changing in ways that work against participation in elections. And this may, in fact, be part of the problem with the political system. When people are not actively engaged, keeping a watchful eye and standing ready to vote against those undermining the public interest, politicians have a freer hand to engage in mischief and malfeasance without facing significant consequences.

The changes giving rise to this generational disengagement from politics can be described in different ways. But at the most fundamental level, they reflect changing norms and practices of citizenship driven by the ascendance of adolescent character traits and values.

Consider participation in elections. Newer generations fail to vote in part because their democratic values differ from those of older generations. When asked whether they see voting as a duty, for example, younger generations—in just about any country where the question has been asked—are less likely to agree. In Canada, for example, a survey after the 2011 federal election asked people whether voting was a duty or a choice. Three-quarters of those sixty and over said it was a duty, compared to just over half (52 percent) of those under age thirty.

However, the decline in voter participation is not just a reflection of diminished commitment to civic principle. It is equally a function of a personality less exercised about sticking to principle. Political surveys have only more recently started to probe this part of the equation. The same 2011 Canadian survey that identified low levels of civic duty among young Canadians found that 42 percent of those sixty and over would feel "very guilty" if they did not vote, compared to just 16 percent of those under age thirty. Even among young people who say they believe voting is a duty, only a quarter say they would feel very guilty for failing to vote.[6] In other words, younger generations are less likely to be inwardly troubled when they fail to live up to principles they themselves acknowledge to be legitimate in the abstract.

We can go further down this road of linking adolescent character traits and declining involvement in politics by looking at other results emerging from recent research on voter turnout. Two leading researchers, James Fowler and Cindy Kam, start from a premise that has informed voting research for many decades: looking beyond feelings of civic duty, there can also be a basic cost-benefit calculation that individuals make in deciding whether to vote. Is it worth the time and effort to get out to the polls for any contribution my vote might make to the outcome of the election? They then offer a new twist on this old idea by inviting us to think about what this cost-benefit calculation might mean for people of different temperaments:

> Several empirical studies suggest that voter turnout is influenced by the costs of processing information and going to the polls, and the policy benefits associated with the outcome of the election. . . . However, none of these studies considers the fact that the costs and benefits of turning out to vote are borne at different times. The costs of voting are paid on or before Election Day, while policy benefits may not materialize until several days, months, or even years after Election Day. If an individual must bear the costs of participation long before the benefits are received, then an individual's level of patience should also affect the decision to turn out. Patient individuals—that is, those who place greater value on the future benefits of participation—should be more likely to vote, while impatient individuals, who place greater value on the immediate costs of participation, should be less likely to vote.[7]

Fowler and Kam tested their theory by first measuring how patient people were. They asked their research subjects to choose between two potential prize options: a $100 prize that would be received in thirty days, or slightly larger prizes of varying amounts that would be received in sixty days. Those who opted for the more immediate gain were deemed to be less patient individuals. The political connection lies in the fact that those same immediate-gain individuals were substantially less likely than the other research subjects to have voted in a recent primary election. The potential linkage to turnout decline in our adolescent society is clear: for citizens of today, more impatient and impulsive in character and therefore demanding of immediate benefit, voting has become a less worthwhile form of political participation.

Another problem arising from the spread of adolescent proclivities is that many people are in no position to vote, because they know virtually nothing about politics and public affairs. Levels of knowledge about politics, as revealed through surveys that administer mini-civics quizzes to citizens, are abysmal, especially among younger citizens. In a November 2010 poll by the Pew Research Center, fewer than half the respondents (46 percent)—and barely a quarter of those under age thirty—were able to recall the result of recent midterm elections (that the Republicans had gained control of the House of Representatives but not the Senate).[8] In another study reported in *Newsweek* in 2011, it was discovered that the average respondent believed the federal government spends 27 percent of its budget on foreign aid—just a shade over the true value of less than 1 percent![9] It's no better in Canada, where a 2011 poll revealed that barely half (53 percent) of those under age thirty could identify the premier of their province, an officeholder who should be familiar to any citizen paying the least bit of attention to what is going on in politics.[10]

Knowledge of these basic political facts tracks closely with news media consumption habits, which have been steadily eroding for several decades. If we go back far enough, we can find a time when most people read the newspaper on a daily basis. When television came along in the 1950s, newspaper reading took a hit, but most who stopped reading the news at least tuned in to watch Walter Cronkite and other authoritative voices delivering the news of the day on TV each evening. Gradually, however, this audience diminished as well, and now regular news followers are in the minority, most of them sporting more than a touch of gray. Many younger adults might skim the headlines on the internet, but do not engage with politics and current events in any depth. People who know little about politics represent a growing part of the population, a surprising trend in a society where levels of formal education have been steadily rising.[11]

People attribute this knowledge deficit and seeming indifference to the news of the day to various shortcomings. Some think there is inadequate teaching of civics in schools, which may be true, but this doesn't really explain why many adults pay so little attention to what is happening in the world around them in the here and now. Others feel the brave new world of electronic media and gadgetry is to blame, providing people with so many riveting diversions (Angry Birds, Candy Crush Saga) that they have little time left over for keeping up with the news. But the timing for this explanation is off, since the erosion in news reading and news viewing is not something that coincides with the advent of our wired world but instead dates back several decades.

The explanation I favor is simpler and more direct: people don't keep up with news because we live in a society where there is a sharp preference for the frivolous and entertaining over the serious and mundane. Unless there is some compelling reason for giving attention to something that is not intrinsically enjoyable or relevant to one's own interests, people typically don't bother. This has long been true of adolescents, inclined to focus on the lighter side of life and issues of relevance in their immediate social setting—but it has, like so many other adolescent proclivities, slowly migrated upward to much of the population at large.

It is worth quoting again from the Elmtown study of adolescent life from the early 1940s and what it had to say about the news consumption habits of American teens at a time when reading newspapers was the widely accepted norm and stories about the war in Europe should presumably have provided compelling, if sobering, reading for all interested citizens:

> The front page of *The Bugle* is scanned hastily, the reader often reads nothing more than the headlines and local news of personal interest, but the comic page is read carefully. To be well informed, a high school boy has to know the standing of the major league baseball teams in the summer and fall, the major college teams in October and November, and the basketball scores in January and February. . . . Girls read the women's page and the society column with almost as much relish as the boys read the sports page. Their concern is focused upon clothes, cosmetics, hair styles [and] publicity on motion picture stars.[12]

These 1940s teenagers were not distracted from world events because of iPads, smartphones, Facebook, and Instagram. They were distracted because they were teenagers living in an adolescent social cocoon where they were free to follow their own natural impulses to focus on the lighter side of life and educate themselves about "important" developments accordingly.

As with other adolescent behaviors, inattention to the serious world of politics and world events is not so troubling in itself but has become problematic as it has gradually drifted upward from teenagers to older age categories as the adolescent society has evolved over time. When adults don't pay attention to adult matters, it represents a major problem for democracy. The failure of many citizens to maintain a basic level of what one author calls "civic literacy"[13] is strongly connected to low voting rates: one study found turnout in presidential elections to be just over 20 percent among those at the bottom end of the civic literacy spectrum, compared to nearly 90 percent for those at the top end.[14] And increasingly the problem is not simply that people fail to vote from time to time, but that they drop out of electoral politics altogether. The percentage who never vote has been steadily growing and now represents, in Canada at least, roughly one-third of younger citizens.[15] The premium placed on entertaining diversions leads many people in the adolescent society not just to tune out intermittently but to ignore politics altogether.

For those who do still turn up at the polling booth, the penchant for entertainment has pernicious consequences of another sort. It influences how they look upon politics and elections—as a form of spectacle and competition rather than serious deliberation and public choice. Again, the blame for this trend is often pinned elsewhere: on a media that likes to emphasize the horse race dimension of campaigns, or on politicians who prefer to keep it light, hoping to win their way to power with a wink and a winning smile. But many voters lap up this style of politics, treating elections as spectacle and allowing sentiment as much as reason to influence how they vote. This same downgrading likely contributes to our willingness to tolerate bad behavior on the part of politicians; like the fights in professional hockey, the barbs and insults are treated as part of the game, in fact the most entertaining part for at least some of the fans. Instead of getting angry, we just shake our heads at their shenanigans.

Selecting who will govern us through democratic elections is a preeminently adult activity that used to be taken more seriously. People were motivated in part by a widespread belief in their civic duty to vote and character dispositions that made them feel guilty if they failed to live up to that obligation. Voting was also undertaken with a view to the long-term consequences of electoral decisions and was facilitated by broad awareness among citizens of public policy issues and political leaders. Now many don't participate, too impatient to be bothered with electoral politics or distracted by more personally engaging matters. Or if they do vote, they take the election process casually, treating it as sideshow spectacle. Individuals imbued with adolescent qualities are lightweight citizens, failing to provide the necessary grounding and steadying influence to keep our politicians and political system on track.

Popular Agitation

It's an exaggeration, of course, to suggest that everyone is turning away from politics these days or doesn't take it seriously enough. In addition to those who do still vote consistently and thoughtfully, there are pockets of active and engaged citizens who seek to take further action that they hope will lead to change on the issues they care about. There are many ways to do this, but those who do participate beyond the ballot box often do so in forceful and adamant ways. One of the signature trends of political life over the past several decades has been the rise of protest politics. Instead of expressing grievances quietly through traditional political channels—contacting an elected representative, attending a local meeting, working for a political party—many people prefer more direct action: demonstrations and marches, petitions and sit-ins. They rally and march, wave signs and shout, and generally kick up a stink as they seek to instigate change.

Grassroots mobilization and protest have been a part of politics throughout history, overthrowing kings and dictators, sending oppressors to the guillotine, bringing corrupt regimes to heel. But in our day and age, this activity is less an occasional eruption and more a constant rumble. There is a strong generational wave to this development, as protest politics took off with young people in the 1960s and has only expanded further as new generations have come along with their own set of issues to rally around—globalization, environmental concerns, human rights, and so on.

The turn to protest politics partly stems from the goals people are seeking to achieve. In the minds of protesters, the issues they care about are being ignored by the powers that be and won't be properly addressed unless they are given a forceful airing. Working quietly behind the scenes to achieve change isn't a viable option. But the direct style of politics also has a lot to do with protesters themselves, their personality and character, and again it is fair to characterize these as reflections of an ascendant adolescent temperament.

The connection between character traits and political protest would have been difficult to make just a few years ago because political scientists have traditionally paid little attention to personality traits when investigating factors that influence how and why people become involved in politics. But as the Big Five typology has gained wider currency, political scientists have jumped on the bandwagon and are now revisiting a lot of old ideas as they take a look at connections between personality and political participation. Their research helps us see why protest politics would become a more popular option among an increasingly "adolescent" citizenry.

One relevant finding is that it is the extroverted among us who are most likely to engage in political activities that involve interacting in large groups. This includes both traditional forms of engagement, such as attending campaign meetings and rallies at election time—in one study, extroverts were six times more likely to have attended such an event[16]—as well as protests, marches, demonstrations, and the like. Being in a noisy crowd with enthusiastic others is something that appeals to those who are energized by this kind of social interaction and stimulation. As would be expected, the effect of extroversion on political participation diminishes for actions that are done solo, such as voting.[17] The essence of protest politics, however, is to organize and mobilize collectively, and therefore extroversion is an important personal quality that aids and abets this kind of grassroots political activism.

A second personality trait conducive to political activity of this sort is openness. In general, openness implies amenability to that which is new and different; in the political realm, this translates into a willingness to consider initiatives that disrupt the status quo, including policies designed to bring about greater equality in society—in other words, a liberal and progressive political agenda.[18] One key example we saw in chapter 5 is that openness has been strongly and consistently linked to attitudes of social equality and political tolerance; those who are open in temperament tend to look favorably on marginalized, outsider groups and to be sympathetic to their concerns and claims for redress. Since the issues taken up through protest politics often are liberal causes that involve challenging the status quo in favor of inclusion and equality, it is not surprising to see these kinds of movements flourish as openness has emerged as a more prominent character trait in today's society.

As political activists seek to disrupt the status quo, however, things can become heated, especially when the methods used are highly confrontational and disruptive. And so a third important result from recent research on personality and politics is that high levels of agreeableness (and in some studies conscientiousness) tend to discourage personal involvement in contentious political action, while low levels work in favor.[19] One scholar whose work builds on the premise that political involvement is as much a social act as a political one offers this insightful observation: "So long as people do not care about offending others or provoking heated discussion in their social environments, or about differentiating and potentially distancing themselves from others, then passionate political participation can thrive."[20] But, of course, many people do care about giving offense in these ways. Such individuals simply aren't comfortable participating in "passionate" actions that lay bare their political sentiments or that cast them in the role of hostile opponents. It is only those not hamstrung by such hesitation who are likely to take to the streets.

One important example of impassioned protest in recent times is the Occupy movement. Starting in September 2011, people protested for months against rising economic inequality, made all the more glaring by the financial collapse of 2008, by occupying public spaces throughout North American cities and other urban centers around the world. This was definitely in-your-face protest; camping out in parks and town squares for extended periods was a highly visible action that attracted a great deal of public attention and upset daily routines. While the main motivation for taking part was presumably caring about the issue of inequality, the tactics employed meant that participation was also favored by having a thick skin—the capacity to remain unperturbed about breaking with social norms or enduring dirty stares from people who could no longer use their favorite park to walk Fido. The same was true of another movement around the same time that attracted wide attention, the months-long student protests in Quebec in 2012 to oppose tuition fee increases in the province. Taking place just after the Arab Spring uprisings, the protests in Quebec were dubbed the Érable (maple) Spring. The demonstrators again were strident and noisy in their tactics, as they took to marching in their underwear and banging pots and pans as they paraded through the streets of Montreal bringing attention to their concerns. These unorthodox tactics were certainly not ones that would sit well with someone anxious to be an agreeable citizen conforming to social expectations.

To observe that there is a confrontational mind-set and style behind certain political actions is not to suggest that we should think poorly of such efforts. Those who feel the cause being pursued through such means is just—be it fighting inequality, stopping environmental degradation, or championing minority rights—would certainly see great merit in protest politics. Instead of being deferential and acquiescent, these brash and bold citizens are not shy about standing up for what is right.[21]

One important example of forceful contributions from those on the front lines of political protest involves the fight for civil rights in the American South in the 1950s and 1960s. In this period, legal victories alone were not enough; to make equal rights for African Americans a reality, it was necessary for some individuals to insert themselves into places where they had a legal right to be— desegregated schools, buses, and lunch counters—yet faced harassment and intimidation nonetheless. One study captures the character of these often young protagonists with the observation that "the civil rights movement depended on *aggressive, adventuresome* teenagers to make legal victories a practical reality in the South." Not everyone was so inclined, the same study notes: "'They were brave kids,' a woman who remembered the struggle said . . . 'I knew the kind of personality I had. . . . I would not [have been] able to withstand that kind of abuse.'"[22] Similar qualities can be detected in the young people who have spearheaded efforts to mobilize students across the United States to fight for stronger gun-control laws following the high school shooting in Parkland, Florida, in February 2018. As a profile in *Time* magazine observed, these young activists are not afraid of adopting a "bombastic style" as they call out politicians for their anemic legislative efforts and suffer abuse from NRA wingnuts who send them vulgar and threatening messages.[23] If the battles for civil rights and gun control have been aided by the brash and bold character of young activists, then clearly this should be marked as a positive outcome of the growing influence of adolescent qualities—and in these cases, adolescents themselves—in the political arena.

Yet while the flourishing of protest over the past several decades has provided new opportunities for citizen engagement and some notable victories for progressive causes, there are important questions sometimes asked about its overall effectiveness. The mentality that emboldens citizen activists and makes them willing to be strident in their actions also means that they can be categorical in their demands. When people protest forcefully, they typically want a positive response from the powers that be, and they want it *now*. Sometimes it works out that way. The Quebec students demonstrating in their underwear against tuition hikes largely achieved their goals, as a new government was elected that rolled back the bulk of the proposed increases. More often, however, protesters are disappointed, as governments don't capitulate to their demands. Governments resist, either for their own reasons or because the cause being pursued doesn't resonate with the wider public, at least not immediately. Even the most impressive protests sometimes fall flat. The Occupy movement beat the drums on the issue of inequality for months, but despite all the noise and fury it was to no real avail. It was popular to say the occupiers drew attention to growing inequality through their efforts, but once the tents were taken down and the protesters dispersed, the issue was quickly forgotten—not by the protesters themselves perhaps, but certainly by most politicians and by citizens at large, many of the latter still trying to figure out which party controls Congress or who the premier of their province might be. Similarly, despite the best efforts of the Parkland youth activists, serious gun-control legislation still seems a long way off even as mass shootings remain an all too common occurrence in the United States.

In short, protest politics often requires other elements of citizen engagement in order to be truly effective. Confrontational action highlights issues that greatly agitate some, but for change to occur, this must be joined by larger pools of attentive citizens willing to take the issue seriously—talking about it, thinking about it, tucking it away in their memory banks until the next election. It is this that makes politicians take note and think seriously about the consequences of inaction. Protests, in the absence of a wider base of attentive voters ready to engage with the cause, are often ineffective and can seem more like the griping of a disaffected minority than the angry voice of the people. For this reason, the broader political disengagement that has seen many citizens turning away from voting and paying little attention to current affairs has not only diminished the realm of electoral politics. It has also undermined the force of political protest, as it conveys the sense that many out there really do not care much one way or the other about whatever it is the rabble-rousers are squawking about. The democratic system as a whole is weaker for it.

Populist Foment

A few years ago, this would have been the end of my account of the principal features of democratic politics in the adolescent society: sophomoric and self-serving behavior on the part of politicians, combined with growing disengagement on the part of many citizens and combative agitation from others that is sporadically effective, has created a democratic system where accountable and responsive government is often lacking. New developments now require further analysis, as a different kind of contentious politics, populist in nature, has emerged in many places. In contrast to the protest politics of activist citizens seeking change on targeted issues, populism is marked by more amorphous discontent with the state of the country and its politics, coupled with an appetite for demagogic leaders who promise to take control of government and deal firmly with various groups—privileged elites, special interests, coddled minorities—on behalf of the supposedly downtrodden people. Concern has rightly been voiced about where this rising populism might lead and whether core democratic norms and principles could come under threat.

A warning bell was sounded by two papers by Roberto Foa and Yascha Mounk appearing in the *Journal of Democracy* in 2016 and 2017.[24] Utilizing the World Values Survey data set, the authors examined questions that probed respondents' attitudes toward core democratic principles and practices in the developed democracies, with particular attention to the United States. These particular questions had not been closely scrutinized previously, perhaps because it has typically been assumed that all is well with Western democracy: there might be opposition to specific policies from critical citizens, but the democratic system itself remains on solid footing. Foa and Mounk's analysis suggested otherwise. They found evidence of significant and steady erosion in support for basic democratic norms and argued that there was, in fact, a real danger of what they called "democratic deconsolidation" in the established democracies.

Figure 6.1 compiles some of the WVS results highlighted by Foa and Mounk for the United States, focusing on the two particular measures that tested people's democratic resolve by asking how they felt about governance options clearly deviating from democracy: (1) having a strong leader who does not have to bother with Congress and elections; and (2) army rule. As shown in figure 6.1, one-quarter of US respondents in 1995 thought the first of these, a strongman leader, was a good idea; by 2011, this had climbed to more than one in three (35.1 percent). For army rule, the increase in support over this same period was nearly threefold, jumping from 6.5 percent to 17.5 percent.[25] The clear upward trend on these two measures undermines the optimistic assumption that where democracy has the deepest roots there is no threat of reversal.

While the two papers inspired a number of responses, most were critical of the core findings, arguing that they were overstated, the authors' concerns about democratic deconsolidation overblown. There was surprisingly little effort expended trying to analyze what might be driving these disconcerting trends in attitudes toward democracy.[26] Foa and Mounk, for their part, focused their efforts on documenting the pattern rather than unpacking and explaining it. Where they did allude to the underlying forces at play, their principal suggestion,

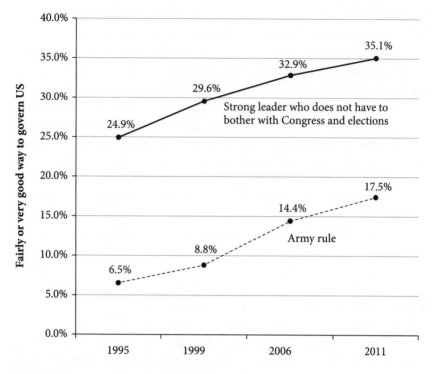

FIGURE 6.1   Support for autocrats and army rule in the United States
Source: US World Values Survey, waves 3–6. N ranges from 1,179 to 2,170.

in line with the common wisdom on these matters, was that it was deep discontent with democratic institutions causing support for democracy to erode.[27] Those most unhappy with sniping politicians, a dysfunctional Congress, and an out-of-touch government would naturally be the ones most likely to be questioning the value of democracy itself. This assumption certainly seemed to resonate with events in the United States, where Donald Trump's success has commonly been attributed to widespread discontent with what is seen as a dysfunctional and corrupt political system controlled by Washington elites and insiders.

This then was one hypothesis that needed to be examined empirically. Was it in fact the case that those unhappy with the operation of democratic institutions were the ones most apt to be questioning democracy itself? This was the first question I considered in my own reply paper to Foa and Mounk, which focused on the United States.[28] Part of that analysis, based on the 2011 WVS survey, appears in figure 6.2. The graph displays support for nondemocratic alternatives among respondents expressing varying degrees of confidence in core democratic institutions: Congress, political parties, and the government in the

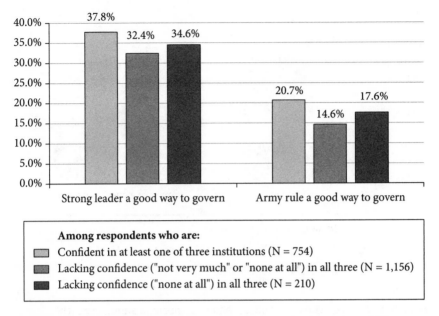

FIGURE 6.2 Institutional confidence and undemocratic alternatives (US)
Source: US World Values Survey, wave 6.

nation's capital. It reveals the rather surprising result that confidence in institutions seems to have little impact on attitudes toward undemocratic methods of governing. Those with the lowest levels of confidence in Congress, parties, and the national government are no more likely to support nondemocratic alternatives than those who are most content with the current system—in fact, they are slightly less likely. The commonsense proposition that people will only start to support nondemocratic alternatives when they are deeply dismayed at how democracy is currently operating does not find support in these numbers.

An alternative proposition that might be derived from the current political climate in the United States is that the rise of undemocratic attitudes could be connected instead to the deep political polarization that has taken hold of the country over the past twenty years[29]—that those on the extremes, both left and right, would be the ones questioning the value of democracy while the center is holding firm. Vocal partisans on both sides of the political divide express such deep frustration with the current political system and animosity toward their opponents that one wonders if they would be open to dispensing with democracy altogether in order to achieve their political goals and ideological vision. The idea is certainly plausible; but again the survey evidence from the WVS is not supportive. As figure 6.3 demonstrates, those Americans who place themselves at

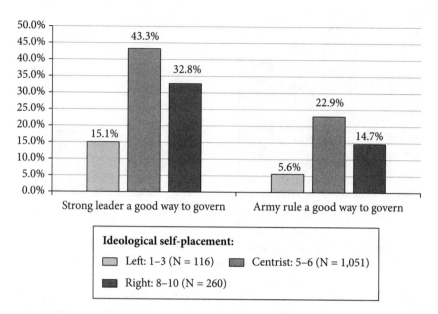

FIGURE 6.3 Ideologues, moderates, and undemocratic alternatives (US)
Source: US World Values Survey, wave 6.

the ideological poles—responding either 1–3 or 8–10 when asked to place themselves on a 1-to-10 ideological scale running from left to right—are *less* likely to
voice support for strong leaders or army rule than those who place themselves
squarely in the center of the spectrum (5 or 6). Oddly enough, it is political
centrists, those who are supposed to be moderate and pragmatic in their views,
who are more extreme than ideologues in their attitudes concerning democracy.

A related finding that helps make sense of this surprising result is that respondents who report they are relatively uninterested in politics are, by a sizable
margin, the ones most likely to support the notions of a strong leader or army
rule. Among those saying they were "not at all interested" in politics, nearly half
(48 percent) liked the idea of a strong leader untroubled by elections or Congress;
among those very interested in politics, only 21 percent agreed. A similar difference between those less and more politically interested is evident for the army
rule question: 31 percent versus 10 percent support. The connection to political
ideology lies in the fact that ideologues tend to have high levels of interest in
politics, whereas those in the center of the political spectrum are less interested.
Caring about politics is partly what leads people to develop strong opinions
on political matters and also makes them more invested in democracy; in the
absence of this kind of engagement, many drift toward the indifferent middle,
caring little about politics or even (in some cases at least) democracy itself.

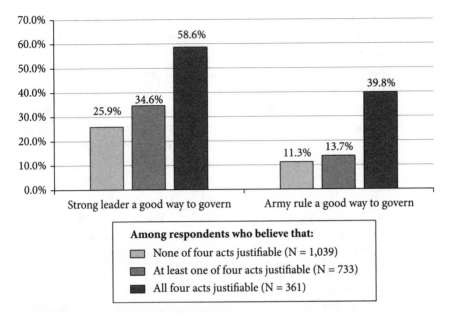

FIGURE 6.4   Antisocial attitudes and undemocratic alternatives (US)
Source: US World Values Survey, wave 6.

If we add up these findings about those who are willing to entertain undemocratic options—that they are not especially critical of current democratic institutions; that they are not ideologues and instead sit more in the middle of the
political spectrum; that they are relatively uninterested in politics—it is fair to
say that they are simply not very political individuals, and that their dim views
concerning democracy do not appear to be politically driven. But if not a politically motivated set of attitudes, then what? In my prior analysis, the place I naturally turned next in seeking to explain the rise of undemocratic attitudes was to
consider hypotheses of a more social or cultural nature, ones in keeping with
the larger pattern of an increasingly adolescent society. This exploration brought
me back to the set of questions considered previously that tap into antisocial
attitudes in the American population, and led to the results presented in figure 6.4. The right-hand bars represent WVS respondents who expressed consistently antisocial attitudes—those believing that tax evasion, bribery, wrongfully
claiming government benefits, and evading a fare on public transit are actions
that can sometimes be justified. The left-hand bars are the pro-social respondents who said that none of these actions was ever justifiable. The middle bars
represent an intermediate group who said that one to three of the four actions
could be justified.

Clearly, the antisocial group stands decisively apart from the rest. Nearly three in five (59 percent) support the idea of a strong leader, compared to just one in four (26 percent) of the most pro-social respondents. Forty percent like the idea of army rule, nearly four times as many as the pro-social group (11 percent). More than any political variable, this bundle of antisocial views successfully discriminates between those committed to democracy and those willing to consider nondemocratic "alternatives," a finding that places undemocratic attitudes in a rather different light. Rather than a reflection of political discontent, it instead casts them as part of a broader constellation of antisocial dispositions and transgressive attitudes.

It is worth recalling from chapter 4 that this antisocial mind-set is substantially more common among younger generations. This helps explain why Foa and Mounk consistently found in their analysis that young Americans were the ones most likely to express skepticism about the value of democracy and support for nondemocratic alternatives. The finding from their papers that received the greatest attention was the striking statistic that only 30 percent of Americans born since 1980 felt that it was essential for them to live in a democracy, compared to 72 percent of those born before World War II.[30] Consistent with this result, young people expressed greater openness to specific undemocratic governance options. On the 2011 WVS survey, nearly half (49 percent) of those under age thirty thought a strong leader unbothered by Congress and elections was a good idea, compared to 27 percent of those sixty and over. Nearly a quarter (24 percent) of young respondents were favorably inclined toward army rule, compared to just 10 percent of older respondents.

Tracing relationships over time offers further insight into these worrying trends. The connection between antisocial attitudes and undemocratic views in the United States has become much stronger since 1995 (figure 6.5). At the start of the time series, the antisocial were somewhat more likely than their pro-social counterparts to prefer a strong leader and army rule, but the differences were relatively moderate. The gap has grown much wider since that time. It is as if antisocial sentiments have diffused to encompass a wider set of targets, now undermining belief in democratic principles in a way that was not the case twenty years ago. Rather than burgeoning authoritarian attitudes—a common way of characterizing recent political trends—this evolving constellation of attitudes among a sizable minority of the population might better be described as creeping nihilism: that is, growing disregard for an extensive range of norms and principles that hold us together as a polity and as a society.

Donald Trump, it must be said, is an entirely fitting representative of this social constituency. He is, like many of his more ardent followers, contemptuous of core elements of democracy. Prior to being elected in 2016, Trump questioned

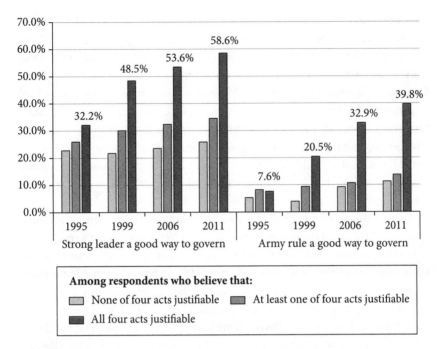

FIGURE 6.5 Antisocial attitudes and undemocratic alternatives: a growing connection (US)

Source: US World Values Survey, waves 3–6. Total N per wave ranges from 1,179 to 2,170.

whether he would accept the legitimacy of the election result and threatened to jail his Democratic opponent if victorious. Now as president, he casts aspersions on any body or unit of government that threatens his position or disrupts his agenda—be it the courts, Congress, the media, or the Justice Department. One suspects he would happily dispense with certain agencies altogether if he could so without causing a political crisis and potentially losing power. At the same time, Trump consistently displays antisocial behavior in both his political and personal life. These transgressive actions include bullying political opponents, encouraging violence at political rallies, boasting about assaulting women, and incessant lying. It is reasonable to interpret Trump's contempt for democracy as a reflection of a more pervasive disregard for basic social norms rooted in his intemperate and adolescent character—and nothing much to do with any political concerns or motivations.

Much of this contrasts rather sharply with the behavior and mind-set of the traditional conservative. One consistent finding in the literature on personality and politics is that the strongest Big Five predictor of conservative ideology is conscientiousness[31]—a personality trait implying respect for conservative virtues such as prudence, sobriety, and lawfulness. It is clear that Trump and those who applaud his transgressive behavior do not fit this description. Of course, many traditional conservatives still held their noses and voted for Trump as the Republican nominee for president in November 2016, and many have continued to support him through his raucous time in office. But it is clear that Trump's supporters represent a motley coalition, not only in terms of policy priorities, but also—so this analysis would suggest—in terms of temperament and disposition. How long it will all hold together is one of the burning political questions of the day, one that has, for the time being, supplanted other issues and concerns pertaining to the state of modern democracy.

These patterns of underlying dispositions and attitudes help us to better understand the social context that abetted Donald Trump's rise to the presidency in the United States. What about other cases, including the European countries where populist leaders with some affinity to Trump have been gaining support in the past several years? It would require another chapter or more to properly review the relevant evidence, not least because there is variation within the European countries that is papered over when all are considered together as one. However, the aggregate results from the most recent wave of the EVS (2008–2009) are worth summarizing succinctly.[32]

In brief, the same story about democratic deconsolidation and its social underpinnings loosely holds in the European context, but most of the empirical relationships are muted compared to the United States, making strong conclusions inadvisable. Sizable numbers in the European countries say that strong leaders unbothered by legislatures or elections are a good thing (27 percent), an increase of 3 percentage points since the previous EVS wave in 1999–2000. Support for the idea of army rule is much lower (6 percent), though this too nudged upward from the previous wave (by 2 points).[33] As in the US, lack of confidence in current political institutions has a surprisingly weak effect on these undemocratic attitudes, while antisocial attitudes have a stronger impact—though not to nearly the same degree as in the United States. Among pro-social respondents, for example, 24.2 percent support a strong leader, compared to 36.6 percent of antisocial respondents; for army rule, the respective figures are 4.8 percent and 12.3 percent. As in the US, it is also the case that those with little interest in politics are the most likely to support undemocratic propositions, consistent with the notion that indifference to democracy is not necessarily the product of any deep political reflection or calculation.

Overall, the European data suggest a more nuanced story, while at the same time confirming that, as in the United States, a social account featuring the combined role of detachment from politics and rising antisocial attitudes appears to play some part in explaining democratic deconsolidation. Further investigation would be needed to reveal in which countries the social dimension of democratic deconsolidation is most salient and why this aspect of the problem is more acute in some places than others.

A Broken System

Democracy, and the principles of freedom and equality on which it rests, remains one of our most important collective achievements. But the full potential of democracy has been undermined by the rise of an adolescent ethos and culture, to such a degree that the democratic system may be imperiled in places. This runs counter to the widespread assumption underlying many assessments of the problems of contemporary democracy, which is that politics itself is to blame. If politicians act disrespectfully toward one another, so the thinking goes, it is because of the profound political divides separating partisans of different stripes. If some citizens have given up on voting, it is because they have grown weary of self-serving politicians, hyperpartisanship, and a dysfunctional political system. If some are turning to political protest, it is because they see this as the most effective way of achieving policy change given the blockages in the current system. And if some are questioning democracy altogether, it is due to some blend of all of the above—a broad-based discontent arising from various forms of political malfeasance and dysfunction.

But when we examine some of the relevant trends, there is evidence of an important social dimension that helps explain shifting democratic norms and patterns of political behavior. Self-government requires effort and restraint on the part of politicians and citizens, including the willingness to engage and work through differences, the capacity to think long-term and with an eye to the public interest, and the maintenance of a basic level of respect for one another and for the principles that underlie the democratic system. All of these have come under stress, as people increasingly behave in ways that reflect an adolescent mind-set: brash, impulsive, belligerent, and short-sighted. If the health of democracy is suffering, it is not only because of flawed political mechanisms, but also because of erosion in the social foundation that helps sustain a strong democracy.

GETTING AHEAD

Economic Life in the Adolescent Society

If the pervasive influence of the adolescent character sheds light on our often dysfunctional politics, it also provides insight into the workings of another sector of modern life relevant to us all: the economy. Less of a collective undertaking than politics, economic activity is guided primarily by individual decisions and actions in the free market system; so many of the relevant effects are seen first and foremost at the individual level. But these individual effects can multiply and cascade to generate patterns that do have important consequences for the general economic and social fabric.

Like political scientists, economists have not traditionally dwelled much on personality or character traits in seeking to understand people's behavior in economic affairs. The dominant model in economics, informing the pages of virtually every Economics 101 textbook, is grounded in the assumption that people are "rational actors," making efficient Spock-like decisions about all sorts of economic matters: consumption choices, employment options, investment decisions, and more. Their principal motivation is to maximize personal "utility" through the pursuit of economic activities that offer personal benefits outweighing the personal costs.

Real people, however, are more like Captain Kirk than Mr. Spock, failing to conform to the rational actor model posited by economists. Emotions, misperceptions, intangible costs and benefits, influenced in many instances by underlying character traits, lead people to act in ways that the traditional models don't anticipate. As in other fields, it is only recently that some researchers have started to link personality to economic behavior in interesting and enlightening ways to dig deeper into what makes people tick when it comes to economic decision making and activity.[1] When we combine some of these findings with ideas about the changing contours of character in the adolescent society, we can develop new understandings of some of the more salient economic trends of the past number of years.

Consumers

One unfortunate feature of economic life in the adolescent society is excessive consumerism—excessive in the sense that many people get too wrapped up in material possessions and seek to live beyond their means. This observation is seconded by other authors who draw links between personality and everyday behaviors. Daniel Nettle, looking at impulsive behavior in general, notes that it is helpful to "distinguish between the reasons for starting something, and the reasons for not being able to stop." Extroversion provides the impulse to start, as those who score high on this trait tend to get a "bigger buzz" from stimulating activity. Conscientiousness supplies the brakes, as careful and cautious individuals are "able to decide not to do it again, however big the buzz was."[2] High levels of extroversion and low levels of conscientiousness are a dangerous combination; people of this temperament seek pleasure from various sources of material gratification and lack the control mechanisms to resist going back for more time and time again.

Survey data reveal that younger generations embodying this set of personal traits commonly display strong materialist appetites. On the European Social Survey (2002–2016) younger respondents are substantially more likely to indicate that they are the kind of person for whom it is important to be rich and to have a lot of expensive things. Thirty-eight percent of those under age thirty say that this is an apt personal description—that it is at least "somewhat like me"—versus just 16 percent of those age sixty and over. Moreover, these materialist attitudes are, as Nettle suggests, strongly linked to the extroverted personality type. The latter are those who say they are apt to look for "adventures" and "risks" and want to have an exciting life, like to have a "good time" and "spoil themselves," and who seek "every chance to have fun." Among respondents on the ESS who feel that all these statements capture something of their character, 39 percent also say they are the type who hankers after riches and material gratification. At the other end of the scale, among those who say that none of three extroversion measures is an accurate personal descriptor, only 10 percent express materialist inclinations.[3]

It will be recalled that these three extroversion measures from the ESS are the same ones used in chapter 5 to make the case that extroverted dispositions have been rising over the long haul, as successive birth cohorts for many years have shown a heightened propensity for adventure, risk, and the pursuit of pleasure. It follows that the increased emphasis on consumption and material goods nowadays is, partly at least, embedded within this broader transformation that has seen greater emphasis on adventurous, hedonistic, and carefree ways of living. If we sometimes think of the materialistic attitudes prevalent in today's society as a reflection of narrowly acquisitive values focused on accumulation and social status, the connection to fun and adventure casts them in a somewhat different light, painting consumerism as a product of excitement seeking and exuberance as much as avarice.

Jean Twenge and Keith Campbell make related observations as they draw connections between core personality traits and consumptive behavior in their account of the economic meltdown of 2008. Citing rampant spending by reckless consumers prior to the crisis, they note that "shopping addiction [is] linked to impulsivity, a trait that . . . involves favoring short-term pleasures at the expense of long-term gains."[4] But they also explore other dimensions of modern culture that help explain the rapacious demand and desire for material goods. They hit on an important point when they note that gradually over time "there has been a giant transfer of time, attention, and resources from reality to fantasy."[5] Advertisers and marketers stoke this tendency as they flog their wares with glossy advertisements and celebrity endorsements promising a luxuriant lifestyle to all who possess them. The adolescent character of the current age makes consumers all too vulnerable to these attempts at beguilement. A penchant for fantasizing, tinged with the narcissistic tendencies of youth, renders modern consumers highly susceptible to empty promises of material fulfillment.

A similar perspective is articulated at greater length in an insightful study from 1987 that identifies a "romantic" spirit at the heart of modern consumerism. Sociologist Colin Campbell writes,

> The spirit of modern consumerism is anything but materialistic. The idea that contemporary consumers have an insatiable desire to acquire objects represents a serious misunderstanding of the mechanism which impels people to want goods. Their basic motivation is the desire to experience in reality the pleasurable dramas which they have already enjoyed in imagination, and each "new" product is seen as offering a possibility of realizing this ambition. However, since reality can never provide the perfected pleasures encountered in day-dreams . . . each purchase leads to literal disillusionment, something which explains how wanting is extinguished so quickly, and why people disacquire goods as rapidly as they acquire them. What is not extinguished, however, is the

fundamental longing which day-dreaming itself generates, and hence there is as much determination as ever to find new products to serve as replacement objects of desire.[6]

So the appetite for material goods is never fully sated, as we are always craving something new that will live up to our fantasized reality. The consumption treadmill keeps on turning, fueled by character traits that have become ever more common with rising generations.

Another way in which our voracious consumption is leading to serious troubles is through the ongoing depletion of resources and growing dangers to the environment. Wealthy nations have built prosperous economies over the centuries by harvesting and accumulating natural riches from around the world. Developing nations, their populations in the billions, hope to do the same; major players, such as China and Brazil, are well on their way. Resources are being depleted rapidly, fossil fuels burned at a prodigious rate. Stern warnings have been issued by the most reputable scientific bodies that the earth cannot sustain a rise in global temperatures of more than two degrees Celsius without suffering a series of profound consequences and potentially triggering major feedback effects as icecaps and permafrost melt and diminish the earth's capacity to cool itself. Yet still we push on in what may eventually prove to be the ultimate risky behavior.

Dealing with the issue is a challenge for various reasons. All countries must pitch in with reductions in greenhouse gas emissions to make a difference, but there is no one with the power or authority to ensure that this happens. And if some don't contribute, it becomes harder to persuade others to stick with the program. However, our reluctance to take decisive action is also grounded in character traits that make us willing to roll the dice and enjoy the good life while we can. We can live well now, the thinking goes, and take a chance that we will be able to manage the many problems created by a rise in global temperatures—everything from rising ocean levels to violent and unpredictable weather to severe drought conditions. Thomas Homer-Dixon, a scholar deeply concerned about our failure to understand the interconnectedness of systems in the modern world and the cascading impact that shocks can have, echoes these concerns. He sees common character traits at work in both the 2008–9 economic crisis and the looming environmental one. His sage advice: We "need to grow up. Collectively, we have been behaving like adolescents—believing we're invulnerable, living for today while ignoring tomorrow, and sneering at anything that smacks of prudence. But grownups do take life seriously, and they pay attention to their fears."[7] Our adolescent selves, immune to such warnings, are poorly equipped to devise and adhere to the more sustainable economic models sorely needed at the present time.

Creators

On the consumption side of the economy, we haven't been particularly well served by attitudes and behaviors linked to the ascendance of the adolescent character. Consumers who are pleasure seekers, dreamers, and risk takers put significant strain on themselves and their bank accounts, the economic system at large, and the planet's ecosystems. But on the other side of the coin, the production side of the economy, it's fair to say that dreaming and risk taking can be valuable assets. These qualities underwrite entrepreneurial vision and innovation, facilitating the development of new products and methods of production that can lead to a more efficient and prosperous economy—and perhaps (hopefully sooner rather than later) a greener one as well.

One of the best-known thinkers on the topic of economic innovation is Richard Florida. An urban economist, Florida focuses particularly on understanding what has allowed certain cities and regions to be economic dynamos, including larger centers like San Francisco, Seattle, and Boston and smaller hubs such as Austin and Boulder. His first and probably better-known work on the subject, now nearly two decades old, is *The Rise of the Creative Class.* The book focuses on a particular group, the creative class, that Florida believes is the driving force in the modern, postindustrial economy and responsible for much of the rising prosperity of the twentieth century. This class is represented in many occupations, not just the obvious ones such as artist and musician, but also in science and engineering, as well as "creative professionals" in business and finance, law, and health care. All "engage in complex problem solving that involves a great deal of independent judgment," as well as sharing "a common creative ethos that values creativity, individuality, difference and merit."[8] The creative class has helped alter the structure of work and workplace norms (casual dress, flexible work hours, greater autonomy), as well as lifestyles more generally. Uncomfortable with a strict division between work and personal life, the creative class seeks an alignment of the two and a more varied "experiential lifestyle."[9]

Florida came up with some colorful measures to assess the potential of different areas to attract and retain members of the creative class: the gay index and the bohemian index. The first, based on the prevalence of gay individuals in a city, was deemed to be a measure of both diversity and openness to diversity, important factors in generating creativity and economic dynamism.[10] "Diversity increases the odds that a place will attract different types of creative people with different skill sets and ideas. Places with diverse mixes of creative people are more likely to generate new combinations . . . to be [places] where newcomers are accepted quickly into all sorts of social and economic arrangements."[11] The bohemian index measured "the number of writers, designers, musicians, actors and directors, painters and sculptors, photographers and dancers" as an indirect means of gauging the cultural amenities available in different cities.[12] The key finding of his work was that those cities scoring highest on the gay and bohemian indices tended to be the most economically dynamic places and the ones with the greatest concentration of high-tech industry.

This exploration of the creative class and its contribution to modern economic life continued in Florida's more recent book from 2008, *Who's Your City?* But now there was an important twist, as Florida became aware of work being done in the field of psychology, in particular personality psychology. One project in particular caught his eye. Using data collected from more than six hundred thousand people spread throughout the United States, a group of researchers had created "personality maps" showing where different types of people tend to congregate geographically—the Pleasantvilles where agreeable people are more likely to dwell, the big-city, bright-lights locations where extroverts prefer to congregate and let loose, the culturally diverse hubs where those open to experience migrate to enjoy new encounters and experiences. Florida started to sense that this was relevant to his ideas about urban geography and economic growth. "All my professional life, I've looked at how social and economic factors shape the world. I'd never really been into psychology—never thought about how personal proclivities might affect innovation or economic development. But all of a sudden it was dawning on me that psychology plays a central role."[13] He teamed up with the psychology researchers to look at some of the connections between their personality maps and his results on innovative cities. The linkages, Florida reports, were startling. "The strongest results by far were those that looked at my gay and bohemian indices and the correlation with openness to experience—the results were literally off the chart. . . . This makes me think my earlier measures of gay and bohemian concentrations are really proxies for regions with large concentrations of open-to-experience people."[14] After many years of thinking and research on this issue, Florida has come to this important conclusion: it is people of a particular temperament and character, defined by openness and its allied qualities, who are the leading force in fueling innovation and moving the economy forward in different places.[15]

Florida's main mission throughout his work is to understand why some regions fare well and are leaders in economic innovation, while others lag behind. But the title of his first book points to a different question that is equally intriguing: what is it that explains the *rise* of the creative class *over time?* Despite the title of that book, Florida did not spend much time trying to probe the question. He certainly demonstrates that this class has grown by leaps and bounds over the course of the past one hundred years (now representing about 30 percent of all employed Americans) and that the effects have been wide-ranging, touching not just the working world but life more generally. But he doesn't really try to unpack the root causes of this economic and social transformation.

He does, however, offer a few relevant observations. First, Florida doesn't believe in technological determinism. The dominant economic activities of a given age—be they agriculture, manufacturing, or today's information, communication, and service sectors—clearly have some impact on the way we work, but there are always different ways to organize any given economic activity, and choices to be made.[16] In reflecting on reconfigurations connected to the creative economy, he writes, "By insisting that these social changes are somehow imposed on us . . . commentators avoid the real question of our age: Why are we *choosing* to live and work like this?"[17] Florida also sees the creative economy not as the product of any single catalyst but as the long-term outcome of a subtle evolutionary process: "The deep and enduring changes of our age are not technological but social and cultural. They are thus harder to see, for they result from the gradual accumulation of small, incremental changes in our day-to-day lives. These changes have been building for decades and are only now coming to the fore."[18]

All of Florida's thoughts and observations are consistent with the adolescent society perspective on our changing world: It is the slow, steady rise of openness to experience that helps explain the premium that has come to be placed on creativity, flexibility, and innovation in the workforce over time. The emergence of openness as a core character trait represents one of the critical changes stemming from the growing influence of the adolescent experience on the adult world. Building for decades, openness to experience has slowly become a more dominant trait in the population and has deeply affected how people approach the world of work, including the capacities and dispositions we bring to the job as well as our expectations for workplace fulfillment. The sea change represented by the rise of the creative class, underwritten by enhanced levels of openness, represents one of the more noteworthy economic effects of the adolescent recasting of modern society.

Workers

As with its impact on social and political tolerance, the influence of the adolescent trait of openness on the working world has been primarily positive, with many beneficial consequences. Members of the creative class do well for themselves, earning high incomes and enjoying a work-life balance that is stimulating and engaging; if we all could enjoy such lives, the world would be a happier place. More important for Florida, they are key drivers of the economic prosperity that benefits us all. We have unlocked a great deal of creative wealth by allowing more people to work in flexible ways that allow for the exploration and expression of new ideas and innovation.

But if the rise of the creative class is a positive development in the adolescent society, there have been challenges in the workplace as well. Not every job meets the criteria desired by the creative class—a flexible and autonomous environment with work that is challenging and stimulating. Moreover, virtually no job meets these standards *all the time*. Inevitably, there are rules and restrictions and some pedestrian tasks to be completed. Most jobs involve at least some mundane work that draws more on reserves of perseverance and tenacity than lateral thinking. When people who prefer tasks involving creativity run up against these restrictions, problems sometimes ensue.

The demographic group most often pegged as craving a creative and stimulating work environment and resistant to any hint of drudgery are younger generations of workers. Jeffrey Arnett, who coined the term "emerging adulthood," writes about the workplace experiences of the twenty-somethings he has studied: "They expect work to be not just a job but an adventure, not just a way to put bread on the table and a roof over their heads but a venue for self-development and self-expression."[19] When work fails to be a nonstop voyage of creative discovery, younger workers sometimes have trouble adjusting—or at least more trouble than used to be the case.

A TV show a few years back called *From the Ground Up* offered a glimpse of these challenges. The show focused on a group of twelve young people, under the guidance of an experienced designer, Debbie Travis. They were put to work on a house-building and design project, which required a mix of manual labor and creative input from the group. The hope was that they would come away with both a sense of accomplishment and some portable job skills. Things did not proceed smoothly, however. The constant complaint from Travis was that these young workers had a very poor work ethic and did not take kindly to being asked to carry out some of the more mundane tasks involved in completing the project. They were not willing to pay their dues to gain the experience and skills that would allow them to become the kind of workers who could be given greater responsibility and autonomy down the road.

As with many changes in the adolescent society, what is most salient among the youngest adults is revealed, on closer inspection, to be connected to a more gradual generational shift. This, at least, is the pattern suggested by the results of a survey question posed on a series of Canadian values surveys from the 1990s that asked respondents whether they agreed: "At work, with everything I undertake, I stick with it until I am satisfied with the result." The percentage that "totally agreed" shows a familiar pattern: steady drops as we move down the age categories from seventy-plus (53 percent) to under age thirty (33 percent). Diligence in the workplace, it seems, is less likely to be seen as an absolute necessity among younger generations.

The upshot is that a balance of qualities is needed for success in the working world, including creative energy as well as traditional virtues of focus and dedication—in other words, some traits linked to openness and others reflecting high levels of conscientiousness. To say this, and to suggest that younger generations sometimes come up short on the latter count, is not to pin all the negatives of their work experiences on their shoulders. Many young adults—too many in these days of widespread unemployment and underemployment—find themselves stuck in dead-end jobs unlikely to lead anywhere, however diligent they might be. It is understandable when young people have trouble dedicating themselves to the finer techniques of cheeseburger preparation or folding clothes at the Gap. But even among those in more promising positions, there is often a failure to appreciate that a certain apprenticeship period is needed to develop the skills and experience that will eventually warrant promotion to more autonomous and creative roles in due course.[20]

Perseverance and dedication, it should be added, are not just valuable traits for young workers trying to get a foothold in the job market and some traction on a career path. As careers progress, it remains the case that conscientiousness is a powerful predictor of job success. Summing up the findings of dozens of studies, Daniel Nettle reports that "the correlation [between conscientiousness and occupational success] shows up more or less identically whether the criteria for occupational success is ratings of job proficiency, speed of promotion, income, or success in completing training. Similarly, the correlation is found among professionals, managers, salespeople, police officers, and more routine occupations, so it cannot be put down to the specific demands of any one job type. The more conscientious you are, the better you will do in the workplace, however better is defined and whichever workplace it is."[21]

These claims are corroborated by the ascendancy of the company and the individual that many would see as the epitome of modern innovation: Apple and its cofounder Steve Jobs. The popular image of Jobs and his company is that they were all about creativity—developing sleek new products and inventive ways of doing things that excited countless consumers and revolutionized the tech industry. But detailed accounts of Jobs's life and his time at Apple reveal that for all his ingenuity and imagination, he also was incredibly focused and exacting, demanding the same of those who worked under him. Yes, they dreamed big under his leadership at Apple, but behind the scenes the attention to detail, down to every last pixel and font choice, was extraordinary.[22] The success of Jobs and his company underlines how creativity and perseverance are both essential ingredients to achieve greatness in the business world.

Students

Interestingly, the same combination of traits has also come to be identified as critical for individual success in earlier stages of life—particularly in the school setting. As research on the determinants of academic success has evolved over time, we have started to gain a more holistic understanding of what is needed to excel in the classroom, with many of the key findings mirroring what is known about success in the working world.

The traditional line of thinking in education research focused on two qualities that help children achieve academic success: innate cognitive ability, along with the social advantages enjoyed by children from stable and well-to-do families. But more recently, researchers have started to examine the character traits that influence how youngsters fare in their studies. The best synthesis of this research is presented in Paul Tough's *How Children Succeed*. Tough draws on the work of various researchers and educational practitioners, including one whose work is most central to his theme, Nobel Prize winner James Heckman. After winning the Nobel in economics for the development of complex statistical techniques that only an economist could love, Heckman turned his attention to a subject outside the normal boundaries of his field. This later work has helped uncover important factors often overlooked in the traditional study of educational success.

One of Heckman's pioneering studies, recounted by Tough, involved taking a fresh look at an older research project launched back in the mid-1960s. A group of young children from disadvantaged backgrounds were recruited and randomly split into two groups; one was given the opportunity to enroll in a top-notch preschool program, the other was not. The expectation was that the enriching preschool experience would boost children's IQs compared to peers who did not have the same opportunity, and from there lead to greater educational success down the road. As it turned out, the effects of the program on IQ levels were small and ephemeral—by the third grade, the cognitive advantage gained from their preschool experience had disappeared. But as the children were tracked further, it became apparent that some sort of tangible benefit had been acquired: they were more likely to graduate from high school and more likely to find steady employment than their counterparts who had not attended preschool all those years ago. Reanalyzing some of the data collected during their school years, Heckman found that the preschool group scored higher on certain personal qualities, including self-control and curiosity, that substantially aided their efforts in the classroom. It was these effects that were long lasting and critical to their success in both the school setting and beyond.

Paul Tough summarizes the conclusions that can be drawn from this and similar studies that followed Heckman's pioneering work: "What matters most in a child's development . . . is not how much information we can stuff into her brain in the first few years. What matters, instead, is . . . a very different set of qualities, a list that includes persistence, self-control, curiosity, conscientiousness, grit, and self-confidence. Economists refer to these as noncognitive skills, psychologists call them personality traits, and the rest of us sometimes think of them as character."[23]

In Tough's review, the character traits that emerge as the most critical to academic success are grit and curiosity, corresponding to the personality traits of conscientiousness and openness.[24] These qualities not only support learning independently; they also work together to produce optimal learning outcomes. The synergy between grit and curiosity is evident in virtually any area of intellectual endeavor. When physicists make a monumental breakthrough, coming up with a new theory about the origins of the universe or some such thing, it isn't curiosity and creativity alone that lead to success. The eureka moment typically comes after many grit-filled years of relentless probing and pondering. On a smaller scale, when children come up with the solution to a challenging math problem, it normally requires a few minutes of hard intellectual labor. Those who give up after fifteen seconds don't solve the problem and don't develop the same mathematical aptitude. But just as perseverance supports curiosity, so does curiosity aid persistence. A powerful desire to understand something better provides the necessary motivation to push through any obstacles that might stand in the way of enlightenment—be it the three minutes needed to solve a grade-school math problem or the many years of training and dedication required to crack the deepest riddles of the cosmos. In this way, a blend of different personal qualities is required to help sustain intellectual development and achievement.

Moving Up, Moving On

From these various examples and bodies of research, we could say there is something of an emerging consensus: that character matters a great deal across various areas of human endeavor, and that openness and conscientiousness in particular are critical traits that help us get ahead in the world, contributing to both individual advancement and collective well-being. In the adolescent society, one of the two has been widely encouraged and has helped produce a flourishing creative economy and society, but the other, conscientiousness, has suffered from some neglect, and its degraded condition may be holding us back. As we reflect on the consequences of the adolescent society for different aspects of our lives, it's fair to say that the effects on economic advancement and individual achievement have been decidedly mixed—reflecting the combination of the good and the not-so-good embodied in the character changes of the adolescent society.

With this, our analysis of the adolescent character of modern society draws to a close. Having consistently made the case across the past few chapters that adolescent traits and values have been steadily infiltrating diverse areas of modern life, we are left with a couple of important additions and amendments to consider. We first consider whether there is more to this story than simply the ascendance of adolescence character traits over time and identify some other important factors that need to be added to the explanatory mix. We then finish off by presenting evidence suggesting that the steady march forward of the adolescent society has been slowing down considerably in recent years—a puzzling development on its face, but one that makes more sense when we probe deeper into the social dynamics giving rise to this transition.

ADOLESCENCE ALONE?

In surveying the landscape of the adolescent society, I've taken us on a whirlwind tour of notable landmarks scattered far and wide, from the brashness of reality TV and real life, to declining voter turnout and climbing obesity levels, to the onset of delayed adulthood and the rise of the creative class. At the same time, I've drilled down on one particular process supposedly responsible for these diverse features of today's social topography: the steady infusion of adolescent character traits into the fabric of contemporary adult society. Surely, many will say, this isn't explanation enough. There must be other factors at play producing this diverse medley of social, political, economic, and cultural change.

My response: true enough. Other forces of change have been at work, and something should be said about those as well. But I don't just want to rhyme off a long list of additional or alternative explanations for the various trends that we've seen—be it the uprooting effects of industrialization and urbanization, the disruptive impact of new technologies, or the erosion of traditional buttresses of social cohesion, such as religion and family. Instead, I'll focus on some key forces reshaping society over the past century (or more) that have *combined* with the rise of adolescent character traits in interesting and often unexpected ways to produce the adolescent society we see all around us today.

Liberalism and Capitalism: Backdrop to the Adolescent Society

The basic concerns voiced in this book are far from unique. Many analysts of modern society see problems arising across diverse areas of modern life and offer similar characterizations of current conditions. More and more we fail to act with moderation and maturity, and instead fall into shallow, impulsive, and sometimes narcissistic ways of living. We lament the personal and collective consequences, even as we ourselves, to varying degrees, indulge in these widespread practices and ways of being.

Observers searching for a deeper understanding of these far-reaching changes offer different accounts of how we arrived at our current pass. Some think we can get to the heart of things by probing the philosophical underpinnings of Western society. Charles Taylor, one of the leading philosophers of our time, expresses this viewpoint in his 1991 book *The Malaise of Modernity*. To understand life today, Taylor believes, we have to look back through the past several centuries at the emerging ideological foundation of modern Western society. The critical development was the articulation and dissemination of a philosophy that rejects entrenched privilege and tradition in favor of individual freedom. We must not, this pervasive doctrine holds, force people to conform to society's goals but instead should create an organized social order in which each person can fashion a life as he or she sees fit. This powerful idea led to the toppling of kings and autocrats, the rise of modern democracies, and the dismantling of traditional institutions of authority such as the church. Personal autonomy and freedom of choice for all—or more simply liberalism, in the classical sense of the term—became the defining principles of the modern age.

The ideology resonated deeply and over time has penetrated ever deeper into our consciousness and the fabric of everyday life. What began as an abstract principle has evolved into a pervasive way of being. Over time, people have come to exercise their personal autonomy in increasingly diverse ways. Some use it to live their lives in ways that philosophers of earlier centuries might have anticipated—developing personal aptitudes and talents, building lasting relationships with significant others, fashioning a personal legacy of their own design that will survive their passing and lend greater meaning to their time on earth. In short, they make the kinds of choices and commitments that allow them to look back on their life with a sense of accomplishment and fulfillment. Others use their freedom to do as they wish in ways that sages of the past likely didn't foresee—to play X-Box in their sleepwear all day long, to buy an endless array of material goods that ostensibly give expression to their individuality, to jump from one relationship or job to the next without any sense of commitment or purpose. As these superficial applications of the principle of personal autonomy have become more common, they have, according to Taylor, crowded out more edifying pursuits. This is the essence of what he labels our modern malaise: we have a philosophical ideal that remains powerful and persuasive, but countless examples of its everyday application that make us wonder about its true value.[1]

Other leading thinkers seeking to understand the state of today's society focus less on abstract philosophical ideals and more on the material realities that shape our lives. One prominent perspective holds that the main force of change is capitalism, now the dominant economic system in most parts of the world. Capitalism embodies and reinforces narrow, self-regarding values in the production, accumulation, and consumption of material goods. It concentrates our attention too much on material acquisitions and gives little heed to higher-order aspirations and goals.

Benjamin Barber is one critic struck by the pernicious effects of capitalism on the character of modern society. He is particularly scathing on the practice of advertising. As capitalism has evolved, it has increasingly made products that serve no genuine human needs. The manufacturers of baubles and trinkets have turned to advertising to create demand for these superfluous extras by making us feel we simply *must* have them. We have, Barber argues, been "infantilized" by these commercializing forces, no longer able to make sensible decisions in the manner of mature adults. Instead, we are conditioned to act impulsively on our materialistic desires, seeking quick fulfillment in a wide range of consumer goods. Barber sees a variety of pernicious habits emerging from this impulsive consumer mind-set. When life presents us with choices between that which is easy or hard, fast or slow, simple or complex, we unthinkingly opt for the quick and superficial option.[2] As these habits permeate other aspects of our lives, not just our consumption decisions, we find ourselves drifting away from adult practices toward more "infantile" ways of living.[3]

While offering different accounts, Taylor and Barber also share certain key assumptions. Both point to the impact of ideologies and systems with a very long history in their efforts to better understand the state of today's society. While both believe the impact is profound, they also see considerable variation in the social fabric produced by these systems down the years. Things haven't been as they are now since the inception of liberalism and capitalism; it is only recent decades that have seen various kinds of social malaise growing at an accelerating rate. Both also believe that substantial improvements are possible without overthrowing the "system"—either the philosophical system that enshrines individual autonomy or the capitalist economic system grounded in self-interest and materialism. Taylor thinks we can become more thoughtful in the exercise of our personal freedom, making more meaningful and considered life choices— that we can retain our philosophical ideal but shed some of its more trivial applications. Barber believes we can temper capitalism's more pernicious effects, rein in the excessive consumerism, and become more adultlike in our consumption decisions and life choices more generally. In short, neither thinker believes that liberalism or capitalism must inevitably bring out the worst in us. These background conditions establish broad parameters for the shape of modern society and create certain challenges to the retention of important values, but they do not determine our collective fate.

It is at this point that notions of character can and should enter the picture. The adolescent society argument helps us better understand the thoughts and actions of adults living in a society rooted in liberal ideals of personal autonomy and capitalist values of material gain and economic self-interest. People who retain adult qualities will favor certain choices, taking advantage of personal liberties and economic opportunity in a careful and considered manner. Those more adolescent in nature will make other choices, reflecting their more free-spirited and impulsive character. The relative balance between the two has significant implications for the lives of individuals and for the texture of society as a whole.

The way in which philosophical and economic underpinnings interact with character traits can be demonstrated with concrete examples—one example in particular. The country where many of the trends I've pegged as "adolescent" have gone furthest, the place that has furnished the greatest number of examples in previous chapters, is the United States. The US stands out on various counts. For example, the exceptionally brash and bold character of Americans, while something of a stereotype, is backed up by a certain amount of concrete evidence. Antisocial behaviors are generally more prevalent, crime being one leading indicator. Certain risky behaviors are more common as well: the number of teenage pregnancies in the United States, for example, is unusually high, more than four times the average rate in European countries.[4] Likewise, the decline in social trust in the United States has been steeper than in most other places. One unfortunate symptom is the growing segregation of the American population, with the more advantaged sections of society tucked away in gated communities, while the least fortunate tough it out in dilapidated ghettos. Adolescent qualities reflecting impulsiveness also seem more prevalent. Exuberant consumerism runs rampant in the United States, as anyone who has spent any time at a Walmart on Black Friday will attest. The problem of rising obesity levels, present throughout the developed world, has reached super-size proportions in America, where one in three adults and nearly one in five children is now considered obese.[5] Entertainment values are also paramount throughout the land, from the escapist movies of Hollywood, to the glam and glitter of Las Vegas, to the family-oriented fun of the Disney empire. On the other side of the adolescent coin, Americans are also widely seen as among the most open and uninhibited of peoples, with positive consequences for innovation and freethinking. Americans are not held back by inner caution or societal constraint, and their society is structured to foster this creative energy. The result has been cutting-edge thinking and creative achievement in a wide variety of fields over the years—science, business, arts and entertainment, technological innovation. If these various trends, both the good and the bad, can reasonably be linked to the spread of adolescent qualities throughout the population, then the United States can be rightly deemed the most adolescent of modern societies.

This way of summing up the American social landscape diverges considerably from other accounts. Common wisdom holds that the critical influences on the nation's long-term development have been its distinctive philosophical and economic underpinnings. From colonial times to the present, it is said, the United States has embraced the doctrines of liberal individualism and capitalism more unreservedly than any other country. The founders of the nation developed a uniquely powerful attachment to notions of individual rights and liberties. These principles were enshrined in the country's constitution, which helped ensure the United States would remain a place committed to liberal values and the fullest freedom of thought and action for its citizens. This same spirit influenced approaches to economic development of the continent, a spirit reinforced by the rugged and freewheeling frontier conditions in which that development took place. Free market ideals took root and have flourished ever since. The US is seen as a place where dedication to personal freedoms and capitalist economic principles runs deep and has shaped all aspects of the country's development.

I wouldn't completely discount this traditional interpretation. However, I would point out that in addition to its uniquely strong attachment to particular philosophical and economic ideals, the United States is also the country where adolescent influences have been most powerful over the past one hundred years—simply because it is here that adolescence in its modern form first took shape in the early years of the twentieth century. A system of universal secondary education was established at an early date, as new secondary schools were built throughout the land and laws governing mandatory attendance were established and enforced. Enrollment levels grew rapidly, well in advance of other countries, with the greatest leap forward occurring between 1910 and 1940. Over that period, the percentage of fourteen- to seventeen-year olds attending school jumped from less than 15 percent to over 70 percent. "Secondary-school enrollment and graduation rates increased spectacularly in much of the United States from 1910 to 1940," notes one study. "This increase was uniquely American; no other nation underwent an equivalent change for several decades."[6] There was also, in the United States, little filtering into different schools based on academic streaming, some students destined for postsecondary education, others for early entry to the workforce. Instead, all were brought together in the generalist high school, where they created a relatively complete adolescent society.

In other countries it remained the norm for only a select group to attend school through their teenage years and for secondary schooling to focus on the preparation of this social elite for university education.[7] In the mid-1930s, Germany and France had secondary enrollment rates below 10 percent; in Britain around the same time, 38 percent of fourteen-year olds were still in school, and only 4 percent of seventeen-year olds.[8] Other adolescents were out in the working world, learning trades, earning a living, interacting with adult society all the while. All of this meant that the distinctive character of adolescents, and the emergence of an adolescent group mentality, became apparent in America earlier than elsewhere. It is for good reason that the word "teenager" was an American coinage, first appearing in the early 1940s, and that the American teenager of the 1950s became a widely recognized global icon. Other societies followed suit, as secondary schooling for everyone gradually became the norm after World War II. But the United States was at the forefront of these important changes that fostered the emergence of the adolescent character.

In gauging the impact of these developments, it's worth noting that many early observers of the United States—people writing in the nineteenth century *before* the educational and social infrastructure of the adolescent society was put in place—were impressed by the upright character of the citizenry and their principled adherence to values reflective of the adult society of the time. Americans, in the eyes of one nineteenth-century European observer, were a people "habitually correct in their actions."[9] Similar sentiments were expressed by Frenchman Alexis de Tocqueville. One section of *Democracy in America*, his seminal analysis of American society and government appearing in 1835, was headed "How the Enlightenment, Habits, and Practical Experience of the Americans Contribute to the Success of Democratic Institutions."[10] Americans, Tocqueville observed after months of traveling the country, enjoyed more extensive liberties and freedoms than people elsewhere, but did not use them wantonly. Instead they were guided in their behavior by the maxim of "self-interest properly understood"— self-interest tempered by a sense of the public interest and shared civic values. Despite fewer external restraints on their behavior than elsewhere, the Americans he met on his travels impressed him as "orderly, temperate, moderate, careful, and self-controlled citizens."[11]

The evidence from the American experience helps in formulating a more nuanced version of the adolescent society argument. The philosophical and economic underpinnings of a society matter a great deal, but so does the character of the individuals who make up that society. If the United States were not a nation wedded to liberal principles and dedicated to capitalist practices, the inculcation of adolescent traits would not have had such far-reaching effects. It is primarily in conditions of extensive personal liberty and economic freedom that character shines through as a powerful influence on individual life outcomes and the condition of the social fabric. But shine through it does. As the content of the American character has become more deeply tinted with adolescent coloring down the years, there have been major changes in what Americans choose to do with their extensive freedoms, with wide-ranging societal consequences.

The United States led the way in all of this, but other countries have followed suit. Throughout the Western world, liberal ideals and capitalist practices have become more deeply entrenched over time. Meanwhile, changes to schooling systems have created a more sharply defined adolescent stage of life and encouraged the cultivation of adolescent qualities. The same combination of permissive background conditions and gradual transformations in character has resulted in trends that were evident first in America slowly emerging across many different countries over time.

Sense and Sensibilities

In thinking about other factors that can help us better understand the evolution of the adolescent society, there is one that deserves special extended attention: the dramatic expansion in educational opportunities for people of all backgrounds. It used to be that primary education at most was the norm for most people. Nowadays, secondary education is considered the basic minimum, and many go on to receive extensive postsecondary education. The education received in these additional years covers many bases, but stated most generally the goal is quite simple: to equip people with the knowledge, skills, and wherewithal to be competent, thoughtful, and contributing adults in modern society. And it appears to do all these things remarkably well. Across many indicators of personal capability and commitment, those spending more years in school come out ahead of those with less formal education under their belts. Yet on a number of measures where education produces positive outcomes, the general trend over time has been in the opposite direction. The vast expansion in educational attainment over the past one hundred years has produced clear individual benefits but has failed to deliver the aggregate gains we naturally expected to follow. Where did things go wrong?

I'm not the first to remark on this puzzling pattern. James Côté, focusing on issues of personal growth and maturation, observes that we have "opened the door for a greater proportion of the population to seek higher and more fulfilling forms of personal development." Yet, he continues, "it does not appear that the bulk of the population is doing so. Given that the adult populations of Western countries are more highly educated than any previous citizenry, it is indeed a puzzle why so few people are reaching the heights of personal development."[12] A more specific example involves political participation. One of the most consistent findings in the relevant research is that those with higher levels of education are more likely to participate in various forms of political activity. So why haven't we seen a more active and engaged citizenry emerging as average education levels have shot upward over the years?

A compelling answer to this and similar questions lies, of course, in the effects of the emergent adolescent character—a major unintended consequence of keeping young people in school for a longer time. Extending educational opportunity by making secondary education a universal experience—as well as enlarging the pool of individuals with postsecondary education—*did* equip more people with the knowledge, skills, and wherewithal to be empowered and contributing adults. But it simultaneously created the teenage enclaves that incubated adolescent qualities and triggered *other* forces of change that slowly undermined potential educational benefits. Simply put, the educational and social effects of schooling have often worked at cross-purposes.

As I've argued throughout, the social effects are basic and elemental. Immersion in a society of adolescent peers reinforces core character attributes and values of adolescents, extending their influence into the adult years. The educational effects of education are potent in their own right, but they operate on a different plane, primarily in the realm of rational and deliberate thought. Education improves us in a variety of ways, making us more knowledgeable and discerning, more skillful and adept, but it doesn't fundamentally change who we are.

Or at least not as much as some might hope. Martin Luther King Jr. echoed a common aspiration when he wrote, "Intelligence plus character—that is the goal of true education." This laudable ambition has informed the efforts of administrators and teachers who have placed character education on the agenda of their schools down the years. The idea comes and goes, but in the past two decades it has come back into vogue with the backing of Presidents Clinton, Bush, and Obama and has reappeared on the curriculum in many places. Typically the identified goal is to make students good citizens, meaning not just people active in politics, but individuals of sound motivation and judgment who will make positive contributions to their communities across the board.

The problem is that character education delivered through the school system often tends to be a formal and artificial process quite different from the organic character formation that takes place through intensive interaction with peers. The deliberate attempts schools make to instill "character" can have difficulty competing with the pervasive social conditioning that takes place in the adolescent environment. Teachers and textbooks tell young people one thing, while another is subtly and persistently conveyed by youthful friends and acquaintances. People schooled in these contradictory ways sometimes experience a tension between what they have been told is the "right" course of action—the one reflecting principles they have been explicitly taught in the classroom—and the one they are instinctively drawn to by temperament and disposition. It is a classic battle of sense versus sensibilities, with adolescent sensibilities often winning out over the correct course of action suggested by formal lessons. As a result, the substantial societal benefits we might have hoped to see from steadily rising education levels over the past one hundred years have, in many instances, failed to materialize.

Benefits Lost: Political Engagement

We can see the tug of war between educational effects and adolescent social influence in a number of areas of modern life. In most cases, the benefits of education are widely recognized, but the countervailing effects of the rising adolescent character are not, leaving us struggling to understand why we seem to be spinning our wheels on different fronts instead of making steady advances over time.

One trend that has puzzled many observers is the long-term decline in political engagement even as education levels have risen steadily over time. The most in-depth study of the linkages between education and citizenship starts by noting the consensus on the powerful boost education gives to political engagement: "The notion that formal educational attainment is the primary mechanism behind citizenship characteristics is basically uncontested. A half-century of empirical evidence in American politics points to the consistent and overwhelming influence of 'the education variable' on various aspects of democratic citizenship." There is also, according to the same work, broad agreement on the mechanisms that underlie this tight connection: "People who have been in school for more years absorb civic values and develop interest in politics, which then facilitates increased participation."[13]

Evidence of these positive educational effects is not hard to find. Surveys suggest that those who spend longer in school do in fact show greater absorption of civic values. In the Canadian election study of 2011, for example, 80 percent of those with a graduate degree said that voting was a "duty" and not a "choice," compared to just 59 percent of those who hadn't finished high school. In the 2008 American national election study, there was a similar education gap, with civic duty topping out at over 90 percent for the most educated Americans and bottoming out at 70 percent for the least educated. The second linchpin, interest in politics, is also clearly linked to years spent in the classroom. On that same 2008 American election study, 42 percent of college-educated Americans said they followed politics and elections "extremely" or "very" closely, compared to only 21 percent of those with a high school education or less.[14]

The survey record also suggests these positive educational effects have held steady over time. Within each generation, more-educated individuals express greater interest in politics and are more apt to believe in the idea of civic duty. There is nothing to suggest that the impact of education on various components of engaged citizenship has somehow become less potent in recent times.

So we are left with what has been rightly described as "the puzzle of stagnant or declining political engagement amidst a period of increasing educational attainment."[15] To solve the puzzle, the natural reaction has been to search elsewhere for some counterweight that has been working against the rising tide of positive educational effects. Various ideas have been advanced. Some think it's a simple matter of practicalities: life is a lot busier these days than it used to be, so we have less time for politics. Others point to the relative comfort and affluence of the postwar years, which have made most of us more secure in our day-to-day lives and perhaps more complacent about democracy. Others think that politics itself is to blame. We don't feel any connection or commitment to a system overrun with special interests, spin doctors, and career politicians.

Probing educational effects more closely isn't an obvious approach, since the positive effects of schooling on political engagement seem so well established. But we need to take a broad view of how educational experiences shape us, looking not just at the educational impact, but also the social consequences of the years spent in various educational settings.

In the case of political engagement, we can see how the environment of secondary schooling, the social world of teenagers and their influential peers, would work against the very benefits the education system aims to deliver. Even as students are being introduced to notions of civic duty in the classroom, their social environment is one where ideas of duty and obligation are looked upon with considerable skepticism, where the character trait of conscientiousness is in short supply. The formal lesson presented in the classroom is undermined by the social environment in which it is received.

The same holds true for political interest. Education does a great deal to spark interest in politics: we learn about our society and the world, about how things work and where they fail to work; we are enlightened about alternative approaches to social and political issues; we gain relevant skills that help us to imagine ourselves being politically active and influential. Yet even as we are acquiring some of these building blocks of political interest and engagement, we are surrounded by peers little enthused about politics. Their attention is elsewhere, in the priorities and preoccupations of the teenage realm. In a prior study I looked at survey samples of European citizens and found that levels of political interest and discussion of politics with friends were dramatically lower for fifteen- to eighteen-year olds than for adults—about half the level.[16] There may be a few teenagers who are keen on politics and happy to discuss it with friends, but in general the social environment of adolescence is not one conducive to stoking interest in politics.

So we can see how an education system designed to help young people become empowered adults ready to participate energetically in modern democracy had a basic contradiction at its heart: seeking to teach young people adult roles by institutionally isolating them from adulthood. In the case of political involvement, the system gave rise to powerful effects tugging hard in opposite directions—educational dynamics serving to instill feelings of civic responsibility and cultivate political interest, coupled with a social environment where notions of duty are treated with skepticism and peers are, relatively speaking, quite uninterested in politics. As a result, the citizenship dividends that would be anticipated from rising education levels over the decades have simply not been realized. The best that can be said is that educational gains have likely staved off greater declines in citizen engagement than might have otherwise occurred—though this still implies a significant benefit lost.

Benefits Lost: Social Trust

Other social goods have also been subject to these contradictory forces emerging out of the modern education system. Social trust—the trust we have in those directly around us and in people more generally—is an important example. In the past twenty years or so, there has been a great deal of discussion among economists, political scientists, sociologists, and others about the role of trust in society. Trust has come to be seen as an indispensable good that makes society work more smoothly and effectively, as people lean toward giving one another the benefit of the doubt in all sorts of situations—social interaction, economic exchange, political negotiation, and so on.

Like political engagement, there is little doubt that this social good is positively connected to education. When asked the most common survey question designed to probe trust—Generally speaking would you say that most people can be trusted, or that you can't be too careful in dealing with people?—those with more years of schooling are much more likely to display faith in their fellow humans. On surveys done in the United States, for example, the trusting response climbs from 16 percent among those who did not finish high school all the way up to 56 percent among those with a graduate degree, with steady increases between these two endpoints of the educational spectrum.[17] The same linkage is evident in surveys done in Canada and in various European countries. Trusting individuals are at least twice as numerous at the upper end of the education spectrum as they are at the bottom end.[18]

The connection between education and trust probably comes from a variety of sources. Life experience may be the first that comes to mind. Those who spend more years in school often come from more privileged backgrounds, and the education they receive enables them to live relatively prosperous and secure lives. The better educated are less likely to suffer the kinds of deprivations and hardships that can cause people to be wary of others. This experiential explanation suggests it is not so much education itself that generates trust as it is other life advantages that go along with educational attainment.

However, there are other sources of social trust that suggest more direct educational effects. Our trust in others is not simply based on how the world treats us. Like civic duty, it is a pro-social norm that we can choose to affirm or not—and the educational environment tends to be one in which pro-social norms of this sort are very much promoted. Education also makes us more aware of the social and legal mechanisms that help make a trusting society workable and allow for the detection and punishment of those who break the rules. In short, education conveys the understanding that a trusting society is both desirable and viable. As one study notes, "A college education increases individual knowledge of the cultural environment, economic environment, and legal environment. High [sic] educated people are more likely to share a social consensus on normative values that create an incentive to honor trust, and they are more affirmative of the competence and willingness of social arrangements in the enforcement of trustworthiness and fairness."[19] This same study concludes that it is these perceptions and beliefs—not positive life experiences—that are the most important source of the education-trust connection. In other words, education is not just a proxy for agreeable life experiences; people do actually learn to be more trusting as a result of their years of schooling.

Given this connection, the logical expectation would be that rising education levels should have made us a more trusting society over time. But in fact social trust has moved in the other direction. Robert Putnam provides evidence that the United States has suffered a substantial decline in social trust over the years due to steady erosion in trust levels among rising generations.[20] Many other countries have also seen a drop, while in others trust levels have been more or less stagnant—still an unexpected outcome, given the tremendous rise in average education levels over time. Cases of substantial increase are very much the exception among European and North American countries.[21] So we face a similar mystery to the political engagement conundrum. Why in an era of steady advances in educational attainment are we not seeing the emergence of ever more trusting societies?

Again, the first reaction would be to look for something other than education that has been undermining positive educational effects. One culprit often cited is television. As this medium came to dominate our leisure time, we spent less time out in the community, socializing and interacting with others, and therefore failed to develop the strong social connections that underlie social trust. Instead, we were spending too much time absorbed in the artificial world of television and came to suffer from the "mean world syndrome"—believing that the violence and mayhem seen in TV dramas, police procedurals, and nightly news broadcasts were actually an accurate reflection of the world outside our doors.

I wouldn't totally discount such ideas. But I would highlight another important dynamic stemming from changes to our educational system. We've grown less trusting because we have become, as a result of the rise of adolescent values and behaviors, less trustworthy. As with so many other changes associated with the emergence of the adolescent society, the changes have been gradual and subtle while they are occurring, but striking and undeniable over the long haul.

As we saw in an earlier chapter, there are a number of indicators from the World Values Surveys—questions asking whether it is ever justifiable to cheat on taxes, accept bribes, and so on—that suggest younger generations have slowly been leading society in a more antisocial direction over time. These antisocial attitudes and behaviors affect trust in two ways. One is that we would presumably encounter untrustworthy behavior more often, or hear stories about such behavior from family, friends, and acquaintances. The other is that if we ourselves have absorbed antisocial attitudes, thinking that lying is sometimes justified, for example, or that wrongfully claiming government benefits is OK, then we may believe that others have as well. As Robert Putnam nicely puts it, distrusting attitudes sometimes reflect "projections of one's own dishonest inclinations."[22]

The evidence from the World Values Surveys suggests both dynamics have been slowly draining the reservoirs of social trust as fast as they can be replenished by positive educational infusions. Consider first how our own levels of honesty and rectitude influence our perceptions of the trustworthiness of others. In examining this relationship in the European countries and the United States together, it turns out that a negative effect on trust is mainly evident among those who express rather strong antisocial attitudes—those with an average score of 5 or more (across four items) on the response scale running from 1 (never justifiable) to 10 (always justifiable). Among this group, 32 percent say that "generally speaking, most people can be trusted," compared to 46 percent of those who consistently offer the principled response.[23] On another question about trust in others within one's own country, the effect is stronger still—a trust gap of about 23 percentage points between the most antisocial respondents (49 percent) and their pro-social counterparts (72 percent).[24]

So, in part, declining trust derives from changes in our own underlying character. But it also has to do with our assessment of others. In the 1999 wave of the European Values Study, respondents in the European countries were asked: How many of your compatriots do you think cheat on their taxes? Or claim government benefits to which they are not entitled? The responses were eye-opening. A solid majority (57 percent) felt that "all" or "most" of their fellow citizens cheat on their taxes. Another 40 percent said that "some" compatriots do this, leaving only a minuscule number (4 percent) who believed this wrongful action was committed by "almost none" of their fellow citizens. The picture was not much better for wrongfully claiming government benefits: 42 percent said all or most compatriots do this, while a further 51 percent said some. Only 7 percent said almost none.[25]

Clearly, the people in these surveys believe that antisocial acts are rampant in today's world. And it is not surprising to learn that these beliefs are connected to the trust held in others. Among those who feel that almost all their compatriots are guilty of wrongfully claiming government benefits, only 24 percent express general trust in others. This doubles to 49 percent among those who believe that either some or almost none of their fellow citizens engage in this conduct. For cheating on taxes, the effect runs in the same direction but is weaker: a difference of 8 percentage points (37 percent versus 45 percent) between those who see this behavior as widespread and those who believe it to be more limited. In the smaller set of countries where we can link up questions about the behavior of compatriots and trust in compatriots specifically, both these effects are greater: a yawning trust gap of 36 percentage points (41 percent versus 77 percent) for the government benefits question, and a still sizable difference of 18 percentage points (58 percent versus 76 percent) for the tax-cheating item.[26]

When we stitch together these results, what we see is another unfortunate irony. Our massive investment in education over the past hundred years should have made us a much more trusting society, since further years of education do reliably produce greater trust in others. But changes to the education system have also fostered adolescent character traits and values, setting in motion a parallel process of rising antisocial behaviors that has weakened adherence to important social norms and gradually undermined social trust. The net effect of these two processes has varied from place to place, but the most common outcome has been either a significant decline or stagnation in trust levels—both of which clearly fall short of the substantial gains we might reasonably have expected to see.

Benefits Lost: Personal Empowerment

The same logic can be applied, and similar conclusions derived, for actions and life-style choices that have implications first and foremost for our personal well-being. All else being equal, those possessed of greater formal education are equipped to make better life decisions, ones that serve them well in the long run, than those who have spent fewer years in the classroom. Education cultivates awareness of consequences and knowledge of alternatives; it gives us the capacity to access relevant information and to reason through decisions. Rising education levels down the years should have greatly expanded the pool of individuals with the necessary knowledge and wherewithal to make smart life choices for themselves.

In practice, however, this is not always the case, and problematic life choices continue to plague us. The argument could be applied to any number of trends, but consider just one earlier example: the issue of rising obesity levels and the many health problems that go along with this—increased rates of diabetes, hypertension, and heart disease, to name but a few. As with political engagement and social trust, education is clearly connected to the positive side of the ledger when it comes to weight levels (and indeed healthy living more generally). The more years of education people have under their belt, the less likely they are to be carrying extra pounds.[27]

Again, this education effect partly reflects underlying socioeconomic realities. Those with higher education levels also tend to be better off financially and can afford the gym memberships, healthier food choices, and leisure time that make it easier to live a healthy life. Poverty undoubtedly presents real obstacles to physical well-being. But researchers also believe there is a genuine education effect underlying the differences in weight problems across educational groupings. Greater awareness of potential health risks and consequences, along with better understanding of dietary and nutritional issues, make the better-educated more likely to maintain a healthy weight.[28]

Studies demonstrating the connection between education and positive health outcomes have not generally pondered why we have seen a growing obesity epidemic over the same period that people have become ever more educated. One report highlighting the link between obesity and education mentions only in passing that "it is interesting that . . . a trend towards a higher education in the survey populations has been observed."[29] It's more than just interesting—it is both disturbing and perplexing that widespread educational gains have not seen more people taking some of the personal steps necessary to address one of the major contemporary causes of poor health and early morbidity.

Clearly we can't hold individuals solely responsible for this state of affairs. The food industry itself must carry much of the blame for stocking grocery store shelves with unhealthy fare packed with sugar, salt, and fats and enticing us to add it to our shopping carts through incessant advertising. But studies also show that personal habits and decisions around diet and lifestyle make a very significant difference to weight problems. The consistent finding is that the most important character trait driving these decisions is impulsiveness, linked to a more general lack of conscientiousness.[30] An appetite for risk has also been implicated, suggesting that some who are carrying extra pounds may be aware of the potential health dangers lurking ahead yet indifferent nonetheless.[31] As with other trends in our adolescent society, a potential educational benefit—more health-aware individuals and a healthier society—has been at least partly undone by the countervailing impact of rising adolescent character traits and behavioral proclivities.

Obesity is just one example of our failure to make advances in important areas of personal well-being. If we extend the idea to ask broader questions about life choices, we come back to the conundrum raised by James Côté, author of *Arrested Adulthood* and other works that question the life decisions and sense of purpose among grown-ups of today, both young and old. We have "opened the door," Côté observes, "for a greater proportion of the population to seek higher and more fulfilling forms of personal development," yet "it does not appear that the bulk of the population is doing so. Given that the adult populations of Western countries are more highly educated than any previous citizenry, it is indeed a puzzle why so few people are reaching the heights of personal development."[32]

Côté's concern is grounded in the understanding that education has the potential to empower us in so many ways. It is seen, quite rightly, as an all-purpose transformative agent. Extending educational opportunity should have served to strengthen our individual capacities and to create a more empowered adult society—socially, economically, politically, personally. Instead, decades later, too many of us are caught up in impulsive ways of living that offer immediate gratification at the expense of long-term well-being. Adolescent character traits mean that too often we opt for the quick and easy option rather than drawing on our knowledge and reasoning capacities to make more fully informed and considered decisions.

Benefits Amplified: Tolerance and Creativity

All is not doom and gloom, however. On the other side of the ledger, there are areas where adolescent sensibilities, rather than undermining educational benefits, have instead tended to reinforce them. Rather than a tug of war, the two have worked together to produce greater and more rapid social change than might have been expected from simple education effects alone.

These ramped-up benefits are mainly connected to the adolescent quality that is typically seen as a boon to modern life: openness to experience. In adolescents, this openness is often directed inward, toward goals of self-exploration and the cultivation of personal identity. Education injects important new dimensions to this temperamental openness, as it expands our horizons and directs our attention outward to the richness and diversity of the world. Social studies classes teach us about other cultures and different ways of living. History lessons demonstrate that ideas and practices of the present are not universal and timeless by introducing us to events and societies of the past. Literature likewise broadens our perspective, as we are drawn into the lives of fictional characters whose circumstances and experiences differ vastly from our own. All these learning opportunities cultivate an awareness of human diversity and difference, of possibilities beyond our present reality. When combined with temperamental openness, this helps to produce individuals who have their eyes wide open to the world around them.

Following this reasoning (which echoes ideas presented back in chapter 5), it's fair to say that one of the principal benefits of greater educational opportunity, aided and abetted by the adolescent quality of openness, has been the emergence of a more tolerant society—a society where different groups and ways of living are acknowledged and accepted, sometimes even celebrated. The gains achieved on this front have been substantial and, in a historical context, amazingly rapid. In the 1950s, segregationist laws were still in effect in the southern United States; a mere half century later, Barack Obama won the presidency in the historic election of 2008. In a similar vein, the traditional line of thinking was that native peoples should be assimilated into the dominant culture, for their sake and for ours; now there is much greater respect accorded to indigenous traditions and practices, as well as considerable sympathy for claims to some form of self-governance. In the past, LGBTQ individuals remained in the closet for fear of humiliation and persecution. Since the 1970s, their right to the same opportunities as everyone else, most recently the right to marry, has come into effect at a rapid pace. As we saw back in chapter 5, these postwar victories were built on a gradual increase in tolerant attitudes that had begun among cohorts born prior to World War II—cohorts that received the combined benefits of greater education and the openness-enhancing effects of adolescent socialization experiences. Smaller steps in this earlier era gradually gave way to larger leaps forward in the postwar period. Our current attitudes and policies may not be fully enlightened toward all marginalized groups on all counts, but we have gained a deeper appreciation over time of the need to acknowledge and respect basic human differences.

The educational contribution to this happy story is widely recognized—many studies of expanding tolerance over time attribute the bulk of this change to the enlightenment acquired through higher education levels in the population.[33] What is missing from the story is the added momentum generated by our increasingly adolescent character. If we have made great strides in the area of tolerance and acceptance, we have a potent combination of educational edification and adolescent sensibilities of openness to thank for this important advance.

Another example of adolescent qualities working in combination with educational gains to produce impressive change lies in the economic sector. The most common explanation for the strong economic growth that marked large swaths of the twentieth century is the enormous increase in "human capital"—that is, the massive investment in education that has created a smarter and more capable workforce. But as Richard Florida has shown, the twentieth century also witnessed the steady rise of the creative class, a broad category of people contributing to economic advancement through the application of creativity across a wide range of occupations. Underlying the rise of this class, the adolescent society theory suggests, has been the ascent of openness as a character trait in society at large, and by extension in the working world specifically. In other words, the past century has witnessed a potent synergy of character and "human capital" effects, adolescence furnishing the trait of openness that underwrites creativity and innovation, education giving people the skills and knowledge that have allowed this creativity to be adeptly applied in the real world. Educational advances alone might have given us more competent thinkers and workers, but an infusion of adolescent openness meant that these adept individuals were also open-minded creators. The result has been sustained periods of economic growth, fueled jointly by heightened capability and creativity, unparalleled in human history.

In both these cases, where education effects have worked in concert with adolescent influences to produce positive social change, the pattern of forward progress over time has been steady, strong, and unidirectional. In the case of tolerant social and political attitudes, this is indeed the pattern suggested by the prior analysis of growing tolerance in the United States, which was traced back as far as cohorts born in the 1920s. By contrast, in cases where adolescent influence and education effects are working at cross-purposes—such as political participation and social trust—the tug of war between the two is unlikely to produce steady, one-way change. What we will see instead is a back-and-forth battle between opposing forces of social transformation. Putnam's analysis in *Bowling Alone*, for example, identifies an upward surge on certain key measures in early decades followed by a more recent period of decline: "The best evidence suggests that social trust rose from the mid-1940s to the mid-1960s just as many other measures of social capital did.... In the mid-1960s, however, this beneficent trend was reversed, initiating a long-term decline in social trust."[34] Likewise, his extensive analysis points to rising civic and political participation through the earlier decades of the twentieth century, followed by a slow, steady decline since the 1960s.[35] One basic benchmark is voter turnout: participation in US presidential elections trended upward from 1920 on, reaching its high-water mark in the Kennedy-Nixon contest of 1960 before starting a gradual downward slide thereafter.

The long-term pattern of rise and decline suggests that the positive impact of education effects on the population outpaced negative adolescent influences for some time, as student enrollments at both the high school and university level expanded rapidly from the 1920s onward. At this stage, the adolescent society was in its infancy; adolescent qualities were quietly incubating in the social circles of the teenage world but did not yet exert broad influence on adult behavior. Several decades later, the accumulating effects of adolescent peer socialization, growing more pronounced with successive generations, became more substantial and began to outweigh the positive effects linked to a more educated populace. A downward trend on social indicators negatively affected by adolescent character traits started to become apparent and has been outpacing—in some cases, overwhelming—the effects of educational uplift ever since.

A Divided Society: Education Gaps and the Social Fabric

The interplay of educational effects and adolescent influences points to a further important refinement of the adolescent society thesis: the effects may have been sweeping, but they have rippled unevenly through different sections of the population. The negative consequences of an infusion of adolescent qualities are evident first and foremost among those who have not received some of the offsetting benefits of extended education. Those same negative effects are muted among those with abundant schooling, while the more beneficial adolescent qualities that are embellished by educational experiences—openness and its education-enhanced offshoots, creativity and tolerance—are apparent in spades. The adolescent society looks quite different depending on where you focus your attention.

A number of writers have identified sections of American society lying on different sides of the deep demarcation line now represented by educational attainment. One contributor is Charles Murray in his 2012 work, *Coming Apart*. His book is inspired by a theoretical framework more conservative than mine. Murray's starting point is the idea that America was built around the "founding virtues" of honesty, industriousness, religiosity, and marriage and that these need to be recovered to make the nation whole once again. Yet many of the empirical patterns of social change he identifies are consistent with my analysis.

Much of the book is dedicated to examining how life has been evolving on the proverbial wrong side of the tracks. Murray observes that since the early 1960s America has seen serious declines in social trust and rising rates of divorce; over the same period, there has been a drop-off in civic involvement, along with a rise in antisocial acts, including criminal activity. This is familiar terrain, characterized above as some of the more pernicious effects of a burgeoning adolescent temperament in the adult population. The point Murray adds to my story is that all these trends are disproportionately concentrated among those with below-average levels of education, or what he calls the new lower class in American society. It is in this section of society that a number of social problems have grown quite dramatically over the course of time.[36]

Back on the other side of the tracks, among well-educated Americans, Murray sees evidence of the same worrisome trends, but all are considerably muted. To put this in my terms, these highly educated individuals are as much the product of the adolescent society as those at the lower end of the education spectrum, but they possess important skills, knowledge, and cognitive habits that have helped mitigate those negative adolescent influences. For the most part, they do participate politically, are trusting of others, and make shrewd life choices that serve them and their families well, owing to important capacities gained through their educational experiences. That same educational background has also amplified the more positive patterns of the adolescent society. The well-educated are highly tolerant and creative, involved in meaningful work, and eagerly partake of the varied cultural amenities and opportunities that modern life has to offer. Moreover, as Murray observes, they congregate together, creating communities that are vibrant and well-functioning, including convivial neighborhoods in large urban centers and smaller, upscale hamlets that teem with civic and cultural life.[37] Extensive schooling and adolescent sensibilities have come together to create a societal upper crust experiencing a few of the stresses of the adolescent society but generally enjoying lives as rich and fulfilling as any ever have. Given these trends, Murray's principal concern is that this divergence in fortunes points to the emergence of two Americas, separated not just by occupation and wealth but by a deeper division encompassing social mores and broader life outcomes— which has weakened Americans' affinity for those on the other side of the tracks and undermined their commitment to the common good.

Similar themes echo throughout Robert Putnam's follow-up investigation of the American social fabric, one that updates the picture of general social decline he outlined in *Bowling Alone* fifteen years earlier. In his 2015 work *Our Kids*, Putnam documents the diverging fortunes over the past half century of those growing up with college-educated parents and those whose parents have a high school education at best. The title picks up on an important shift in public thinking: caring about "our kids" used to mean paying heed to the future of all young people in one's community and the nation as a whole. Now it means nurturing and promoting our own offspring, something highly educated parents do very effectively and strategically compared to their poorly educated counterparts.[38] Where Murray emphasizes the loss of traditional virtues, Putnam is more sensitive to the practical challenges facing those at the lower end of the social ladder: economic hardship leads to family strife and frequent marital breakdown, which damages communities and reduces the social supports kids need as they are developing. Social advancement is blocked, contributing to widespread attitudes of disillusionment and distrust. Not only is life harder for kids starting at the bottom; it is much tougher for them to transcend their life circumstances.

The two studies together offer a sense of the varied factors that have transformed life on different sides of the tracks and contributed to a widening gulf in American society. To summarize this social division in my terms, one America embodies the downside of the adolescent society, where a variety of social ills—distrust, disengagement, disempowerment—have fully manifested as unfortunate consequences of the rising tide of adolescent character traits and values. Difficult socioeconomic conditions only exacerbate these effects and amplify the consequences of personal missteps and misfortune. The other America embodies the upside, where educational resources and skills have mitigated negative adolescent influences and enhanced other, more positive, adolescent qualities to create a vibrant, creative, and open society. Affluent circumstances provide a generous cushion against any pressures and stresses that might come along to threaten this happy arrangement. The two Americas are growing apart, with no catalyst in sight that might help bring them back together. Murray corrects those who lament the general social corrosion of recent decades by underlining that what we are really seeing is the "*selective* collapse of American community"[39]—or as Putnam puts it, a "split-screen American nightmare . . . in which kids from the wrong side the tracks . . . can barely imagine the future that awaits the kids from the right side of the tracks."[40]

Further evidence of this deep division within American society came to the fore during the 2016 presidential election campaign. Donald Trump's policies were certainly different (from both Hillary Clinton's and those favored by the Republican establishment), but it was his angry and aggressive demeanor that really set him apart from prior presidential candidates. Time and again he broke with established political and social norms, as he lied on a regular basis, encouraged violence at political rallies, bullied and belittled political opponents, and used offensive language to cast aspersions on various minority groups. News stories during the campaign revealed earlier instances of egregious conduct, including numerous allegations of sexual assault. The divergent reactions of Americans to Trump's transgressive behavior, both past and present, were revealing. Some—especially Trump's much beloved "poorly educated" cohort—cheered him on and voted him into office, while others were stunned and mortified that so many of their fellow Americans could find him an acceptable candidate for president. Rarely have the political worldviews—or perhaps more so, the social sensibilities—of Americans seemed so starkly at odds. Of course, the Trump phenomenon, or something like it, is not unique to the United States. Populist leaders in a number of countries have taken a similar path, not only proposing more nativist immigration, trade, and security policies but also adopting a more belligerent and unrestrained manner of politicking that flouts established social and political norms. This approach to politics has won them surprising electoral success in many places, especially among the less fortunate sections of society.

These troubling developments offer striking evidence that the fissures run deep in modern society, with education looming large in the equation. Education has emerged as a key divide in the current age, not simply because it opens the door to better jobs and higher incomes for those who have the privilege of staying in school longer, but also because of its complex interactions with adolescent characteristics and the distinctive social fabric that has emerged on different sides of the educational divide.

The Plot Thickens

To come back to the opening question at the start of this chapter, the answer is clearly yes: other factors have influenced the evolution of the adolescent society in important, intriguing, and sometimes lamentable ways.

The driving force behind the change was the creation of adolescent enclaves that lent special influence to peers in the formative teenage years and promoted the rise of the adolescent character. But the effects have been felt most fully in places where a general commitment to principles of personal autonomy and economic freedom ensures that individual character has a profound impact on the texture of our lives. This is why the United States and other Western countries, places where the prevailing public philosophy and economic model are centered on the individual, have witnessed the greatest social transformations in the wake of the advancing adolescent character.

The progress of the adolescent society is also intimately connected to the changes in the education system that created adolescent enclaves in the first place—changes that elevated the education level of the population, which itself has been a significant source of social transformation over time. Over the course of the past century, these educational effects have interacted with adolescent character trends to produce diverse and sometimes surprising outcomes in wide-ranging areas of modern life. Our understanding of the changing contours of modern society, and the divisions within, is extended and deepened by looking beyond straightforward educational effects to consider the adolescent society dynamics that have been inextricably linked to twentieth-century reforms to the education system.

BUCKING THE TREND
The Millennials and Beyond

To avoid undue complication, I've left aside the most important qualification and update to everything I've said in this book. Until now. It turns out that the evolution of the adolescent society is not a simple one-way street where adolescent qualities become ever more prevalent and influential in the adult population over time. More than a decade into the new millennium there are important counter-trends, evident for some time now, that cry out for some acknowledgment and explanation.

These developments are embodied in the attitudes and values of today's younger generation, a group that has been given various labels, most commonly "generation Y" or the "millennials." A number of observers have suggested there is something quite different about today's young adults and teenagers. These new cohorts are bucking trends—undesirable trends for the most part—that had been moving steadily in the wrong direction for a great many years.

Among the first to sing the praises of the millennials were American authors Neil Howe and William Strauss. Their 2000 book, *Millennials Rising*, offered a sweeping portrait of the youth population at the dawn of the new millennium. Their overarching theme, since picked up by many others, was that the millennials are more careful, conscientious, and considerate than young people have been for a very long time—not entirely adult perhaps, but certainly more grown-up than earlier generations of postwar adolescents at the same age and stage of life.

The demographic cut-off Howe and Strauss use to define the millennials is concise: they are those born in 1982 and later, who would have been eighteen or younger at the turn of the millennium. My definition is a bit looser: the "millennials" are those coming of age *after* the adolescent society was in full flight—roughly, in other words, those born from the late 1960s onward, the decade when adolescent norms and traits became fully manifest. I agree with Howe and Strauss that the millennial transformation has been most apparent among those born in the 1980s and later, but would suggest that the mechanisms of change were already quietly operating at an earlier date. In other words, millennial qualities have emerged gradually rather than abruptly, and paradoxically from within the very citadel of the adolescent society.

Definitional differences aside, Howe and Strauss present a variety of persuasive evidence to suggest new ways of thinking and acting on the part of the millennials, with more recent data confirming the continuation of many of these trends:

- The sharp drop in the crime rate among young people is a widely known and welcome trend. Howe and Strauss report that since 1993 "America has enjoyed a plunge in youth crime, the speed and distance of which has no precedent since the birth of modern data."[1] The youth rate for the most serious violent crimes, for example, fell by 45 percent from 1993 to 1998. Since then, the decline has continued across most categories of crime, albeit at a slower pace, to reach new historic lows.[2]

- Mirroring the declining crime rate, the National Youth Risk Behavior Survey found that the percentage of high school students who had been in a physical fight in the past twelve months fell from 42 percent in 1991 to 23 percent in 2015.[3] In a similar vein, Steven Pinker reports that rates of violent victimization at school have declined from about 9 percent in the early 1990s to less than 2 percent by 2010.[4]

- The use of harmful substances among young people has fallen off substantially after peaking in the late 1970s. In 1979, half of those ages twelve to seventeen reported having drunk alcohol in the prior month; by 1998, Howe and Strauss reported, this was just under 20 percent.[5] The downward trend has continued, and by 2011 the rate of alcohol use among teens was just over 13 percent. Cigarette smoking in this same group has plummeted from the 30 percent level in the early 1980s to just under 8 percent by 2011.[6]

- Around the mid-1990s, the percentage of teenagers reporting that they were sexually active began to fall. Accompanying this was a sharp rise in the use of contraceptives among those who were active; the proportion of teenage girls using birth control at first intercourse jumped from 48 percent in 1982 to 77 percent in 1995.[7] The result of these changing behaviors has been a sharp drop in the rate of teen pregnancy. By 2012, the US Department of Health and Human Services was reporting the lowest teenage birth rate in seven decades,[8] with the birth rate for girls fifteen to seventeen sitting at one-half the 1991 level.

- On the educational front, Howe and Strauss saw signs of looming improvements in the results of international standardized tests conducted in 1995. Grade 12 students were struggling, comparatively speaking, but grade 8 and especially grade 4 students were doing much better.[9] Long-term tracking suggests mixed results on this front. After suffering across-the-board declines from the 1960s through to the early 1980s, SAT scores for high school students have recovered on the mathematics side, but stagnated, and more recently declined further, on the reading component of the test (which I suspect may be connected to something else entirely—the impact of pervasive electronic gadgets on reading habits).[10] A different educational outcome showing clearer and sharper improvement is the high school dropout rate, which fell from 14.1 percent in 1980 to just 6.6 percent by 2012—a trend suggestive of improved perseverance among marginal students in the millennial generation.[11]

- Signs of renewed civic-mindedness have also been emerging—what Howe and Strauss called a "new Millennial service ethic."[12] This partly reflects new service learning and volunteer requirements in high school and middle school, but Howe and Strauss also saw evidence of a more vibrant civic spirit in the actions of the most committed teenagers in the 1990s. The rate of regular volunteering, as opposed to the onetime activities usually required by schools, has been steadily climbing among grade 12 students—from below 10 percent in the early 1990s to about 13 percent by 2005.[13]

- As the millennials have become eligible to vote, they have shown further signs of renewed civic spirit. Following a turnout rate of 40 percent for the eighteen-to-twenty-nine age group in the 1996 and 2000 presidential elections, participation increased to 49 percent in 2004 and 51 percent in 2008, before dipping down to 45 percent in 2012.[14] While there is undoubtedly some "Obama effect" in those most recent numbers—the euphoria of 2008 followed by reduced enthusiasm in 2012—the fact that the upward turn began in 2004 when John Kerry was the Democratic nominee suggests there may also be a more general millennial trend at work.[15]

- One final adultlike shift on the part of millennials: more are interested in becoming parents. In 2012, 74 percent of college freshmen said "raising a family" was an important life goal, compared just to 59 percent back in 1977.[16]

All in all, it's a fairly impressive record extending across many different sectors of youth activity and behavior. Howe and Strauss sum it up this way: "The

Millennials . . . are demonstrably reversing a wide array of negative youth trends, from crime to profanity to sex to test scores, that have prevailed in America for nearly half a century. In other words, Millennials are reversing the long-term direction of change."[17]

Given these auspicious beginnings, the outlook for the future seems promising. As the millennials age and mature further, they have the capacity, Howe and Strauss believe, "to become America's next great generation"[18]—the phrase newsman Tom Brokaw coined to describe those who came of age during the Depression and World War II, the stalwart generation that overcame and achieved so much. Whether that grandiose title is deserved remains to be seen. Up to this point, millennial changes have been most pronounced in the area of personal conduct, rather than public engagement and achievement; they are quietly marking out new footpaths for themselves as individuals in a world where adolescent-inspired norms are deeply entrenched in the wider culture. And most of the millennial trends, at this stage, are J-turns rather than U-turns: a reversal of prior trends to be sure, but not a complete turnaround. Still, this could be the harbinger of greater things to come, from both the millennials and subsequent generations following in their footsteps. They are certainly developments worth tracking.

The notion that a new generational spirit is in the air is reinforced by trends in other countries. A Canadian version of the millennials argument has been advanced by sociologist Reginald Bibby. Bibby has been surveying large samples of Canadian teenagers at eight-year intervals since 1984. Comparing today's teens to the youth of past decades, he finds evidence of similar changes taking place north of the border, with personal conduct and attitudes again leading the way.

As in the United States, one notable shift lies in millennial attitudes toward the future and expectations around family formation. In 1992, 15 percent of the teenagers in Bibby's sample did not anticipate getting married later in life. By 2008, this had fallen to 10 percent.[19] Similarly, 16 percent in the earlier survey indicated they did not anticipate having children, but by 2008 this was only 5 percent—a threefold decrease in a fairly short period.[20] These changes suggest a more adult orientation among Canadian teens, again representing the reversal of a long-standing trend.

These attitudinal changes are mirrored in behavioral patterns similar to those in the United States. Teen pregnancy rates in Canada have followed a sharp downward path, falling by 40.8 percent from 1994 to 2006 before leveling off more recently. Canadian millennials may anticipate having children down the road but seem to be taking the necessary precautions to avoid this for the time being.[21] Property crime arrests among those twelve to seventeen have dropped to about one-quarter the level of the early 1990s, while violent crime rates, much

lower to start with, have also declined by a modest degree.[22] High school dropout rates across the country have likewise greatly improved, now sitting at half
the 1990 level.[23] As these various indicators demonstrate, the US is not alone in
seeing a host of positive behavioral changes among today's younger generation.

While the main focus of millennial research has been on their distinctive behavior, assertions about character typically follow. The millennials, it is suggested, are
unusually conscientious, as evidenced by their avoidance of risky behavior and
generally temperate conduct. They are more agreeable than teenagers or young
adults of the past and consequently less rebellious, delinquent, or generally difficult to get along with. They are not the spoiled narcissists some have claimed
them to be; instead, Howe and Strauss write, the millennials "have much greater
regard for each other, their parents and the community than Gen X'ers or baby
boomers had at the same phase of life."[24] A leading Canadian newsmagazine sums
up this optimistic assessment this way: "After spending the past 50 years fretting
that each successive generation is more depraved and uncontrollable than the
one previous, perhaps society can finally rest easy. This [the millennial cohort]
appears to be a generation with its collective head screwed on right."[25]

If it all sounds too good to be true, there is another angle to consider. While
the millennial reversal of long-term trends may have mitigated some of the negative consequences linked to the emergence of the adolescent society, it also has
dampened the positive effects. In particular, openness to experience and its allied
qualities, the most attractive feature of our adolescent society, seem to be less
prominent among the millennial generation.

A couple of Reginald Bibby's findings hint at this change. He finds a decrease
in the propensity of young Canadians over the past thirty years to hold mystical
beliefs, beliefs connected to one of the constituent elements of openness, the tendency to fantasize. In a 1984 survey, for example, 53 percent of Canadian teenagers reported believing in astrology; by 2008, this had fallen to 47 percent. In 1984,
69 percent of Canadian teens agreed that "some people have psychic powers." By
2008, it was only 43 percent.[26]

No one, except perhaps those in the palm-reading business, will be overly
concerned about these particular changes. However, other openness attributes of
greater consequence also seem to be flagging. A research paper published in 2011
caught public attention when it announced evidence of a "creativity crisis" in the
United States.[27] The paper drew on the results of a widely used test, the Torrance
Test of Creative Thinking, that has been administered to tens of thousands of
students of various ages over the past forty years. The test is an hourlong series of
creative exercises (listing alternative uses for an everyday object like a paper clip,
for example) that has proven to be a reliable gauge in predicting creative activity
and achievement later in life.

The 2011 study sounded alarm bells when it found evidence of a decline across various components of the Torrance Test that was "steady and persistent, from 1990 to the present."[28] This was not simply a decline in habits of lateral thinking. The study's findings suggested a broader erosion in qualities linked to the personality trait of openness, as well as those elements of extroversion most closely tied to openness. Over the twenty-year period covered by the study, young people had become "less emotionally expressive, less energetic, less talkative and verbally expressive, less humorous, less imaginative, less unconventional, less lively and passionate"[29]—a series of changes that can be seen as the flip side, and downside, of the buttoned-down nature of the millennials.

Howe and Strauss make similar observations when they suggest that the respect for rules and convention exhibited by the millennials may have the unfortunate side effect of making them "more bland [and] less creative." They flag a related concern: this disposition could give rise to inflexible thinking and a reduced willingness to "tolerate deviation from the group norm."[30] Just a year after *Millennials Rising* was published in 2000, the events of 9/11 triggered developments in which concerns of this very sort came to the fore. Americans rallied behind their government even as actions of questionable legitimacy and necessity—the American-led invasion of Iraq, the torture of prisoners of war, the establishment of a beyond-the-pale military prison at Guantanamo Bay— were carried out as part of the "war on terror." Concerns about excessive group-think and intolerance of dissent on the part of Americans were rightly expressed by various observers, both inside and outside the United States. Wherever one stood on these actions, it seems clear that American millennials were much more quiescent in the face of controversial government action than the youth of earlier periods—the sharp response of young Americans to the Vietnam War, for example, offers a stark contrast. For those who believe that democracy sometimes benefits from a more expressive and critical youth who push us to take a hard look at ourselves and our government's actions, the millennials may just be a bit too well behaved.

The cautious and practical bent of millennials also manifests itself in the place I spend my workdays—the university. The educational choices being made by young people today tilt sharply toward professional and technical fields. Enrollment in the liberal arts, where creativity and critical thinking are more heavily valued, has been steadily declining in recent years. No doubt the uncertain state of the economy makes millennials nervous as they think about their job prospects after graduation. But research also shows that character traits guiding young people in their decisions generally have a strong impact on their choice of major, with those low in openness and high in conscientiousness opting for the more practical fields.[31] The critical and creative thinkers who used to fill our

philosophy, history, and sociology classrooms are, it would seem, slowly diminishing as a proportion of the younger generation.

As these diverse examples suggest, the actions and inactions, the priorities and
preferences, of the millennials raise a host of important questions about where
we are headed as a society. The same trends also make us wonder how we got
here. How is it that the gradual spread of adolescent qualities has slowed down
and even reversed itself over the course of the past thirty years?

The popular answer to this question (focused on the positive side of the
millennial coin) is simple: we came to our collective senses. As the 1960s gave
way to the 1970s, the excesses that were resulting from an effusion of youthful
qualities—unfettered individualism, hedonism, skepticism toward conventional
norms and social order—started to become more apparent. We were slow to move
on this, however, and continued on a downward spiral through the rest of the
Me Decade—until finally we saw the light. "The early 1980s," Howe and Strauss
write, "is when the national rates for many behaviors damaging to children—
divorce, abortion, violent crime, alcohol consumption, and drug abuse—reach
their postwar high-water mark. This was also when the well-being of children
began to dominate the national debate over family issues."[32] The charge was led
by a resurgent conservative movement decrying the social upheaval that liberals
had purportedly unloosed on the nation. Riding this wave of righteousness, Ronald Reagan moved into the Oval Office preaching messages of personal responsibility and family values that resonated with many Americans.

Liberals were reluctant to jump on the family values bandwagon but nonetheless recognized some of the problems as urgent and pressing. By the 1990s,
as Democrats came back to power, they had come around to their own version
of how to address the problems facing young people and the nation as a whole.
Instead of parents alone taking care of their children's upbringing, the liberal
view was that it "takes a village," as Hillary Clinton argued in her 1996 book
(the title borrowed from an African proverb). It is for society as a whole, liberals
argued, to ensure children receive the support and guidance they need to become
responsible, competent, and contributing adults.

But if liberals and conservatives differed over methods, a consensus had
emerged on the need to be more attentive to children in their formative years.
As a result of this agreement, parenting styles, along with schooling policies
and practices, changed considerably. Howe and Strauss remark, "Not since the
Progressive era, near the dawn of the twentieth century, has America greeted
the arrival of a new generation with such a dramatic rise in adult attention to
the needs of children."[33] Following the laissez-faire parenting styles of the 1960s
and 1970s, parents in the 1980s started to be more focused on their children (in
varied ways to be sure: conservatives emphasizing monitoring and discipline,

liberals respectful listening and gentle guidance). This attentiveness to children was mirrored in policies adopted in schools, though here the emphasis was probably more on the stick than the carrot. These included a back-to-basics curriculum to ensure all were developing core academic skills, along with zero tolerance for disciplinary infractions and a renewed emphasis on character education. The impact, so the thinking goes, was apparent in various positive trends: less risky behavior, better academic results, greater civic engagement, and stronger moral commitment. As a result of our collective determined efforts, young people were developing into more responsible and upstanding members of society.

This same shift in parenting practices and schooling philosophy has been linked to negative trends connected to the rise of the millennials. If there has been a creativity decline, critics say, it is because we have been structuring our kids' lives too much, both at home and in the school setting.[34] From 1981 to 1997 alone, according to one study, the amount of time children ages three to twelve spent in "unstructured" activity fell from fifty-two to thirty-three hours per week.[35] To develop open, creative minds, children need free play and opportunities to explore, not rules and tight schedules. For some, these stifling effects go further than the suppression of creativity to a greater incapacitation of the young. They see children, teenagers, and even young adults having become reliant on parents for support of all kinds—financial, moral, emotional—and utterly unable to think or act for themselves. Examples of so-called helicopter parents and their coddled offspring abound, including parents who shadow their children during college orientation week or who undertake contract negotiations on their behalf when they land their first job. One psychotherapist writing in the *Atlantic* reports encounters with twenty-something patients who seem to have everything going for them on the surface but feel anxious and disoriented as they try to navigate the world on their own. Parents who have supported them unfailingly from day one are largely to blame.[36]

Clearly there are various angles to consider in this wave of millennial change, but there is also a common core of agreement. Significant changes representing a reversal of earlier trends have been occurring among teenagers and young adults for a number of years now, and this is largely because of conscious decisions we made as a society and as individual parents to stop leaving young people to their own devices and instead provide a stronger guiding hand in their development.

It is the second part of this common wisdom that I would question. It's not that greater attentiveness to the young isn't part of the story behind the rise of the millennials. But there is more to it than this. Beneath the surface, and probably a bit prior to the early 1980s, developments were quietly unfolding that help explain why the millennial generation came into being. As with earlier changes that mark the rise of the adolescent society, it is too simple to characterize the emergence of a new ethos in a particular era as a conscious change of course by those embracing it at the time. The millennial generation is as much a natural and predictable consequence of the ongoing evolution of the adolescent society as it is the result of deliberate efforts to rethink how we shepherd young people into adulthood.

To see how this is so, we first need to take a step back and take a fresh look at the different forces that influence character development and help shape the kind of people we become. We can then sort through how these forces have been at work molding the distinctive character of the millennial generation.

Who We Are: Nature and Nurture

All human traits and characteristics originate in two basic sources: genes and the environment. Back in chapter 2, the genetic contribution to personality formation was briefly discussed and then set aside. But the point raised was an important one: a series of studies over a number of years have led to the surprising conclusion that there is a substantial heritable component to personality. For each of the Big Five traits, roughly half of "who we are" represents the genetic contribution of parents. The effect is so powerful that some, including Judith Harris in her influential book *The Nurture Assumption*, suggest it undercuts any notion of parents as active agents in the process of personality development.

Like many parents, I would resist going quite that far. But it is certainly fair to say that the environmental influence of parents is less than we might have previously imagined—which means, of course, that others in our social circles have a greater environmental impact than we commonly assume. Back in chapter 2, this conclusion was the starting point for an argument focused on environmental effects on who we are—specifically, the impact of a critical environmental change that decisively influenced the character of rising generations over the course of the twentieth century. The creation of a social milieu in which peers were the dominant influence during the adolescent years represented a sharp break with the past. Our provisional adult character was henceforth shaped largely by adolescent peers rather than adults, with wide-ranging consequences for the personality of individuals and the character of modern society as a whole.

Having spent most of the book on this theme, I now want to go back and revisit how the intimate ties between parent and child do, in fact, have important molding effects. For it is family dynamics, touching on both the nature inherited from parents and the nurturing parents provide, that help explain the distinctive character of the millennial generation.

These new family dynamics are connected to an important trend of the past few decades: changing fertility patterns in the adolescent society. People have fewer children nowadays as birthrates have fallen over time, especially since the 1960s. In the United States, it now sits at 1.8 children per woman, a bit below the replacement level of 2.0; in other developed countries, it has fallen further, as low as 1.3 in some European countries.[37] In all these places, having children has become a more limited and selective process than used to be the case. There are now certain filters in place—self-chosen filters for the most part—that affect childbearing, and these have served to dampen or even reverse the steady diffusion of adolescent qualities.

To Be or Not to Be a Parent

To see how these filters operate, we have to look more closely at factors that affect the decision to have children. It's helpful to break down the final outcome—how many children people end up having—by looking at the various decisions and circumstances that affect the end result.

First there is the question of general inclination: do I want to be a parent? A variety of personal traits can influence this orientation, with some seeing parenthood as an integral part of their personal life plan and others finding it an unappealing proposition. There is then the immediate follow-up question: how many children do I want to have? Family size varies a great deal nowadays, the variations again primarily a reflection of personal preference. People who have one or two children often look at those who choose to have a minivan's worth with a mix of wonderment and disbelief, as if they had five heads rather than five kids—suggesting that the mind-set of those content with a smallish family differs markedly from those preferring a bigger brood.

Another important choice in the procreation process is deciding when to start a family. This has been pushed later and later, with many now delaying parenthood well into their thirties or even early forties. In the United States, 2009 marked the first time that women in the thirty-to-thirty-four age bracket had a higher birthrate than women twenty to twenty-four.[38] Postponing parenthood has implications for the number of children borne, as those who delay often end up having fewer kids. So factors that affect when someone chooses to begin a family indirectly influence family size.

Meanwhile, many of the decisions around becoming a parent are contingent on being in a stable relationship, far from a given in this day and age. This too is partly a function of various personal qualities, including some that affect whether individuals wish to be in such a relationship and others influencing whether anyone is lining up to be their significant other. Obviously, this is not an essential condition of parenthood: some people choose to be single parents, and others inadvertently find themselves in that situation. But it remains the case that couples in stable relationships tend to have more children than others. So personal qualities that affect the formation and stability of relationships indirectly affect the number of children someone has.

How many children, if any, someone has is also affected by potential decisions around the termination of unwanted pregnancies. This is a more sensitive area for obvious reasons. But with 17 percent of pregnancies ending in abortion in North America and 30 percent in Europe,[39] it is another potential factor to consider in seeking a fuller understanding of who has children these days and who does not.

Reproductive Choices: The Influence of Doctrine and Ideology

As birthrates have declined across the Western world as a result of procreation decisions and broader life choices being made by millions upon millions of individuals, researchers have turned their attention to the question of who exactly is having kids these days. There are a couple of prominent ideas floating about, ones that might seem to have some bearing on the emergence of the millennial generation.

One well-established finding is that those who are more religious tend to have more children than those who are not. The argument is sometimes made that this has the potential to reshape society profoundly, as the religiously devout will become more numerous as time wears on, and religiously inspired values will grow more influential—reversing the long-term movement toward the secularization of Western society. Such a trend could have potential relevance to the distinctive character of the millennials, since some traits they display could be loosely linked to a religious outlook on life, such as being a relatively conscientious and community-oriented individual. Others, such as sexual abstinence prior to marriage, could be a direct result of adherence to religious doctrine.

One exploration of these ideas can be found in Eric Kaufmann's book *Shall the Religious Inherit the Earth?* The answer to the book's question, Kaufmann tells his readers, is yes. To make his case, Kaufmann focuses mainly on those who are zealous in their religious belief, who tend to marry strictly within their faith and to propagate with great zeal. These twin factors allow their numbers to grow rapidly over just a few generations. He offers compelling examples of this process in action, including ultra-Orthodox Jews in Israel who were "once a trace element in the population" but "now make up a third of the country's schoolchildren and are on track to becoming a majority group in the second half of this century."[40] The implications of this demographic shift have been significant for both domestic Israeli politics and the larger geopolitics of the Middle East.

Tight-knit religious communities of devout adherents can demonstrate the potency of the argument, but also reveal its Achilles' heel. Another case, the French-speaking Catholic population of Quebec, is instructive. The example is mentioned briefly by Kaufmann but not followed through to its surprising conclusion.[41] When New France, as Quebec was then called, passed from French rule into British hands in 1760, the French Canadians were a small population of no more than seventy thousand scattered along the shores of the Saint Lawrence River. After the British takeover, many promptly left; for those who remained, the future was uncertain. With Britain in control, it was clear that future arrivals to the colony would be primarily of British background. New immigration from France or other French-speaking locales would grind to a halt. The long-term prospects for survival of the French Canadian culture and language looked decidedly dim.

Encouraged by the Catholic Church, however, the French in Quebec quietly fought back with what came to be known as "revenge of the cradle." In many households, the cradle was a constant hum of activity: the average number of children per family in nineteenth-century Quebec was six to seven, and families of a dozen were not uncommon.[42] High fertility rates continued into the twentieth century even as other countries saw a sharp decline. When families reach this size for sustained periods, the magic of compound growth produces dramatic results. In just over two centuries, the French population of Quebec grew to six million, with demographers estimating that two-thirds of the current gene pool can be traced back to a mere twenty-six hundred settlers from the earliest days of French settlement.[43]

Yet none of this procreative enthusiasm actually ensured that the "religious would inherit the earth"—or that Catholicism would reign supreme in Quebec ever after. It took longer than elsewhere, but French Canadians eventually started to question the dominance of religion within their society. In the 1960s, Quebec experienced the so-called Quiet Revolution, a modernizing transformation that affected virtually all sectors of society. Among other changes, Quebecers abandoned the church in droves, becoming for the most part nominal Catholics, attending at Christmas and Easter only. Apart from these ceremonial affirmations, most are now happy to live their lives without religious guidance and often in complete disregard of basic tenets of the church. The province now has more common-law marriages, more out-of-wedlock births, and a higher rate of abortion than anywhere else in Canada.[44] Among all Canadians, Quebecers express the highest level of support for gay rights, including same-sex marriage.[45] Contrary to the doctrinal sanctity of life, the first euthanasia law in Canada was introduced by the provincial government. In short, Quebec is now number one among the Canadian provinces in essentially every practice or tenet that is anathema to the Catholic Church. In the end, then, the revenge of the cradle was a hollow victory: Catholicism fueled dramatic population growth, but the final result was to create a populous province of superficial adherents and nonbelievers.

The Quebec example underlines both the potency of the argument and its weak link. As one critical reviewer of Kaufmann's book put it, "Secularism and fundamentalism are not ideas stitched into people's DNA. They are, like all values, absorbed, accepted, rejected."[46] It is the relative rates of absorption, acceptance, and rejection by new generations that determine the capacity of religious belief to propagate itself through time.

At this point in time, in the adolescent society, where matters of belief and conviction are very much the product of individual choice, rejection seems to be slowly winning out. Despite the fact that the religious do have more children across virtually every country in the Western world, religiosity continues to decline in those same countries as younger generations move away from the church. In Reginald Bibby's study of Canadian teenagers, he found the percentage *never* attending religious services jumped sharply from 28 percent in the early 1980s to 47 percent in his 2008 survey.[47] Similar surveys of high school seniors in the United States show religious attendance down since the late 1970s. The percentage never attending church has gone from about 10 percent to 20 percent (with a further 25 percent rarely attending). The same surveys show that over the same period young people have become more likely to consider religion either "not important" or just "a little important" in their lives—an increase from roughly 40 percent to 45 percent.[48]

It's fair to say that the decline in religiosity over the past few decades would have been greater still if it weren't for the fact that religious adults tend to have more children; the religious birth advantage has slowed the pace of decline, particularly in the United States, where the evangelical movement is vibrant and growing.[49] Be that as it may, the decline in religiosity among the young has not been reversed—not in the United States, and certainly not in other countries like Canada that have witnessed the rise of their own millennial generation. So clearly we can't say that the change in attitudes and behaviors among the millennials is somehow a product of heightened religiosity, when the millennials are actually less religious than young people were in the past.

The same critique can be directed at another argument about a belief system that is said to promote large families and therefore has significant growth potential: conservatism. The idea is voiced most often in the United States, where conservatism is strongly tied to the idea of family values (in contrast to Europe, where the conservatism is more often focused on individual freedoms, free markets, and small government). The argument is similar to the religious one—in fact in some ways it is the same argument, given the significant demographic overlap between conservative ideologues and the religiously devout in the United States. Conservatives have more children these days, the thinking goes, so conservative ways of thinking are set to grow over the long haul.[50] The millennials could be seen as the first wave in this process, their ways of thinking and acting, their more conventional and cautious behavior, a reflection of the conservative leanings imparted by parents.

Yet once again, the argument doesn't seem to hold water. It's true that conservatives have more children and have done so since the 1980s,[51] but this does not mean that their ideology is on the rise among the millennials. Just ask John McCain and Mitt Romney. Both Republican candidates for president went down to defeat when their opponent Barack Obama—a relatively liberal Democratic candidate by recent standards—swept the under-thirty vote by a margin of roughly 2 to 1. Given that adults over age fifty favored the Republicans in both 2008 and 2012, many young people clearly were not voting the same way as their parents.[52] If there was a time when ideology and party identity were passed down with some consistency within families, nowadays political beliefs are transmitted from parent to child with much less fidelity. A birthrate advantage for conservatives does not ensure the gradual ascendance of conservative ideology.

The bottom line is this: In the right set of circumstances, there is potential for a doctrine or ideology to grow by leaps and bounds if it successfully encourages its followers to go forth and multiply. But doctrines are learned, not innate, which leaves them open to challenge and change. They can be rejected virtually wholesale in a single generation (as was the case with Catholicism in Quebec) or fade more slowly with the passing of time.

Reproductive Choices: The Influence of Personality

It is for this reason that bringing personality traits into the mix is very useful. Unlike political ideology or religious doctrine, personality traits are in fact "stitched into people's DNA"—in the sense that people inherit (at least in part) basic personality traits from their parents. If particular personality traits make people more likely to have children, it's more certain—more so than for ideological belief or religious conviction—that these traits will manifest in their offspring and thereby help shape the character of the next generation.

With this in mind, the effects of personality on fertility can be summarized succinctly: adolescent personality traits make people less likely to have children, adult traits more likely. This should come as no great surprise. Having children and raising them is one of the more significant adult responsibilities that can be undertaken nowadays. We live in an era where having children is usually the product of careful reflection and deliberation rather than a given for virtually everyone once a certain age is attained. The character of those who choose to become parents has become more sharply defined in recent decades, with important implications for the nature—but also the nurturing—of their offspring.

To pursue these ideas further, we need to better understand the connections that exist between personality traits and fertility rates. There are not many studies that permit this, but one that is helpful is the Midlife in the United States (MIDUS) study. Focused primarily on issues of health and well-being, this survey of over seven thousand American adults age twenty-five and over was conducted by a team of researchers in the mid-1990s. In addition to questions on health, the study asked about respondents' children—how many they had, when they first became a parent, and so on—as well as including small batteries of questions designed to measure the Big Five personality traits. The results reveal some intriguing findings about the personality profiles of contemporary parents and, by genetic implication, their offspring.

Openness to Experience

On the Midlife in the United States study, the personality trait with the strongest connection to fertility is openness to experience. Those who score high on this trait—one of the important personal qualities rising to prominence in the adolescent society—tend to have *fewer* children than those at the lower end of the scale. The overall difference on the MIDUS study is substantial: those highest on the trait of openness reported having an average of 1.75 biological children, compared to an average of 2.21 for those at the opposite end of the spectrum. And this birthrate differential is very much concentrated among the younger adults on the study, those fifty and under. Since the study took place in the mid-1990s, this means people who were themselves born around 1945 or later—in other words, people who were making decisions about whether to have children from the latter half of the 1960s onward. For these generations, who very much saw procreation as a personal choice, the birthrate gap associated with openness is nearly 0.5.[53] Among older groups, on the other hand, openness has no effect on fertility patterns. For those over age sixty (born in 1935 and earlier) birthrates are virtually identical at opposite ends of the openness scale.[54]

Why has openness to experience come to work against having children? Having kids certainly brings some new experiences to our lives, including such novelties as changing diapers at three in the morning and learning all four-teen verses of "The Wheels on the Bus" (and once those are mastered, invent-ing your own!). More seriously: there is a genuine sense of personal growth and accomplishment involved in taking on the challenge of raising children, in helping them to develop and flourish. Howe and Strauss believe, in fact, that this has become a critical motivator for parenthood, suggesting that for the boomer generation children were "regarded by parents as the highest form of self-discovery."[55]

So the personality trait of openness does not seem fundamentally at odds with the experience of becoming a parent. The key hindrance to fertility rates is that those scoring high on openness often embrace this experience later in life, once they are well into their thirties or sometimes even their forties. After focus-ing on their own personal development for a good number of their adult years, having children becomes the next step in their journey of personal growth and discovery. And this delay in starting a family means they usually end up having fewer children.

This comes out clearly in the MIDUS survey. Among those who scored in the upper range of openness in the under-fifty group, 35 percent didn't get started on having children until age twenty-eight or older, compared to 22 percent of those who scored lowest on openness. That this group would hold off on starting a family makes eminent sense: openness to experience is held to be the key per-sonality trait driving the "emerging adult" trend, the tendency of young people to spend their twenties and sometimes a good part of their thirties figuring out who they are and what they want to do with their lives. Education, new rela-tionships, varied work opportunities, travel and adventure: all these occupy the typical emerging adult for a good many years and lead to substantial delays in having children.

In short, beginning at some point in the later 1960s and continuing ever since, decisions about parenthood have been strongly influenced by the character trait of openness. The effect is not so much a direct impact on the desire to have children, but rather the way the trait shapes important life decisions, which in turn influence the number of children eventually borne. Those who score high on openness do still have children nowadays, but they have fewer than others by a substantial margin.

The effects of this birthrate differential are now popping up in studies that directly examine the personality traits of millennials and compare them to young adults of earlier periods. Jean Twenge and colleagues report, for example, that among US college students, openness to experience scores decreased by about one-third of a standard deviation between 1985 and 2009.[56] This is precisely the change that would be predicted by the birthrate differentials that opened up among those thinking about having children (or not) from the late 1960s onward—as well as a finding consistent with some of the behavioral patterns present among millennials that have led to their being identified as a different kind of youth generation.

Agreeableness and Extroversion

Some of the other personality effects on the Midlife in the United States study are weaker, though still consistent with the proposition that it is the more adult among us who are most likely to have children nowadays. The effects of agreeableness and extroversion are similar to one another: smaller, positive effects on fertility rates.[57] The extroversion questions on the study focus mainly on the sociability dimension of the trait, assessing qualities such as being friendly and outgoing—in other words, the element of extroversion most closely aligned with agreeableness. Given this close connection, it makes sense that these two personality traits would work in the same direction of favoring parenthood.

Finnish researcher Markus Jokela, who has carried out considerable research in the past few years on the connections between personality traits and fertility, suggests some of the mechanisms behind this result. Those who are agreeable are more caring and affectionate, qualities likely to make parenthood seem an attractive life choice. "Temperament and personality traits related to agreeableness . . . [tend] to be associated with higher child-bearing propensity and with more positive views of having children."[58] Those who are sociable also establish relationships more readily. In one of his studies, Jokela explains that "extraverted individuals were more likely to marry and become parents and to have their first child earlier than introverts. These two timing components almost completely explained the positive association between extraversion and total number of children."[59] Adding further to the effect is the impact of agreeableness on marital closeness and stability. Numerous studies have found agreeableness to be an important predictor of strong interpersonal relationships in general, including stable marriages. As one paper on the subject notes, "Agreeable people are less likely to engage in specific interactional behaviors that are deleterious for close relationships."[60]

In an age where relationships are often fragile and easily disrupted, all of these observations make intuitive sense. It seems reasonable that those who are agreeable and sociable would be more likely to end up in the kinds of stable relationships apt to produce children, and likewise that they would look favorably on that prospect, which itself involves building a close and intimate relationship with children. As with openness, decisions around parenthood have come to reflect the influence of other key personality traits that condition the way we choose to live our lives nowadays.

Again, research by Twenge and colleagues suggests that these birthrate differentials are, as we would expect, manifesting themselves in the personality traits displayed by millennials. On one Big Five measurement scale, for example, they find an increase in agreeableness scores among US college students of about one-quarter of standard deviation between 1992 and 2009.[61] A similar study of Dutch college students from 1982 through 2007 likewise revealed significant increases on this particular personality trait over this twenty-five-year period.[62]

Conscientiousness

The MIDUS study produces one result that runs counter to the idea that it is the most "adult" among us who are choosing to have children these days. The more conscientious respondents on the study tended to have fewer children, especially among younger generations of women—this according to a 2012 analysis by Markus Jokela. It's a surprising result, given that raising children is a major, ongoing life responsibility, not to be undertaken lightly—a life choice more suited to the mature and serious, we would assume, rather than the footloose and carefree. Jokela's explanation for the puzzle was similar to the reasoning used to explain why openness hinders high fertility rates. Conscientiousness is a strong predictor of achievement motivation, which is linked to the attainment of higher levels of education and the pursuit of demanding careers. These life choices typically delay parenthood and consequently lead to smaller eventual family size.[63]

Other studies, however, suggest that dimensions of conscientiousness, apart from achievement motivation, do work in the anticipated direction of encouraging rather than discouraging parenthood. One paper finds, for example, that it is the more "socially responsible" among us who are most likely to have children.[64] In another study, Jokela himself used a sample of Finnish adults to examine the impact of "novelty-seeking" on the propensity to have children. This earlier study found that novelty seekers were significantly less likely to have children than others. As he notes, novelty seekers "may prefer a more care-free life and therefore shun [sic] away from the responsibilities of raising children."[65] This points to the conclusion that high levels of conscientiousness should be associated with more children, not fewer.

Evidence concerning levels of conscientiousness among the millennial offspring themselves are a bit conflicting. The same study by Twenge and colleagues that found lower levels of openness and higher levels of agreeableness among millennial youth found no change in conscientiousness scores. A similar study from the Netherlands, on the other hand, found a very substantial increase in conscientiousness levels among Dutch college students between 1982 and 2007.[66]

Overall, the results from the MIDUS study and other relevant studies offer substantial support for the proposition that individuals embodying more adult personality traits are more likely to have significant numbers of children nowadays, whereas those more adolescent in character tend to have fewer. There is also evidence of associated personality changes popping up among millennial populations, changes that are in keeping with their behavioral tendencies to be notably careful and restrained in many aspects of their lives.

Reproductive Choices: The Influence of Social Values

Further evidence and insight into the inherited dispositions of millennials can be found in other data sources that probe qualities closely related to the Big Five personality traits—in particular, some of the social values considered previously in this study. Chapters 4 and 6 made use of the World Values Survey and European Values Study (WVS/EVS) to explore one important manifestation of the growing influence of teenage character traits in the adolescent society: a pattern of rising antisocial attitudes over time. As part of that analysis, it was noted that people holding antisocial views would be those scoring relatively low on the traits of conscientiousness and agreeableness. Since the WVS/EVS surveys also ask people how many children they have, we can use this data set to assess the connection between parenthood and antisocial/pro-social values, and from there to draw inferences about linkages to underlying personality traits.[67]

The earlier waves of the WVS/EVS (1981–1982 and 1990) posed a particularly large array of questions connected to antisocial attitudes. In addition to the five items utilized in the analysis of previous chapters—questions pertaining to self-interested lying, wrongfully claiming government benefits, skipping a fare on public transit, along with cheating on taxes and bribery—there were three others that focused less on cheating "the system" and more on wrongdoing of an interpersonal nature. These asked whether it is ever justifiable to fail to report damage you've done to a parked vehicle; to keep stolen goods; and to keep lost money you have found. In addition to having this larger array of relevant questions, the early waves of the WVS/EVS are also particularly pertinent to questions around the changing character of parents because it was at the start of the 1980s that millennial newborns were first appearing in maternity wards across the land.

Figure 9.1 shows the average number of children reported by US respondents in the first two WVS waves as a function of their level of adherence to these

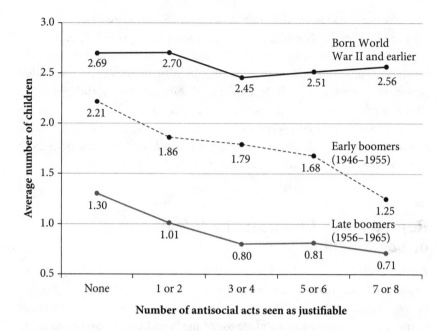

FIGURE 9.1 The pro-social norms of baby boomer parents (US)

Source: World Values Survey, waves 1 (1982) and 2 (1990) combined. Total N = 3,747. Minimum N = 114. Mean N = 250.

basic social norms. On the left of the graph are those who gave the principled response to each of the eight questions concerning antisocial behaviors (that they are "never justifiable"). On the right are those who indicated that most if not all (seven or eight) of these actions could be justified to at least to some degree. Results are shown separately for three age groups: older respondents born before 1946, early baby boomers born between 1946 and 1955, and later boomers born from 1956 to 1965.

Among the older group (who all would have been age thirty-five plus throughout this time period, and therefore largely finished having children), scores on the index of antisocial attitudes show no obvious connection to the propensity to be a parent. The average number of children hovers between 2.45 and 2.7 across the graph, with no sharp upward or downward trend. Among the two baby boomer cohorts, on the other hand, a clear relationship is evident. For the older boomers, who were in their prime childbearing years during the 1980s and were responsible for most of the early crop of infant millennials, the average number of offspring drops from 2.21 among the most pro-social respondents to 1.25 among those harboring the most antisocial sentiments. For younger boomers, who were just getting started on having kids during the 1980s, there is likewise a large gap between the pro-social and antisocial endpoints on the graph (1.30 children on average versus 0.71).

The same pattern holds true for the set of twelve European countries considered earlier in the examination of emerging antisocial attitudes in chapter 4. Among the older generation born during the war and before, the average number of children is 2.34 among the most pro-social respondents and 2.29 among the most antisocial—a minimal difference of no real significance. But among boomers, the respective averages are 1.78 versus 1.35 for the older group and 0.75 versus 0.48 for the younger boomers. This fertility gap among younger generations suggests that personal traits connected to social mindfulness have come to exercise considerable influence on the likelihood of having children in the era where parenthood has come to be seen as an optional life decision.

Looking at the European countries and US together, the WVS/EVS surveys have further questions that help us better understand the pathways that lead pro-social individuals to have more children than their antisocial counterparts—pathways that make sense when we know something about their underlying character. One link lies in the number of children desired: for the full baby boom cohort (1946–1965) on the 1981–1982 and 1990 WVS/EVS surveys combined, the average "ideal" number of children favored by pro-social respondents exceeds the ideal preferred by their antisocial counterparts by 0.17. Also contributing to the fertility gap are issues with long-term relationships: only 63 percent of the most antisocial baby boomers were married or "living together as married," compared to 79 percent of their pro-social counterparts. It probably doesn't help matters that just 67 percent of the antisocial respondents felt that "faithfulness" is very important for a successful marriage, compared to 90 percent of the pro-social group. And finally, there is the sensitive matter of terminating unwanted pregnancies. While there are (understandably) no direct questions on people's personal history in this regard, antisocial respondents were more likely to believe abortion is acceptable under a variety of scenarios, including for the simple reason that one is "not wanting more children"—49 percent of those exhibiting strong antisocial sentiments agreed with this statement, compared to only 29 percent at the pro-social end of the scale.[68]

So there are a variety of factors at play, but the overall result is what most people would probably suspect. In an era where having children is seen as an option, not an obligation, where enduring relationships between couples are less common than before, and where abortion is a readily available option, it is not surprising that people who profess strong antisocial tendencies would tend to have fewer children than the more obliging and congenial members of society. Given the underlying connections between pro-social attitudes and the qualities of agreeableness and conscientiousness, it is reasonable to take these findings as evidence of the more agreeable and conscientious nature of today's parents—and, given what we know about the strong genetic influences on personality, their offspring as well.

But this is not the end of the matter. There is another distinct mechanism that can be identified through the WVS/EVS surveys whereby pro-social parents pass on their pro-social tendencies to their offspring. This is more in keeping with the traditional conception of how parents influence children: nurturing effects. The surveys asked respondents in both 1981–1982 and 1990 to indicate the five qualities from a lengthy list of alternatives that they felt were most important to encourage children "to learn at home." Among pro-social baby boomers, 80 percent included honesty among their top five, while 72 percent included good manners; among their antisocial counterparts, only 66 percent chose honesty, 52 percent good manners. Thirty-seven percent of the pro-social respondents added obedience to their top five, compared to only 25 percent of the antisocial group. On the flip side, the pro-social group were less likely than the antisocial group to favor the promotion of imagination (18 percent versus 31 percent) and independence (39 percent versus 46 percent)—an indication that pro-social individuals who exhibit respect for rules and adherence to norms are, not surprisingly, less likely to encourage their children to be free, uninhibited spirits.[69]

Thus, the explanation commonly used to explain the rise of the millennial generation—that parents began to take a firmer guiding hand in raising their children from roughly the 1980s onward—finds some confirmation in these numbers. But it also suggests a slight modification to the standard argument. Yes, we can see distinctive parenting preferences emerging among the parents of the millennials. However, this is not necessarily because of any broad social transformation in attitudes toward parenting. In part, it simply reflects the fact that certain type of individuals were more likely to become parents as significant birthrate differentials opened up within postwar generations.

Summing Up: Personality, Procreation, and Parenting

We have now seen evidence of important filters at work in the procreation decisions of individuals in the adolescent society, filters that help explain the rise of the millennial generation. Those who choose to become parents these days differ in systematic ways from those who do not. They are less open, more agreeable, and more conscientious than others of the same age cohort; they are more pro-social, apt to respect social norms and to conform to conventional notions of right and wrong. In the context of the adolescent society, these qualities mark them as individuals who retain more traditional adultlike qualities.

There is a twofold effect at work that makes these birthrate differentials a potent source of social change. There is first the genetic effect emphasized in the preceding analysis—the fact that people who are, relatively speaking, less open to experience, more agreeable, and more careful and conscientious will tend to have children who possess those same qualities, owing to the genetic transmission of personality traits. There is also, however, evidence of the environmental effect that is more commonly cited as the source of millennial distinctiveness: parents actively working to inculcate good behavior and respect for social norms in their children (which comes naturally to them, given their own dispositions). The two effects will, of course, work hand in hand, with their combined, interactive effect likely all the greater. That is to say, the genetic effect is likely amplified by the environmental influence of parents, while the environmental effect is likely greater because it is operating on children predisposed to think and act in certain ways.

It's worth pausing for a moment to consider this somewhat uncommon proposition. With most genetically transmitted traits, the idea of environmental enhancements deriving from the genetic trait itself is a bizarre notion. Our eyes don't become a deeper blue because we are raised by blue-eyed parents who encourage blueness at every turn. We don't grow to a taller height than our genetic endowment because we are nurtured by towering parents who treat tallness as a virtue to be cultivated in their offspring. But with personality traits, these kinds of environmental enhancements seem entirely plausible. Parents who are agreeable, conscientious, and mindful of social norms will tend to have children who possess these same qualities. But they will also naturally adhere to the model of the cautious and conscientious parent that has become so common nowadays and thereby reinforce the ingrained personality traits of their children.[70]

This may help explain how it is that the millennial generation managed to emerge in a fairly short time frame. Some of the trends cited at the start of this chapter show rather abrupt and substantial changes in the attitudes and behaviors of young people starting roughly in the early 1990s—among individuals born around the early 1980s or perhaps late 1970s—and continuing to the present day. Nature or nurture effects alone might not have been enough to produce a decisive shift in a compressed time frame. However, the two together, these arguments would suggest, have helped bring about a noteworthy change in dispositions, attitudes, and behavior, which collectively mark the millennials as a distinctive generation.

A Bend in the Path

The rise of the millennials marks a new phase in our social evolution, but one that is connected to a larger historical pattern. The adolescent society expanded and intensified for a number of decades as social influence outside the family during the teenage years came to be dominated by peers, creating a population and a culture that bore important marks of the adolescent character. But as adolescent qualities have become more prevalent, one important effect has been a growing reluctance to engage in that most adult of activities: bringing forth the next generation into the world and nurturing them to adulthood. As birthrates have declined and having children has become a more selective process, powerful forces have been set in motion, all pushing in the same countervailing direction: adult qualities are now favored in the genetics of the procreation process and in the environmental setting provided by contemporary parents and families. The result has been some slowing, and even reversal, of trends tending toward the ongoing expansion of the adolescent society. If this is true of today's younger generation, it may well be the harbinger of further change to come down the road, as the millennials move on toward middle adulthood and subsequent generations potentially follow in their footsteps. Assuming no alteration in the underlying dynamics of change outlined in this chapter, this would indeed be the predicted path.

Conclusion

FINDING BALANCE

In describing the emergence and evolution of our adolescent society, I've told a simple story about our complicated social world. My aim has been to follow one important thread from start to finish to see how it ties together many disparate elements in the complex weave of modern society.

A few core ideas have guided my inquiry. The first is that character matters. Personality traits, and the foundational personal values to which they are intimately linked, wield substantial influence over the conscious decisions and subconscious habits that give shape and meaning to our lives. Over the years, the field of personality research has produced thousands of studies documenting these effects, research I've drawn on liberally throughout these pages. No one claims, of course, that character is the only thing that matters. Social and familial background, economic circumstances, luck both good and bad, have considerable impact as well. But character traits have an important effect on how we deal with the trials and tribulations that come our way, how we grasp opportunity when it presents itself, and the general efforts we make to give form and direction to our lives.

If character matters, then so does the process of character formation. Prior research tells us that nature and nurture have roughly equal impact on who we are: parents provide the basic scaffolding through the genes they pass on to their offspring, but environmental effects are equally important in fashioning the core traits and dispositions that help define us.

The environmental part of the equation opens up the prospect of significant and surprising changes in character if the contours of environment are reconfigured. My focus has been one of the greatest environmental changes of the past hundred years, one less obvious than other social and technological transformations over that same period but equally if not more critical: the alteration in the up-close-and-personal environment provided by the social networks in which we are embedded during our formative teenage years. With peers as our primary companions and guides rather than adults, adolescent traits and values started to take on special significance and to have more enduring resonance as we moved into our adult lives. So it is that the adolescent society, growing by accretion with each new generation, has slowly taken shape since the early years of twentieth century.

Reflection and Inspiration

What does this account of past events entail for the future? My analysis of our evolving adolescent society implies a good deal of social inertia, of steady momentum pushing us forward that is difficult to divert or resist. Like most of us, however, I don't like to think that our future is set in stone. There remains room for reflection, deliberation, critical evaluation, and choice, space to ponder the past, interrogate the present, and set goals for the future. Yes, there are entrenched reflexes and habits to contend with, but conscious of these, we can seek to rise above and consciously decide who we want to be—one by one as individuals and together as a society.

This kind of reflection can partly be prompted by stepping back from the treadmill of current events and our own busy lives to observe larger trends in the social landscape over long periods of time. Books like this one—intended not simply as a detached analysis, but as a tinted lens on the past and present that pushes us to see ourselves in a certain light—can hopefully inform and encourage that process.

Reflection is also prompted by consulting our intuitions and asking if all seems well in our lives. We have, for example, the pithy assessment of Dick Meyer, who says "we hate us" for what we've become. This judgment is severe, though I agree there is a powerful sense of unease with much of what we see around us in today's society and culture. Yet there is also some inner tension. The things we hate about us are connected to things we like about us—or at least to things we like. Many of us are quite happy to live in a freedom-loving, fun-seeking society, and from time to time to indulge in at least some of the guilty pleasures that the adolescent society has to offer—whether it's watching the adolescent-inspired antics of reality TV, impulsively buying something we can't really afford, or letting our ethical principles slip just a tad in order to gain some personal benefit.

Most of us also have a deep attachment to important achievements of the adolescent society—to the sense of adventure and free-spiritedness, to the heightened creativity and social tolerance that have emerged from the openness associated with the adolescent spirit. If we're not entirely content with how our society is evolving, if we are looking to rein in certain adolescent shortcomings, we must also be sure we retain these critically important advances. If we try to take away the things we like and things we like about us, we are certainly doomed to fail.

Moreover, these adolescent qualities that we like and admire, the dynamic attributes of open and creative thought, are resources that we can draw upon to help us imagine a different and better future. Such utopian thinking was prominent in the 1960s, a fertile time for visionary and creative ideas; today, we see it appear more sporadically, but its potency remains undiminished. Social movements ask us to imagine a world transformed as they rally support for important causes in areas such as gender and racial equality or environmental sustainability. Contemporary politicians likewise offer visions for a better world, which, if often lacking in details ("Yes, we can" . . . yes, we can what?) nonetheless sometimes succeed in striking a powerful chord by directing our attention to an unscripted future. The hopeful spirit engendered by such thinking is essential in motivating and energizing people to undertake the hard work involved in addressing difficult social challenges.

Attending to Character

Meanwhile, there is also a need to take a hard-nosed look at contemporary problems connected to our adolescent character. In thinking about the downside of the adolescent society, there are two general categories of concern. One is the people who fall through the cracks, people who are not faring well in a host of different ways. Certain quintessentially adolescent tendencies—impulsiveness, antisocial conduct, narcissistic behavior—lead to problems in people's lives that have become disturbingly pervasive. Then there are problems connected to individual behavior that affect society as a whole: a dysfunctional democratic system, an economy given to consumerist excess, a culture where brazenness wears away at our patience and undermines social cohesion. These things affect us all, and most of us are complicit, to at least some degree, in their perpetuation.

Importantly, these problems are recognized as valid concerns across the ideological spectrum. On the right, they would tend to be seen as self-evident problems, since all involve a downgrading of traditional norms and a degree of social fragmentation that is starkly at odds with the stable social order favored by conservatives. On the left, there would be less inclination to cast judgment on the choices people are making about how to live their lives; yet at the same time, progressives have become increasingly sensitive to the challenges involved in achieving ambitious policy goals in a social and political context marked by division, distraction, and discord. Every issue the left seeks to address—whether it is reducing gun violence, achieving political finance reform, or tackling economic inequality—is rendered more intractable by the fraught and fractured state of contemporary American society. Attending to this social malaise is a necessary component of the left's larger ambition of bringing about a more just and equal society.

Likewise, if conservatives are more obviously inclined to link contemporary social challenges to shortcomings of character, thoughtful liberal voices are adopting this same perspective while eschewing the right's moral righteousness on this score. Richard Reeves and Dimitrios Halikias of the Brookings Institution make what they call "the liberal case for character," highlighting that liberal thinkers have long been concerned about the individual capacity building that allows people to make something of the personal autonomy championed by the liberal creed. These same authors also point out that many modern-day liberal commentators who claim to favor neutrality among life choices and noninterference as abstract principles nonetheless work hard to nurture particular character traits in their own offspring because they recognize their value in underwriting happy, successful, and productive lives.[1]

So if there is not complete consensus, there is broad recognition nowadays that the concept of character is valid and useful and that "strength of character" can be an important asset in overcoming both individual and collective problems. We would be better served if we were all thoughtful, attentive, and engaged members of society, more capable of addressing a wide range of issues, not least those connected to the left's overarching concerns of social justice and equality. This general recognition is an important starting point for developing momentum for positive change.

There is also clear momentum in the rise of the millennials, a natural evolutionary process in the development of the adolescent society, reflecting changes in both the nature and nurture dimensions of who we are. Younger cohorts are shifting certain long-standing trends and behaviors in a positive direction, exhibiting less risky and impetuous behavior along with greater deliberation and maturity. Some of the millennial changes may be less salutary, however, including excessive caution and deference and a lack of independence and audacity. On all these fronts, we are likely to see gradual change in society at large as this generation, and others to follow, carry these traits forward to their later adult years. We can look to build on this momentum and, as best we can, seek to harness it and steer it in preferred directions.

Some of this should involve efforts to foster character development directly. There is a growing body of research and practice that builds on the idea that it is possible to shape important character traits through early interventions in the classroom and elsewhere. In the educational setting, this does not mean simply standing at the front of the room telling young people what it means to be a good citizen and good person and expecting them to follow suit. "It has become clear," writes Paul Tough, a leading chronicler of this research, "that the educators who are best able to engender noncognitive abilities in their students often do so without really 'teaching' these capacities the way one might teach math or reading—indeed, they often do so without ever saying a word about them in the classroom."[2] Instead, what works most effectively are subtle norms and nudges deeply embedded in everyday teaching practices.

Much of this educational work has tended to focus on methods designed to encourage the traits of perseverance and self-control in children or what is popularly known as "grit"; while this can seem like a narrow focus, these qualities have been found to facilitate wide-ranging personal development and are often connected to the development of civic-minded inclinations and capacities.[3] Complementing the educational dimension of character development is relevant work on the effects of early life experiences in the home, which has found that stressful environments and harsh and unpredictable parenting are particularly detrimental to the development of coping mechanisms and self-control in children.[4] Finding ways to mitigate these effects is another general approach that can aid in the project of fostering a strong character base for the greatest number possible.

Meanwhile, a different set of ideas and initiatives targets other dimensions of personal development felt to be in need of attention. Just as grit can be cultivated in schools and nurtured at home, there is also both need and opportunity to encourage openness and creativity in these settings. Researchers have documented the many beneficial consequences of giving children greater time and space for unstructured free play; parents looking for an alternative to helicopter parenting have been putting these ideas into practice with their offspring. In this vein, the "free range" parenting movement, catalyzed when Lenore Skenazy wrote a newspaper column about letting her nine-year-old son travel solo on the New York City subway system, counsels that children be given the latitude to explore their communities independently at younger ages than common wisdom would normally allow.[5] The thinking is that children given this opportunity will learn to be curious and resourceful, while also developing the capacity to make good decisions and exercise prudence—in short, will develop the kind of measured and mature autonomy that serves people well throughout their lives.

This research and these recommendations reinforce the position taken throughout this book that if character runs deep, it is not set in stone and can be greatly influenced by environmental factors at early stages of life. Learning what can be done and applying it in a targeted and deliberate manner should be one part of an agenda to work toward the enhancement of personal qualities vital to individual and collective empowerment.

Education and Social Structure

Another part of that agenda derives from the analysis in prior chapters about where our educational efforts have fallen short in the past: the social structure of the education system has favored the rise of adolescent qualities in ways that have undermined educational benefits. John Dewey, the American philosopher and social reformer, spoke to this theme near the start of the twentieth century, at the time that the modern system of secondary education was taking shape in the United States. Dewey's concern was citizenship, a concept he defined broadly as meaning "all the relationships of all sorts that are involved in membership in a community."[6] He was worried that schools might not be doing all that they could to contribute to this goal, precisely because of the problem identified in this study: the fact that "children were segregated in formal schools that isolated them from adults (other than teachers) and from participation in community activity."[7]

In one of his essays, "The School as Social Center," Dewey presented an alternative vision. The school, he wrote, needs "to operate as a center of life for all ages and classes."[8] Inspired by Dewey's vision, social reformers in the first half of the twentieth century created a handful of experimental "community schools" where this kind of activity and interaction took place, schools that were as much sites of community-wide social activity as they were educational institutions.[9] We've never embraced this model widely, though elements have trickled into the school system over time. New initiatives have seen young people getting out of the classroom to engage with the world outside. Students are asked to participate in service learning or required to do volunteering in the community; they are given opportunities to engage in experiential learning.

All these elements should be further emphasized and enhanced to create a more rounded experience for young people coming of age, an educational experience where they are more fully exposed to ways of acting, thinking, and being different from those encountered in the adolescent realm. The basic aim should be wide-ranging connections between adults and adolescents, a more free-flowing exchange across age groups within the community. This can occur within the education system but also in other social venues that can potentially nurture and sustain such exchanges. There are undoubtedly many ideas to be shared about ways we can alter the conditions under which adolescents come of age to provide fuller exposure to adult ways of thinking and acting.

Such strategies build on the insight that social influence comes in different forms. Hovering in the background is the dominant ethos of a society, characterized nowadays by a pervasive adolescent spirit that one way or another shapes us all. In the foreground, however, are the individuals who are part of our personal social network, people we interact with on a regular basis from whom we take cues and personal guidance. This—the mechanism of interpersonal social influence—is one that can be deliberately employed to widen young people's social exposure and potentially challenge entrenched ways of thinking.

Setting Our Sights

These ideas are largely aimed at finding a renewed place for adult attributes in today's society—a goal that is admittedly hard to pin down. For we've changed a great deal over the course of the past one hundred years, to the point that the defining qualities of adulthood have become more ambiguous and contested. So perhaps the first step, and in many ways the most challenging one, is to initiate a conversation, a serious and wide-ranging conversation, about what it actually means to be an adult in this day and age. If we are to provide guidance for young people moving toward that stage of life, we have to decide what we see as the basic prerequisites of adulthood at this juncture in our social evolution. This won't be a simple reversion to some archetype of the past, but it will likely involve some rekindling of venerable adult qualities—thoughtfulness, respect, restraint, and more—updated for modern times. Yet these must be successfully combined with the liberating attitude and philosophy that our adolescent selves have rightly insisted upon. In the final analysis, adolescent and adult qualities must both have their place, as we search for a healthy equilibrium that can bring out the best in all of us.

Appendix

DATA REFERENCES

Numerous survey data sets originally compiled by other researchers have been used throughout this study. While the generosity of the original investigators in making their data sets available for secondary use is gratefully acknowledged, none bears any responsibility for the data analysis and interpretations presented in this book. The data sets, in order of "appearance" within the text, are as follows:

- British Household Panel Survey: waves 1–17, 1991–2008, 6th ed. [computer file]. SN 5151. University of Essex, Institute for Social and Economic Research. Colchester, Essex: UK Data Archive [distributor]. Funded by Economic and Social Research Council.
- CROP Socio-cultural Surveys, 1989–1996 [computer file]. CROP Inc., Montreal [producer]. Kingston, ON: Canadian Opinion Research Archive, Queen's University [distributor].
- Gallup Polls: Gallup Poll # 1937–0071, February 1937 [computer file], USAIPO1937–0071, version 2; Gallup Poll # 1937–0090, July 1937 [computer file], USAIPO1937–0090, version 2; Gallup Poll # 1939–0146, January 1939 [computer file], USAIPO1939–0146, version 4; Gallup Poll # 1939–0157: May 1939 [computer file], USAIPO1939–0157, version 2. Gallup Organization [producer]. Ithaca, NY: Roper Center for Public Opinion Research, Cornell University [distributor].
- General Social Survey, cycle 17: Social Engagement, 2003 [computer file]. Statistics Canada [producer]. Fredericton: University of New Brunswick, Data Services [distributor].

- World Values Survey 1981–2014, Longitudinal Aggregate v.20150418, 2015 [computer file]. JDSystems Data Archive, Madrid [aggregate file producer]. World Values Survey Association, www.worldvaluessurvey.org [distributor].
- European Values Study 1981–2008, Longitudinal Data File [computer file]. ZA4804 Data file version 3.0.0 (2015–07–30). Cologne: GESIS Data Archive [distributor]. https://doi.org/10.4232/1.12253.
- General Social Surveys, 1972–2006 cumulative file [computer file]. ICPSR04697-v3. Ithaca, NY: Roper Center for Public Opinion Research, Cornell University / Ann Arbor, MI: Inter-university Consortium for Political and Social Research [distributors].
- European Social Survey Cumulative File, ESS 1–8, 2018 [computer file]. Data file edition 1.0. Bergen, Norway: NSD—Norwegian Centre for Research Data [distributor of ESS data for ESS ERIC]. https://doi.org/10.21338/NSD-ESS-CUMULATIVE.
- Canadian Election Study, 2011 [computer file]. Principal investigators: Patrick Fournier, Fred Cutler, Stuart Soroka, and Dietlind Stolle. Toronto: Institute for Social Research, York University [distributor]. Funded by Elections Canada.
- American National Election Study, 2008: Pre- and Post-Election Survey [computer file]. ICPSR25383-v2. Ann Arbor, MI: Inter-university Consortium for Political and Social Research [distributor]. https://doi.org/10.3886/ICPSR25383.v2.
- Monitoring the Future: A Continuing Study of the Lifestyles and Values of Youth, 1976, 1977, 2010, and 2011 [computer files]. Principal investigators: Lloyd D. Johnston, Jerald G. Bachman, Patrick M. O'Malley, and John E. Schulenberg. Ann Arbor, MI: Inter-university Consortium for Political and Social Research [distributor].
- National Survey of Midlife Development in the United States (MIDUS), 1995–1996 [computer file]. ICPSR02760-v8. Principal investigators: Orville G. Brim, Paul B. Baltes, Larry L. Bumpass, Paul D. Cleary, David L. Featherman, William R. Hazzard, Ronald C. Kessler, Margie E. Lachman, Hazel Rose Markus, Michael G. Marmot, Alice S. Rossi, Carol D. Ryff, and Richard A. Shweder. Ann Arbor, MI: Inter-university Consortium for Political and Social Research [distributor]. Funded by John D. and Catherine T. MacArthur Foundation, Research Network on Successful Midlife Development. https://doi.org/10.3886/ICPSR02760.v8.

Notes

INTRODUCTION

1. James Coleman, *The Adolescent Society: The Social Life of the Teenager and Its Impact on Education* (New York: Free Press, 1961), 9.

2. Coleman, *Adolescent Society*, 3.

3. The age of the characters is rarely revealed. According to fan trivia reported on TV.com, there is only one direct mention any of the characters' ages, when Jerry is revealed to be thirty-six in "The Stranded" (season 3, episode 10). George is presumably about the same age, since he and Jerry were at high school together.

4. "Door to Door, season 3, episode 4.

5. In fairness, Barber does stipulate that this is meant only as a "potent metaphor." See *Consumed: How Markets Corrupt Children, Infantilize Adults, and Swallow Citizens Whole* (New York: W. W. Norton, 2007), 5.

6. Barber, *Consumed*, esp. chaps. 2 and 3; Paul Roberts, *The Impulse Society: America in the Age of Instant Gratification* (New York: Bloomsbury, 2014); James Côté, *Arrested Adulthood: The Changing Nature of Maturity and Identity* (New York: NYU Press, 2000); Ben Sasse, *The Vanishing American Adult: Our Coming-of-Age Crisis and How to Rebuild a Culture of Self-Reliance* (New York: St. Martin's, 2017); Gary Cross, *Men to Boys: The Making of Modern Immaturity* (New York: Columbia University Press, 2008).

7. Barber, *Consumed*; Robert Putnam, *Bowling Alone: The Collapse and Revival of American Community* (New York: Touchstone, 2000), chap. 13.

8. The first work to bring this to popular attention was Neil Howe and William Strauss, *Millennials Rising: The Next Great Generation* (New York: Vintage Books, 2000).

1. THE CHARACTER OF ADOLESCENTS

1. Stanley Hall, *Adolescence: Its Psychology and Its Relation to Physiology, Anthropology, Sociology, Sex, Crime, Religion and Education* (London: S. Appleton, 1904).

2. Robert Epstein, *The Case against Adolescence: Rediscovering the Adult in Every Teen* (Sanger, CA: Quill Driver Books, 2007), 9–11. A revised edition was released in 2010 under the title *Teen 2.0: Saving Our Children and Families from the Torment of Adolescence*.

3. Cass R. Sunstein, *Going to Extremes: How Like Minds Unite and Divide* (Oxford: Oxford University Press, 2009).

4. This presumption is supported by a recent research study examining differences between adolescents and young adults in eleven different countries on important adolescent characteristics: sensation seeking and self-regulation. Developmental patterns were largely similar across all countries, but the magnitude of the differences between teenagers and adults varied considerably, suggesting a universal trajectory of human development that can be modified by environment and circumstances. See Laurence Steinberg et al., "Around the World Adolescence Is a Time of Heightened Sensation Seeking and Immature Self-Regulation," *Developmental Science* 21, no. 2 (2018).

5. Total sample size for this wave of the BHPS (2005) is just over 15,000; sample size for those fifteen to seventeen years old is approximately 570 (depending on the number of missing responses for each specific item).

6. We might think that people faced with such questions about their personal habits would fudge the truth or engage in a bit of self-deception to present themselves in a positive light. But when researchers have looked at this issue, they have found that self-assessments are surprisingly reliable, corresponding closely to observer ratings (the judgments others make about our personalities) as well as serving as sound predictors of how we actually behave.

7. For the British Household Panel study and the Canadian CROP surveys cited below, all numbers cited in this section are based on my own calculations using the original data sets. For the American web-based study cited below, results are mainly taken from the published findings in Christopher J. Soto et al., "Age Differences in Personality Traits from 10 to 65: Big Five Domains and Facets in a Large Cross-Sectional Sample," *Journal of Personality and Social Psychology* 100, no. 2 (2011). However, figure 1.1 has been produced using the original study data, kindly provided to the author by Christopher Soto.

8. Ten points on the T-score scale represents one full standard deviation.

9. Patrick Smith, "'The Dude Abides': Twenty Years on How the Big Lebowski Became a Cultural Phenomenon," *Telegraph*, March 7, 2018; Oliver Benjamin and Dwayne Eutsey, *The Abide Guide: Living Like Lebowski* (Berkeley, CA: Ulysses, 2011).

10. Marvin Zuckerman, *Sensation Seeking and Risky Behavior* (Washington, DC: American Psychological Association, 2007), 48.

11. Excitement-seeking measures are from the Canadian CROP Socio-cultural Surveys, 1989–1996. Total N = 20,894; for fifteen-to-seventeen age group, N = 1,187. Risk-taking measures are from the 1989 survey only. Total N = 2,586; for fifteen-to-seventeen age group, N = 154.

12. Daniel Nettle, *Personality: What Makes You the Way You Are* (New York: Oxford University Press, 2007), 93 (emphasis added).

13. Nettle, *Personality*, 82–83.

14. CROP surveys, 1989–1996. Total N = 20,909; for fifteen-to-seventeen age group, N = 1,196.

15. Materialism items from 1989 and 1996 CROP surveys. Total N = 5,096; for fifteen-to-seventeen age group, N = 286. General pleasure and good things in life items from 1989 survey. Total N = 2,587; for fifteen-to-seventeen age group, N = 154. Confirmation of some of these extroversion results, based on much larger sample sizes, can be found in the European Social Survey over the 2002–2016 period. The surveys pose a series of questions about value preferences connected to positive emotion, risk, and the pursuit of pleasure. Specifically, they ask respondents whether they are someone who looks for adventure and likes to take risks; thinks it important to have a good time and spoil oneself; and seeks every chance to have fun and do things that are pleasurable. T-scores for those fifteen to seventeen range from 56 to 58 (total sample size is more than 150,000, with nearly 5,000 in the fifteen-to-seventeen group). These questions are used to support further analysis in chapter 6; results reported here are limited to the ten countries used in this later analysis.

16. Nettle, *Personality*, 88–89.

17. Simine Vazire et al., "Portrait of a Narcissist: Manifestations of Narcissism in Physical Appearance," *Journal of Research in Personality* 42, no. 6 (2008).

18. Jean M. Twenge and W. Keith Campbell, *The Narcissism Epidemic: Living in the Age of Entitlement* (New York: Free Press, 2009).

19. Nettle, *Personality*, 162.

20. CROP surveys, 1989–1996. Total N = 18,199; for fifteen-to-seventeen age group, N = 1,029.

21. Meri Wallace, "Coping with an Angry Teenager," *Psychology Today*, February 25, 2018.

22. Some researchers have explored correlations between the Big Five and concluded that there are one or two "higher-order" personality factors that underlie the Big Five

traits. See, for example, Dimitri van der Linden, Jan te Nijenhuis, and Arnold B. Baker, "The General Factor of Personality: A Meta-analysis of Big Five Intercorrelations and a Criterion-Related Validity Study," *Journal of Research in Personality* 44, no. 3 (2010).

23. Nettle, *Personality*, 183–185.

24. Feelings and fantasy items are from CROP surveys, 1989–1992. Total N = 10,297; for fifteen-to-seventeen age group, N = 646. Experiences items are from 1989 survey only. Total N = 2,011; for fifteen-to-seventeen age group, N = 115.

25. CBS News, December 2, 2007, https://www.cbsnews.com/news/teens-brains-key-to-their-impulsiveness/.

26. Nora Underwood, "The Teenage Brain: Why Adolescents Sleep In, Take Risks and Won't Listen to Reason," *Walrus*, November 2006.

27. Barbara Strauch, *The Primal Teen: What the New Discoveries about the Teenage Brain Tell Us about Our Kids* (New York: Anchor Books, 2003); Frances E. Jensen with Amy Ellis Nutt, *The Teenage Brain: A Neuroscientist's Survival Guide to Raising Adolescents and Young Adults* (New York: HarperCollins, 2015).

28. Laurence Steinberg, professor of psychology at Temple University, cited in "Teens' Brains Key to Their Impulsiveness." More formally, this is referred to as the "dual systems model"; see Steinberg et al., "Around the World."

29. Laurence Steinberg, *Age of Opportunity: Lessons from the New Science of Adolescence* (New York: Mariner Books, 2015), 15.

30. For a general overview of neuroplasticity research see David Doidge, *The Brain That Changes Itself: Stories of Personal Triumph from the Frontiers of Brain Science* (New York: Penguin Books, 2007).

31. Steinberg, *Age of Opportunity*, 33.

32. Jason Chein et al., "Peers Increase Adolescent Risk Taking by Enhancing Activity in the Brain's Reward Circuitry," *Developmental Science* 14, no. 2 (2011).

33. Steinberg, *Age of Opportunity*, 27.

34. Steinberg, *Age of Opportunity*, 122.

35. Steinberg, *Age of Opportunity*, 26 (emphasis added).

36. Steinberg, *Age of Opportunity*, 139.

37. Interview with Tomas Paus in *Generation Boomerang*, directed by Sharon Bartlett and Marie Lerose (Vancouver: Dreamfilm Productions, 2011).

38. Howard Sercombe and Tomas Paus, "The 'Teen Brain' Research: An Introduction and Implications for Practitioners," *Youth & Policy*, no. 103 (2009): 31 and 35.

39. Paul Costa and Robert McCrae, *Revised NEO Personality Inventory (NEO PI-R) and NEO Five-Factor Inventory (NEO-FFI): Professional Manual* (Lutz, FL: Psychological Assessment Resources, 1992), appendix A.

40. Eric Hoffer, *The Passionate State of Mind and Other Aphorisms* (New York: Harper & Row, 1954), 21.

41. David Elkind, "Egocentrism in Adolescence," *Child Development* 38, no. 4 (1967).

2. THE CRUCIBLE OF ADOLESCENCE

1. Israel Zangwill, *The Melting Pot* (Toronto: S. B. Gundy, 1915), 33.

2. Coleman, *Adolescent Society*, 3.

3. Epstein, *Case against Adolescence*, 38–41.

4. Daniel K. Lapsley, Robert D. Enright, and Ronald C. Serlin, "Toward a Theoretical Perspective on the Legislation of Adolescence," *Journal of Early Adolescence* 5, no. 4 (1985): 445.

5. Statistics on education enrollments are from Thomas D. Snyder, ed., *120 Years of American Education: A Statistical Portrait* (Washington, DC: US Department of Education, National Center for Education Statistics, 1993). The cited numbers represent the total number of students enrolled in grades 9 to 12 (table 9) divided by the total population in the fourteen-to-seventeen age group (table 1).

6. Snyder, *120 Years of American Education*, figure 8, p. 28.

7. Howard Chudacoff, *How Old Are You? Age Consciousness in American Culture* (Princeton, NJ: Princeton University Press, 1989), 9.

8. Chudacoff, *How Old Are You?*, 14.

9. Chudacoff, *How Old Are You?*, 18.

10. Chudacoff, *How Old Are You?*, 15.

11. Robert S. Lynd and Helen Merrell Lynd, *Middletown: A Study in American Culture* (New York: Harcourt, Brace, 1929), 212.

12. Lynd and Lynd, *Middletown*, 218.

13. Lynd and Lynd, *Middletown*, 211.

14. Cited in Chudacoff, *How Old Are You?*, 99.

15. Eugénie Dostie-Goulet et al., "The School as a City—Cities in the School" (paper presented at Seminar on Lowering the Age to Vote to Sixteen, Brussels, September 23–24, 2010), 1.

16. Rubén G. Rumbaut, "Children of Immigrants and Their Achievement: The Role of Family, Acculturation, Social Class, Gender, Ethnicity, and School Contexts," in *Addressing the Achievement Gap: Theory Informing Practice*, ed. Ronald D. Taylor (Charlotte, NC: Information Age, 2005), 33.

17. Joseph J. Galbo, "Adolescents' Perceptions of Significant Adults," *Adolescence* 18, no. 70 (1983): 422–423.

18. Joseph J. Galbo, "Adolescents' Perceptions of Significant Adults: A Review of the Literature," *Adolescence* 19, no. 76 (1984): 963–964.

19. Jon Savage, *Teenage: The Creation of Youth Culture* (New York: Viking, 2007), chap. 3.

20. Coleman, *Adolescent Society*, 4.

21. Mihaly Csikszentmihalyi and Reed Larson, *Being Adolescent: Conflict and Growth in the Teenage Years* (New York: Basic Books, 1984), 70.

22. Csikszentmihalyi and Larson, *Being Adolescent*, 71–72.

23. Snyder, *120 Years of American Education*, table 9, p. 36.

24. Robert S. Lynd and Helen Merrell Lynd, *Middletown in Transition* (New York: Harcourt, Brace, 1937), 168, text and footnote 48.

25. Cynthia Comacchio, *The Dominion of Youth: Adolescence and the Making of Modern Canada, 1920 to 1950* (Waterloo, ON: Wilfrid Laurier University Press, 2006), 49.

26. Comacchio, *Dominion of Youth*, 45.

27. Comacchio, *Dominion of Youth*, 28.

28. August B. Hollingshead, *Elmtown's Youth: The Impact of Social Classes on Adolescents* (New York: John Wiley & Sons, 1949), 307.

29. Kelly Schrum, *Some Wore Bobby Sox: The Emergence of Teenage Girls' Culture, 1920–1945* (New York: Palgrave, 2004); Grace Palladino, *Teenagers: An American History* (New York: Basic Books, 1996), esp. chap. 11 on the experience of black teenagers; Comacchio, *Dominion of Youth*, esp. chap. 4.

30. Côté, *Arrested Adulthood*, 168; and Savage, *Teenage*, 452–453. Schrum, however, notes that the words "teen" and "teen-age" had made sporadic appearances in "advice literature" through the 1920s and 1930s. See *Some Wore Bobby Sox*, 18–19.

31. The effects of group identity on processes of mutual influence are described in Sunstein, *Going to Extremes*, 42–43.

32. Judith Rich Harris, *The Nurture Assumption: Why Children Turn Out the Way They Do*, rev. ed. (New York: Free Press, 2009), 22.

33. Harris, *Nurture Assumption*, 19–23. Another helpful summary of this research comes from Nettle, *Personality*, 212–216.

34. Nettle, *Personality*, 216.

35. W. Andrew Collins et al., "Contemporary Research on Parenting: The Case for Nature and Nurture," *American Psychologist* 55, no. 2 (2000).

36. Harris, *Nurture Assumption*, 249.

37. Harris, *Nurture Assumption*, 296.

38. Harris, *Nurture Assumption*, 309–311.

39. Harris, *Nurture Assumption*, 321–322.

40. Harris, *Nurture Assumption*, 185.

41. Epstein, *Case against Adolescence*, 187–188.

42. Jane Kroger, *Identity Development: Adolescence through Adulthood*, 2nd ed. (Thousand Oaks, CA: Sage, 2007), 78.

43. Mary Jo V. Pugh and Daniel Hart, "Identity Development and Peer Group Participation," *New Directions for Child and Adolescent Development*, no. 84 (1999).

44. David A. Kinney, "From 'Headbangers' to 'Hippies': Delineating Adolescents' Active Attempts to Form an Alternative Peer Culture," *New Directions for Child and Adolescent Development*, no. 84 (1999).

45. Rosalind Wiseman, *Queen Bees and Wannabes: Helping Your Daughter Survive Cliques, Gossip, Boyfriends, and Other Realities of Adolescence* (New York: Crown, 2002).

46. M. Brent Donnellan, Kali H. Trzesniewski, and Richard W. Robins, "Personality and Self-Esteem Development in Adolescence," in *Handbook of Personality Development*, ed. Daniel K. Mroczek and Todd D. Little (Mahwah, NJ: Lawrence Erlbaum Associates, 2006), 295.

47. Another research angle that offers confirmation of peer influence effects focuses on what are called "youth bulges"—that is to say, countries, regions, or historical periods where youth make up an unusually large proportion of the population. One application of this concept has involved looking at whether there is a higher incidence of armed rebellion when youth (young men in particular) are more prevalent in a society; most relevant studies confirm that this is the case. Another study discovered that levels of civic knowledge among adolescents were lower in US communities with relatively large populations age sixteen and under compared to communities with smaller populations in that age range. The latter study helpfully draws a distinction between "child-saturated" and "adult-saturated" communities, arguing that young people are more apt to be influenced by one another when there are more of them about. For an overview of youth bulge research and relevant citations see Daniel Hart et al., "Youth Bulge," in *Youth Activism: An International Encyclopedia*, ed. Lonnie R. Sherrod (Westport, CT: Greenwood, 2006), 688–690.

48. Erik Erikson, *Identity, Youth and Crisis* (New York: W. W. Norton, 1968).

49. Joann M. Montepare and Margie E. Lachman, "'You're Only as Old as You Feel': Self-Perceptions of Age, Fears of Aging, and Life Satisfaction from Adolescence to Old Age," *Psychology and Aging* 4, no. 1 (1989). The finding has since been replicated in other studies, such as Nancy L. Galambos et al., "Adolescents' Subjective Age: An Indicator of Perceived Maturity," *Journal of Research on Adolescence* 9, no. 3 (1999).

50. Karl Halvor Teigen et al., "Who Would You Most Like to Be Like? Adolescents' Ideals at the Beginning and the End of the Century," *Scandinavian Journal of Educational Research* 44, no. 1 (2000): 12, 17.

51. Teigen et al., "Who Would You Most Like to Be Like?," 15.

52. Rachel D. Bromnick and Brian L. Swallow, "I Like Being Who I Am: A Study of Young People's Ideals," *Educational Studies* 25, no. 2 (1999).

53. Pugh and Hart, "Identity Development and Peer Group Participation."

54. Montepare and Lachman, "'You're Only as Old as You Feel.'"

55. The ad can be seen at https://www.youtube.com/watch?v=Rt0z6tOGWlU, accessed July 4, 2019.

56. Dan McAdams, "The Psychology of Life Stories," *Review of General Psychology* 5, no. 2 (2001): 110.

57. McAdams, "Psychology of Life Stories," 111.

3. A CENTURY OF CHANGE

1. Susan Cain, *Quiet: The Power of Introverts in a World That Can't Stop Talking* (New York: Crown, 2012).

2. Warren I. Susman, "'Personality' and the Making of Twentieth Century Culture," in *Culture as History: The Transformation of American Society in the Twentieth Century* (New York: Pantheon, 1984).

3. Cain, *Quiet*, 22–24.

4. David Eddie, "How Can I Escape Family Gatherings? The Boredom is Killing Me," *Globe and Mail*, May 30, 2012 (emphasis added).

5. Relevant examples are outlined in chapter 7 of *Quiet*.

6. Cain, *Quiet*, 22.

7. Cain, *Quiet*, 21.

8. Cain, *Quiet*, 24.

9. There are affinities here with Riesman's concept of the "other-directed" personality that he believed was becoming dominant in mid-twentieth-century America. See David Riesman with Nathan Glazer and Reuel Denney, *The Lonely Crowd: A Study of the Changing American Character* (New Haven, CT: Yale University Press, 1950).

10. Cain, *Quiet*, 24.

11. My own calculations based on the original Gallup data sets, available through the Roper Data Archive. The movie attendance question was asked in three 1937 Gallup polls (nos. 65, 67, and 72).

12. Gallup poll no. 71 (February 1937).

13. Gallup poll no. 146 (January 1939).

14. Gallup poll no. 90 (July 1937).

15. Gallup poll no. 157 (May 1939).

16. Schrum, *Some Wore Bobby Sox*, 113.

17. The organic emergence of teen culture is a theme throughout Schrum's work; she notes, for example, "In the realm of commercial beauty culture, as with fashion, teenage girls navigated advice and products . . . before mass marketers sought their attention" (96); and "artists, manufacturers, retailers and marketers did not create a teen market for popular music as much as they responded to one" (113).

18. Walter Buck, "A Measurement of Changes in Attitudes and Interests of University Students over a Ten-Year Period," *Journal of Abnormal and Social Psychology* 31, no. 1 (1936): see table 3.

19. Paul Crissman, "Temporal Change and Sexual Difference in Moral Judgments," *Journal of Social Psychology* 16, no. 1 (1942): see table 3.

20. Paula S. Fass, *The Damned and the Beautiful: American Youth in the 1920's* (Oxford: Oxford University Press, 1977), 157.

21. Fass, *Damned and the Beautiful*, 167.

22. Fass, *Damned and the Beautiful*, 156.

23. Quoted in Fass, *Damned and the Beautiful*, 307 (emphasis in original).

24. S. L. Pressey, "Changes from 1923 to 1943 in the Attitudes of Public School and University Students," *Journal of Psychology* 21, no. 1 (1946): 186–187.

25. Cain, *Quiet*, 27.

26. Comacchio, *Dominion of Youth*, 68.

27. Cross, *Men to Boys*, 56.

28. "Door to Door," season 3, episode 4.

29. Duane Alwin, "From Obedience to Autonomy: Changes in Traits Desired in Children, 1924–1978," *Public Opinion Quarterly* 52, no. 1 (1988).

30. Karen von Hahn, "I Like to Hang Out with My Teenager. What's Wrong with That?," *Globe and Mail*, September 1, 2007.

31. Survey by Synovate reported in "Parents Want to Be Teens' Pals," *USA Today*, October 12, 2004.

32. Tom Wolfe, "The 'Me' Decade and the Third Great Awakening," *New York Magazine*, August 23, 1976.

33. Jean M. Twenge, "Birth Cohort Changes in Extraversion: A Cross-Temporal Meta-analysis, 1966–1993," *Personality and Individual Differences* 30, no. 5 (2001).

34. Jean M. Twenge et al., "Egos Inflating over Time: A Cross-Temporal Meta-analysis of the Narcissistic Personality Inventory," *Journal of Personality* 76, no. 4 (2008).

35. Twenge and Campbell, *Narcissism Epidemic*, 34.

36. Jean M. Twenge and Charles Im, "Changes in the Need for Social Approval, 1958–2001," *Journal of Research in Personality* 41, no. 1 (2007): 185.

37. Jean M. Twenge, *Generation Me: Why Today's Young Americans Are More Confident, Assertive, Entitled—and More Miserable Than Ever Before* (New York: Free Press, 2006), 181.

38. Robert McCrae, "Social Consequences of Experiential Openness," *Psychological Bulletin* 120, no. 3 (1996).

39. Malin André et al., "Cohort Differences in Personality in Middle-Aged Women during a 36-Year Period. Results from the Population Study of Women in Gothenburg," *Scandinavian Journal of Public Health* 38, no. 5 (2010).

40. Aristotle, *On Rhetoric: A Theory of Civic Discourse*, 2nd ed., trans. George A. Kennedy (New York: Oxford University Press, 2007), 151–152 (bk, 2, chap. 13).

41. This comment appeared in an article in the *Dallas Morning News* in 1926. Cited in Sarah Konrath, "The Empathy Paradox: Increasing Disconnection in the Age of Increasing Connection," in *Handbook of Research on Technoself: Identity in a Technological Society*, ed. Rocci Luppicini (Hershey, PA: Information Science Reference, 2013), 204–228.

42. M. Brent Donnellan and Kali H. Trzesniewski, "How Should We Study Generational 'Changes'—or Should We? A Critical Examination of the Evidence for 'Generation Me,'" *Social and Personality Psychology Compass* 3, no. 5 (2009): 775.

43. Robert R. McCrae et al., "Age Differences in Personality across the Adult Life Span: Parallels in Five Cultures," *Developmental Psychology* 35, no. 2 (1999): 466.

44. In fairness to Twenge, some of her academic papers do acknowledge the life maturation perspective as an alternative way of explaining differences between the young and the old; see, for example, Joshua D. Foster, W. Keith Campbell, and Jean M. Twenge, "Individual Differences in Narcissism: Inflated Self-Views across the Lifespan and around the World," *Journal of Research in Personality* 37, no. 6 (2003). But in the two books summarizing her work for a more general audience, this possibility is not discussed at any length.

45. Twenge and Campbell, *Narcissism Epidemic*, 62–63.

46. Twenge and Campbell, *Narcissism Epidemic*, 37.

47. Online appendices to the *Narcissism Epidemic* provide further explanation of how cultural change and individual change interact—but to my mind, these explanations only reinforce the feeling of circularity. Consider this passage: "'Feedback loops' occur when . . . culture shapes individual action, and individual action loops back to change the culture. . . . These feedback loops mean that *culture really changes itself*" (emphasis added). It's then pointed out that this leads to the expectation that cultures should be highly resistant to change. "Because a cultural system is mutually constitutive—a large mass of the individuals shape the cultural ideas and the cultural ideas shape the individuals—it is very difficult to change a culture in a dramatic way." True enough. But since the *Narcissism Epidemic* is all about a dramatic cultural shift in the direction of heightened narcissism over the past few decades, presumably this kind of circular causation can't explain it very well. See appendix C, http://www.jeantwenge.com/wp-content/uploads/2017/08/narcissism_epidemic_appendices.pdf, accessed July 4, 2019.

48. Twenge, *Generation Me*, 49.

4. PROBLEMS OF THE PRESENT

1. As noted in the introduction, there are prior works that liken today's adults to adolescents in various ways, but such work tends to be simply an evocative way of describing contemporary problems rather than a serious hypothesis proposing that adolescent traits have infiltrated the adult world.

2. P. M. Forni, *The Civility Solution: What to Do When People Are Rude* (New York: St. Martin's Griffin, 2009).

3. From an interview with Pier Forni in the documentary film *To Hell with Manners: The Decline of Civility* (Montreal: Kaos Productions, 2008).

4. P. M. Forni, *Choosing Civility: The Twenty-Five Rules of Considerate Conduct* (New York: St. Martin's Griffin, 2002), 5.

5. The first estimate comes from Samuel H. Preston and John McDonald, "The Incidence of Divorce within Cohorts of American Marriages Contracted since the Civil War," *Demography* 16, no. 1 (1979). The second is taken from Betsey Stevenson and Justin Wolfers, "Marriage and Divorce: Changes and Their Driving Forces," *Journal of Economic Perspectives* 21, no. 2 (2007).

6. David Eddie, *Globe and Mail*, July 4, 2012.

7. Brent W. Roberts et al., "The Power of Personality: The Comparative Validity of Personality Traits, Socioeconomic Status, and Cognitive Ability for Predicting Important Life Outcomes," *Perspectives on Psychological Science* 2, no. 4 (2007).

8. Posted by "Kris," November 9, 2010, http://tackyweddings.com/2009/06/30/wedding-cake-face-smashers/, accessed June 23, 2016. A couple of minor spelling errors have been corrected in this quote.

9. Miller McPherson, Lynn Smith-Lovin, and Matthew E. Brashears, "Social Isolation in America: Changes in Core Discussion Networks over Two Decades," *American Sociological Review* 71, no. 3 (2006).

10. Given the magnitude of the change, there was some debate back and forth about how real it was, but more recent research seems to confirm it. See Matthew E. Brashears, "Small Networks and High Isolation? A Reexamination of American Discussion Networks," *Social Networks* 33, no. 4 (2011).

11. Putnam, *Bowling Alone*, chap. 6.

12. Sarah Knapton, "Facebook Users Have 155 Friends—but Would Trust Just Four in a Crisis," *Telegraph*, January 20, 2016.

13. Christopher Carpenter, cited at ScienceDaily, http://www.sciencedaily.com/releases/2012/03/120319194046.htm. The full study is "Narcissism on Facebook: Self-Promotional and Anti-social Behavior," *Personality and Individual Differences* 52, no. 4 (2012).

14. Konrath, "Empathy Paradox." See also Sherry Turkle, *Alone Together: Why We Expect More from Technology and Less from Each Other* (New York: Basic Books, 2011).

15. For further detail on this point see chap. 8.

16. In other countries, such as Canada, rising education levels have helped to keep overall trust levels afloat. Without this educational boost, trust levels would likely have declined in these places as well.

17. The US result can also be held up against the findings from a later American survey that didn't just ask whether lying was justifiable but instead inquired about real-world behavior, asking respondents how often they had lied in the past twelve months. The results reveal the same staircase pattern across age categories. More than four in ten (43 percent) of those seventy and over said they had not lied once in the previous year. For those in their sixties, the figure was 32 percent; for those in their fifties, 23 percent; and so on down the line, until reaching just 8 percent among those under age thirty (my calculations based on the 1998 DDB Life Style survey, a data source used extensively in Putnam's *Bowling Alone* and downloaded from the website for that book, bowlingalone.com).

18. It is only on the lying question that the percentage answering "never justifiable" sometimes dips below 50 percent.

19. A larger set of questions is asked in this section of the WVS surveys, but many speak to moral issues where differences of opinion would primarily reflect liberal versus conservative viewpoints as well as religious belief (e.g., homosexuality, prostitution, euthanasia). The chosen measures more clearly tap into personal probity, pitting potential self-interest against broadly accepted social norms. Other analysis confirms that responses to the items used in my analysis cluster together and are part of a common underlying "self-interest" disposition; see David Halpern, "Moral Values, Social Trust and Inequality: Can Values Explain Crime?" *British Journal of Criminology* 41, no. 2 (2001).

20. The analysis of European countries in this chapter includes the twelve Western European cases that participated in at least three of the four EVS waves, including the first wave and the most recent. These are Belgium, Denmark, France, Germany, Great Britain, Ireland, Italy, Netherlands, Northern Ireland, Norway, Spain, Sweden. Two further possible cases with very small populations (Iceland and Malta) are excluded. For all calculations, the weight variable included in the data sets (s017) was applied in combination with a country weight variable designed to make each survey carry equal weight (by setting $N = 1,500$). However, reported sample sizes (here and throughout the book) are based on unweighted data.

21. To be clear: this is not the same group of respondents interviewed at different points in time but rather a representative cross-section at each point.

22. These results are derived from an OLS regression model based on curvilinear modeling of the life-cycle effect (using a linear and quadratic term for age) and dummy variables for each cohort (with the pre-1920 cohort used as the comparison group). The curvilinear modeling of age allows the model to capture greater change at earlier stages of the life cycle (which would mean, for example, a greater ebbing of antisocial attitudes from age twenty to thirty than from age sixty to seventy)—a common assumption applied when modeling life-cycle effects. Fuller details of this regression analysis are available from the author.

23. The US model also includes a period effect term for the 1995 WVS survey (–0.30). The reasons for this downward shift in antisocial attitudes on this wave of the study are not entirely clear.

24. The case is made stronger by considering other fields of research addressing the same question from different angles and with different evidence. In the area of cultural anthropology, for example, one study of 186 preindustrial societies worldwide discovered that in tribal societies where there is sharper segregation of youth from adults, antisocial behavior (e.g. theft, verbal abuse, destruction of property, drunkenness or misuse of other drugs) is more common. This pattern appears even in cases where the purpose of separating adolescents is deemed valuable and worthwhile by the society in question, such as initiating youth into religious or military activity (just as bringing together teenagers in industrialized societies for the purpose of secondary education is considered a constructive and worthwhile endeavor). The same anthropological study notes a connection between adolescent patterns and adult outcomes, observing that "antisocial behavior occurs among adolescents when it occurs among adults. Part of the *adult character established in adolescence* is a tendency towards misbehavior." All these findings offer support for the interpretation that peer socialization can leave a lasting imprint on individuals as they move forward to adulthood and thereby impart broad social influence. See Alice Schegel and Herbert Barry III, *Adolescence: An Anthropological Inquiry* (New York: Free Press, 1991), esp. 80, 136–137, and 154.

25. While these overall changes are certainly noteworthy and substantial, there are two factors that have likely served to dampen population level change on these antisocial measures despite the presence of strong generational effects. The first is the aging

of populations: the demographic profile of countries in Western Europe and the United States was much younger in the early 1980s (when the baby boomers, the largest demographic cohort, were still young adults) than it was some thirty years later (when the oldest boomers were reaching retirement). If later samples are more heavily populated with older respondents, antisocial attitudes in the aggregate will be pulled downward by this altered age distribution. The second factor potentially dampening estimates of aggregate change over the long haul is survey response rates. These have declined dramatically since the early 1980s. While it used to be possible to secure a response rate of 70 percent, nowadays it can be difficult to achieve 30 percent. In investigating this trend, some have suggested that willingness to participate in surveys is itself a pro-social disposition, which implies that more recent survey samples with their lower response rates would be more heavily biased in favor of pro-social respondents. If so, there may have been a steeper rise in antisocial attitudes in the real world than is apparent from survey-based measures—though it would be difficult to put a precise estimate on how much steeper. Recent evidence concerning pro-social response bias can be found in Scott Keeter et al., "What Low Response Rates Mean for Telephone Surveys" (Washington, DC: Pew Research Center, 2017).

26. American Psychiatric Association, *Diagnostic and Statistical Manual of Mental Disorders*, 5th ed. (Arlington, VA: American Psychiatric Association, 2013), 659.

27. Taya R. Cohen, A. T. Panter, and Nazli Turan, "Guilt Proneness and Moral Character," *Current Directions in Psychological Science* 21, no. 5 (2012).

28. One study providing strong evidence of a connection between low levels of conscientiousness and agreeableness and antisocial tendencies is Joshua D. Miller and Donald Lynam, "Structural Models of Personality and Their Relation to Antisocial Behavior: A Meta-analytic Review," *Criminology* 39, no. 4 (2001).

29. Ulrich Orth, Richard W. Robins, and Christopher J. Soto, "Tracking the Trajectory of Shame, Guilt, and Pride across the Life Span," *Journal of Personality and Social Psychology* 99, no. 6: 1061–1071 (see figure 1). It should be noted that this study presents these age differences as a reflection of life-cycle effects—the notion that people are more likely to experience feelings of guilt as they get older—but it does offer speculation about whether cohort effects could be part of the story as well (1068). Since the study is based on a single cross-sectional survey, it cannot answer this question definitively. My speculation would be that there is a significant likelihood of *both* life-cycle and cohort effects on measures of guilt, much like the pattern for antisocial attitudes analyzed above.

30. Côté, *Arrested Adulthood*, 63.

31. Donald L. McCabe, Linda Klebe Treviño, and Kenneth D. Butterfield, "Cheating in Academic Institutions: A Decade of Research," *Ethics and Behavior* 11, no. 3 (2001): 223.

32. Amy B. Brunell et al., "Narcissism and Academic Dishonesty: The Exhibitionism Dimension and the Lack of Guilt," *Personality and Individual Differences* 50, no. 3 (2011).

33. Zoë Chance et al., "Temporal View of the Costs and Benefits of Self-Deception," *Proceedings of the National Academy of Sciences* 108, Supplement 3 (2011): 15655 and 15657–15658.

34. The video is no longer available on YouTube; however, the cited excerpts appear in the first couple of minutes of *Faking the Grade* (which was shown on the CBC program *Doc Zone* and is currently available through the curio.ca website).

35. *Faking the Grade*, around the 14:30 mark.

36. Joseph Burgo, "How Aggressive Narcissism Explains Lance Armstrong," *Atlantic*, January 28, 2013.

37. Urie Bronfenbrenner et al., *The State of Americans: This Generation and the Next*, quoted in Côté, *Arrested Adulthood*, 67.

38. Dick Meyer, *Why We Hate Us: American Discontent in the New Millennium* (New York: Three Rivers, 2008).

5. LIBERATING EFFECTS

1. Michael Schudson, *The Good Citizen: A History of American Civic Life* (Cambridge, MA: Harvard University Press, 1998), 304.

2. Ronald Inglehart and Christian Welzel, *Modernization, Cultural Change and Democracy: The Human Development Sequence* (Cambridge: Cambridge University Press, 2005); Christian Welzel, *Freedom Rising: Human Empowerment and the Quest for Emancipation* (Cambridge: Cambridge University Press, 2013).

3. Ronald F. Inglehart, "After Postmaterialism: An Essay on China, Russia and the United States: A Comment," *Canadian Journal of Sociology* 41, no. 2 (2016): 218.

4. Inglehart, "After Postmaterialism," 218.

5. Results for items concerning African Americans are limited to white respondents only.

6. The importance of education to tolerance was identified in Samuel A. Stouffer's seminal study, *Communism, Conformity, and Civil Liberties* (Garden City, NY: Doubleday, 1955).

7. Snyder, *120 Years of American Education*, 65–66.

8. Philip Schadwel and Christopher R. H. Garneau, "The Diffusion of Tolerance: Birth Cohort Changes in the Effects of Education and Income on Political Tolerance," *Sociological Forum* 32, no. 4 (2017): 750.

9. John L. Sullivan, James Piereson, and George E. Marcus, *Political Tolerance and American Democracy* (Chicago: University of Chicago Press, 1982).

10. George E. Marcus et al., *With Malice toward Some: How People Make Civil Liberties Judgments* (Cambridge: Cambridge University Press, 1995), 168–170.

11. McCrae, "Social Consequences of Experiential Openness," 326.

12. Fass, *Damned and the Beautiful*, 328–329 and 359.

13. Fass, *Damned and the Beautiful*, 260–326.

14. Anne Case and Angus Deaton, "Rising Morbidity and Mortality in Midlife among White Non-Hispanic Americans in the 21st Century," *Proceedings of the National Academy of Sciences* 112, no. 49 (2015): table 1 and 15078.

15. Eric A. Finkelstein et al., "Obesity and Severe Obesity Forecasts through 2030," *American Journal of Preventive Medicine* 42, no. 6 (2012).

16. Véronique Provencher et al., "Personality Traits in Overweight and Obese Women: Associations with BMI and Eating Behaviors," *Eating Behaviors* 9, no. 3 (2008); Antonio Terracciano et al., "Facets of Personality Linked to Underweight and Overweight," *Psychosomatic Medicine* 71, no. 6 (2009); Angelina Sutin et al., "Personality and Obesity across the Adult Life Span," *Journal of Personality and Social Psychology* 101, no. 3 (2011).

17. One study showing a connection between debt levels and risk attitudes is Sarah Brown, Gaia Garino, and Karl Taylor, "Household Debt and Attitudes towards Risk," *Review of Income and Wealth* 59, no. 2 (2013).

18. Concurring respondents are those who said the description was "very much like me," "like me," or "somewhat like me."

19. Nigel Nicholson et al., "Personality and Domain Specific Risk-Taking," *Journal of Risk Research* 8, no. 2 (2005); Cindy Kam, "Risk Attitudes and Political Participation," *American Journal of Political Science* 56, no. 4 (2012): 821.

20. Barber, *Consumed*, 23.

21. Mark Bauerlein, *The Dumbest Generation: How the Digital Age Stupefies Young Americans and Jeopardizes Our Future* (New York: Penguin, 2009).

22. Chris Hedges, *Empire of Illusion: The End of Literacy and the Triumph of Spectacle* (Toronto: Alfred A. Knopf Canada, 2009), 44.

23. Neil Postman, *Amusing Ourselves to Death: Public Discourse in the Age of Show Business*, 20th anniversary ed. (New York: Penguin Books, 2005), 160.

24. See chap. 3.

25. The same questions were posed on wave 5 of the WVS, which took place in 2006—but this is still not a long enough time frame to measure these effects.

26. These survey questions are part of a larger series developed by Israeli social psychologist Shalom Schwartz as part of his theory of basic human values.

27. The analysis here is based on the ten Western European countries that participated in all eight ESS rounds from 2002 to 2016: Belgium, Finland, France, Germany, Ireland, the Netherlands, Norway, Sweden, Switzerland and the UK.

28. Five-year cohorts are used instead of ten-year (as in chap. 4) in order to reduce collinearity of the age and cohort variables (a greater problem when the time frame analyzed is relatively short).

29. Jennifer Lodi-Smith and Brent Roberts, "Social Investment and Personality: A Meta-analysis of the Relationship of Personality Traits to Investment in Work, Family, Religion and Volunteerism," *Personality and Social Psychology Review* 11, no. 1 (2007): 77.

30. Jeffrey Jensen Arnett, *Emerging Adulthood: The Winding Road from the Late Teens through the Twenties* (New York: Oxford University Press, 2004), 8.

31. Côté, *Arrested Adulthood*, 12.

32. Côté, *Arrested Adulthood*, 34.

33. Zosia Bielski, "Living Alone: A Testament to Freedom or an Erosion of Society?," *Globe and Mail*, January 12, 2013.

34. Côté draws this phrase from another work that explores similar terrain, Robert Bly's *Sibling Society: An Impassioned Plea for the Rediscovery of Adulthood* (New York: Vintage Books, 1997).

6. GOVERNING TOGETHER

1. These examples come from Elizabeth May's *Losing Confidence: The Crisis in Canadian Democracy* (Toronto: McClelland & Stewart, 2009), 68–71.

2. "On Partisanship: Enemies and Adversaries in Politics," delivered at Stanford University, October 15, 2012. Consistent with Ignatieff's observation is the 2014 finding that more than one-quarter of Democrats saw the Republican Party as a "threat to the nation's well-being," while more than a third of Republicans held the same view of the Democratic Party (Steven Pinker, *Enlightenment Now: The Case for Reason, Science, Humanism, and Progress* [New York: Viking, 2018], 372).

3. Alan Wolfe, *The Politics of Petulance: America in an Age of Immaturity* (Chicago: University of Chicago Press, 2018).

4. David Brooks, "When the World Is Led by a Child," *New York Times*, May 15, 2017.

5. Low voter turnout among young adults is common in many countries. So too, in places where the issue has been looked at closely, is the finding that while this may be partly a life-cycle effect (where people tend to vote less when they are younger and more when they are older), it is also clearly a generational effect (where voting is low in a given generation and stays lower than the norm even as they get older). Studies pointing to this conclusion across many of the long-established democracies include Paul Howe, *Citizens Adrift: The Democratic Disengagement of Young Canadians* (Vancouver: University of British Columbia Press, 2010); Martin Wattenberg, *Is Voting for Young People?* (New York: Pearson Education, 2008); André Blais et al., "Where Does Turnout Decline Come From?," *European Journal of Political Research* 43, no. 2 (2004); Yosef Bhatti and Kasper M. Hansen, "The Effect of Generation and Age on Turnout to the European Parliament—How Turnout Will Continue to Decline in the Future," *Electoral Studies* 31, no. 2 (2012); and Maria Grasso, *Generations, Political Participation and Social Change in Western Europe* (Abingdon, UK: Routledge, 2016).

6. Author's calculations based on Canadian Election Study 2011 data.

7. James Fowler and Cindy Kam, "Delayed Gratification and Turnout: Patience as a Political Virtue," *Political Behavior* 28, no. 2 (2006): 113–114.

8. See Tom Rosentiel, "Public Knows Basic Facts about Politics, Economics, but Struggles with Specifics," Pew Research Center, November 18, 2010.

9. Andrew Romano, "How Ignorant Are Americans?," *Newsweek*, March 20, 2011.

10. See R. A. Malatest & Associates, National Youth Survey Report (Ottawa: Elections Canada, 2011), table 3.8.

11. Howe, *Citizens Adrift*, chap. 3.

12. Hollingshead, *Elmtown's Youth*, 307.

13. Henry Milner, *Civic Literacy: How Informed Citizens Make Democracy Work* (Hanover, NH: University Press of New England, 2002).

14. Michael X. Delli Carpini and Scott Keeter, *What Americans Know about Politics and Why It Matters* (New Haven, CT: Yale University Press, 1996), 225.

15. Howe, *Citizens Adrift*, 21.

16. Jeffery J. Mondak, *Personality and the Foundations of Political Behavior* (Cambridge: Cambridge University Press, 2010), 157.

17. Mondak, *Personality and the Foundations of Political Behavior*, 159–160.

18. Dana R. Carney et al., "The Secret Lives of Liberals and Conservatives: Personality Profiles, Interaction Styles, and the Things They Leave Behind," *Political Psychology* 29, no. 6 (2008); Alan S. Gerber et al., "The Big Five Personality Traits in the Political Arena," *Annual Review of Political Science* 14, no. 1 (2011): 269–271.

19. Hermann Brandstätter and Karl-Dieter Opp, "Personality Traits ('Big Five') and the Propensity to Political Protest: Alternative Models," *Political Psychology* 35, no. 4 (2014); Jeffery Mondak et al., "Personality and Civic Engagement: An Integrative Framework for the Study of Trait Effects on Political Behavior," *American Political Science Review* 104, no. 1 (2010): 102; Aina Gallego and Daniel Oberski, "Personality and Political Participation: The Mediation Hypothesis," *Political Behavior* 34, no. 3 (2012): 441–442; Shang E. Ha, Seokho Kim, and Se Hee Jo, "Personality Traits and Political Participation: Evidence from South Korea," *Political Psychology* 34, no. 4 (2013).

20. Diana C. Mutz, *Hearing the Other Side: Deliberative versus Participatory Democracy* (New York: Cambridge University Press, 2006), 138.

21. In support of this viewpoint see Russell J. Dalton and Christian Welzel, *The Civic Culture Transformed: From Allegiant to Assertive Citizens* (Cambridge: Cambridge University Press, 2014).

22. Palladino, *Teenagers: An American History*, 179–180 (emphasis added).

23. Charlotte Alter, "The Young and the Relentless," *Time*, April 2, 2018, 28.

24. Roberto Stefan Foa and Yascha Mounk, "The Democratic Disconnect," *Journal of Democracy* 27, no. 3 (2016); and Roberto Stefan Foa and Yascha Mounk, "The Signs of Deconsolidation," *Journal of Democracy* 28, no. 1 (2017).

25. These numbers differ very slightly from Foa and Mounk's reported results. The difference seems to be due to my use of the weighting variable (s017) provided with the WVS data sets, a procedure I have followed in all my analyses based on this data set.

26. Three critical response papers by Alexander and Welzel, Norris, and Voeten can be found on the website of the *Journal of Democracy* (journalofdemocracy.org).

27. For example, they set the stage for their analysis by noting that "over the last three decades, trust in political institutions . . . has precipitously declined across the established democracies of North America and Western Europe" (Foa and Mounk, "Democratic Disconnect," 6). Further analysis of patterns of eroding confidence in institutions is presented in Foa and Mounk's reply to their critics on the website of the *Journal of Democracy* ("The End of the Consolidation Paradigm: A Response to Our Critics," 12–16).

28. Paul Howe, "Eroding Norms and Democratic Deconsolidation," *Journal of Democracy* 28, no. 4 (2017).

29. Steven Levitsky and Daniel Ziblatt, *How Democracies Die* (New York: Crown, 2018).

30. Foa and Mounk, "Democratic Disconnect," 7. In my earlier paper, I incorporated this question and several others into my analysis. I have omitted some of these additional results, however, since the relevant questions were based on a 1-to-10 response scale (i.e., the same numeric scale as the antisocial attitudes questions). There is a concern that certain respondents might tend to use such scales in a particular fashion (e.g., avoiding "extreme" responses of 1 or 10), thereby artificially creating a correlation between the antisocial response items and the democracy measures. Here I have focused my analysis on democracy questions using a different response format to avoid any such problems.

31. Mondak, *Personality and the Foundations of Political Behavior*, 126–131.

32. These results include fourteen Western European cases that participated in waves 3 and 4 of the EVS: Austria, Belgium, Denmark, Finland, France, Germany, Great Britain, Ireland, Italy, Netherlands, Northern Ireland, Portugal, Spain, and Sweden.

33. More recent analysis by Foa and Mounk indicates a sharper increase on this measure—a jump from 4.9 percent in the mid-1990s to 14.3 percent in 2017 in the eight largest developed democracies combined (which include Germany, France, Italy, Spain, and the UK). See Roberto Stefan Foa and Yascha Mounk, "Democratic Deconsolidation in Developed Democracies, 1995–2018," CES Open Forum Series, Minda de Gunzburg Center for European Studies, Harvard University, 12.

7. GETTING AHEAD

1. For a comprehensive overview see Lex Borghans et al., "The Economics and Psychology of Personality Traits," *Journal of Human Resources* 43, no. 4 (2008).

2. Nettle, *Personality*, 139.

3. Results are based on the same ten Western European countries included in the cohort analysis in chap. 5.

4. Twenge and Campbell, *Narcissism Epidemic*, 135.

5. Twenge and Campbell, *Narcissism Epidemic*, 276.

6. Colin Campbell, *The Romantic Ethic and the Spirit of Modern Consumerism* (Oxford: Basil Blackwell, 1987), 89–90.

7. *Globe and Mail*, April 4, 2009.

8. Richard Florida, *The Rise of the Creative Class* (New York: Basic Books, 2002), 8.

9. Florida, *Rise of the Creative Class*, 13.

10. The index was actually based on couples, not individuals, because the US Census did not ask people to identify their sexual orientation when Florida was first conducting his research. He estimated the number of gay couples based on individuals who claimed to be "unmarried partners" and were of the same sex. Florida, *Rise of the Creative Class*, 255.

11. Florida, *Rise of the Creative Class*, 249–250.

12. Florida, *Rise of the Creative Class*, 260.

13. Richard Florida, *Who's Your City? How the Creative Economy Is Making Where to Live the Most Important Decision of Your Life*, Canadian ed. (Toronto: Vintage Canada, 2009), 215–216.

14. Florida, *Who's Your City?*, 220.

15. These ideas are actually woven together now in the more recent edition of *The Rise of the Creative Class*, which appeared in 2011. I present them here in the way they unfolded over time in Florida's evolving thinking on the subject.

16. Florida, *Rise of the Creative Class*, chap. 3.

17. Florida, *Rise of the Creative Class*, 16 (emphasis in original).

18. Florida, *Rise of the Creative Class*, 17.

19. Jeffrey Jensen Arnett, "Oh, Grow Up! Generational Grumbling and the New Life Stage of Emerging Adulthood—Commentary on Trzesniewski and Donnellan," *Perspectives on Psychological Science* 5, no. 1 (2010): 90.

20. The revised edition of Jean Twenge's *Generation Me* has a chapter on workplace attitudes, which includes a section on the high expectations and impatience among the young workers of today.

21. Nettle, *Personality*, 142.

22. Walter Issacson, *Steve Jobs* (New York: Simon & Schuster, 2013).

23. Paul Tough, *How Children Succeed: Grit, Curiosity, and the Hidden Power of Character* (Boston: Houghton Mifflin Harcourt, 2012), xv. The role of grit in promoting academic success has been researched extensively by psychology professor Angela Duckworth and is discussed in her book *Grit: The Power of Passion and Perseverance* (New York: Scribner, 2016).

24. The tight correlation between grit and conscientiousness is discussed in Marcus Credé, "Much Ado about Grit: A Meta-analytic Synthesis of the Grit Literature," *Journal of Personality and Social Psychology* 113, no. 3 (2017).

8. ADOLESCENCE ALONE?

1. Charles Taylor, *The Malaise of Modernity* (Toronto: House of Anansi, 1991).

2. Barber, *Consumed*, 86–115.

3. Barber's book echoes themes from Daniel Bell's classic work, *The Cultural Contradictions of Capitalism* (New York: Basic Books 1976), which highlighted profound tensions between the Protestant work ethic underlying the production side of capitalism and the hedonistic ethos connected to the consumption side of the capitalist economy.

4. Richard Wilkinson and Kate Pickett, *The Spirit Level: Why Greater Equality Makes Societies Stronger* (New York: Bloomsbury, 2009), 122.

5. Cynthia Ogden et al., "Prevalence of Childhood and Adult Obesity in the United States, 2011–2012," *Journal of the American Medical Association* 311, no. 8 (2014).

6. Claudia Goldin, "America's Graduation from High School: The Evolution and Spread of Secondary Schooling in the Twentieth Century," *Journal of Economic History* 58, no. 2 (1998): 345.

7. A. D. C Peterson, *A Hundred Years of Education* (London: Gerald Duckworth, 1952), 140–141.

8. Fritz K. Ringer, *Education and Society in Modern Europe* (Bloomington: Indiana University Press, 1979), 55 (German data), 221 (UK data), and 316 (French data). See also Goldin, "America's Graduation from High School," 349.

9. Francis Grund, *The Americans in Their Moral, Social and Political Relations* (1837; reprint, New York: Johnson Reprint Corp., 1968), 171.

10. Alexis de Tocqueville, *Democracy in America*, ed. J. P. Mayer (1835; reprint, Garden City, NY: Anchor Books, 1969), 301.

11. Tocqueville, *Democracy in America*, 527.

12. Côté, *Arrested Adulthood*, 45.

13. Norman H. Nie, Jane Junn, and Kenneth Stehlik-Berry, *Education and Democratic Citizenship in America* (Chicago: University of Chicago Press, 1996), 2 and 4.

14. My calculations based on 2008 ANES. The comparison is between those with twelve years of schooling or less and those with sixteen years or more.

15. Nie, Junn, and Stehlik-Berry, *Education and Democratic Citizenship in America*, 106.

16. Howe, *Citizens Adrift*, 246–247.

17. Result calculated from US General Social Survey, 2000–2006 combined.

18. Based on Statistics Canada's 2003 General Social Survey and the World Values Surveys. For further data on OECD countries see Esteban Ortiz-Ospina and Max Roser, "Trust," Our World in Data, 2017.

19. Jian Huang, Henriëtte Maassen van den Brink, and Wim Groot, "College Education and Social Trust: An Evidence-Based Study on the Causal Mechanisms," *Social Indicators Research* 104, no. 2 (2011): 293.

20. Putnam, *Bowling Alone*, 140–141.

21. Trends in social trust, based on World Values Study data, are summarized Christian Albrekt Larsen, "Why Social Cohesion Declines in Liberal Regimes, and Increases in Social Democratic Regimes," paper presented at the International Sociological Association Research Committee 19 conference, Montreal, 2009. Just two countries, Sweden and Denmark, have seen substantial increases in trust. See http://www.cccg.umontreal.ca/rc19/PDF/Albrekt%20Larsen-C_Rc192009.pdf, accessed July 5, 2019.

22. Putnam, *Bowling Alone*, 138.

23. For consistency's sake, this result is limited to the twelve European cases included in the cohort analysis of antisocial attitudes in chapter 4, as well as the United States, for the 2008–2011 survey period. N = 1033 for antisocial category; 6,913 for pro-social category.

24. This result is based on the same set of countries using 1990 WVS/EVS data (N = 1,228 and 6,768), as the question concerning trust in compatriots was not included in the most recent wave of the study. The "trust in compatriots" question was included in a smaller set of the European countries again in 1999 (Denmark, Germany, Great Britain, and Italy) and yielded a similar result: a trust gap of 26 percentage points. Trusting respondents are those who trust compatriots either "completely" or "a little" (as opposed to "neither trust or distrust," "not trust very much," or "not trust at all").

25. A fuller set of questions was posed in several countries. The results were similar. With respect to accepting a bribe and avoiding a fare on public transit, roughly one-third of respondents said "almost all" or "many" compatriots were guilty of these transgressions, while another 60 percent said "some" and 6 percent "almost none." With respect to lying in one's own interest, 67 percent said "almost all" or "many," 32 percent said "some," and only 1 percent said "almost none." The countries asked this fuller set of questions are Belgium, Germany, Great Britain, Italy, and (for all but the "avoiding a fare" question) Denmark.

26. These countries are Denmark, Germany, Italy, and Great Britain.

27. On the education-obesity link see Marion Devaux et al., "Exploring the Relationship between Education and Obesity," *OECD Journal: Economic Studies* 2011, no. 1 (2011); and Silke Hermann et al., "The Association of Education with Body Mass Index and Waist Circumference in the EPIC-PANACEA Study," *BMC Public Health* 11 (2011): 169. On education and positive health outcomes more generally see David M. Cutler and Adriana Lleras-Muney, "Education and Health: Evaluating Theories and Evidence," Working Paper no. 12352, National Bureau of Economic Research, Cambridge, MA (2006); and David M. Cutler and Adriana Lleras-Muney, "Understanding Differences in Health Behaviors by Education," *Journal of Health Economics* 29, no. 1 (2010).

28. K. Parmenter, J. Waller, and J. Wardle, "Demographic Variation in Nutrition Knowledge in England," *Health Education Research* 15, no. 2 (2000); J. A. Swift, C. Glazebrook, and I. Macdonald, "Validation of a Brief, Reliable Scale to Measure Knowledge about the Health Risks Associated with Obesity," *International Journal of Obesity* 30, no. 4; Kylie Ball and David Crawford, "Socioeconomic Status and Weight Change in Adults: A Review," *Social Science and Medicine* 60, no. 9 (2005); Deveaux et al., "Exploring the Relationship between Education and Obesity," 140.

29. Hermann et al., "Association of Education with Body Mass Index and Waist Circumference in the EPIC-PANACEA Study," 2.

30. Sutin et al., "Personality and Obesity across the Adult Life Span."

31. Lisa R. Anderson and Jennifer M. Mellor, "Predicting Health Behaviors with an Experimental Measure of Risk Preference," *Journal of Health Economics* 27, no. 5 (2008): 1267; and Gilly Koritzky et al., "Obesity and Risk Taking: A Male Phenomenon," *Appetite* 59,

no. 2 (2012). This second paper specifies that risk taking has a substantial impact on males, whereas impulsiveness has a greater effect among females.

32. Côté, *Arrested Adulthood*, 45.

33. Nie, Junn, and Stehlik-Berry, *Education and Democratic Citizenship in America*, 120–125 and 159.

34. Putnam, *Bowling Alone*, 139–140.

35. Putnam, *Bowling Alone*, chaps. 2 and 3.

36. To avoid confusion about the role of ethnicity and race in all this, Murray's analysis of these trends looks only at the non-Latino white population—hence the subtitle of his book, *Coming Apart: The State of White America, 1960–2010* (New York: Crown Forum, 2012). Graphs displaying the cited trends are on pages 156, 191, 193, 229, 248, and 249.

37. Murray, *Coming Apart*, 241–244.

38. Robert D. Putnam, *Our Kids: The American Dream in Crisis* (New York: Simon & Schuster, 2015).

39. Murray, *Coming Apart*, 236.

40. Putnam, *Our Kids*, 1.

9. BUCKING THE TREND

1. Howe and Strauss, *Millennials Rising*, 206.

2. Howard N. Snyder, "Arrest in the United States, 1990–2010" (Washington, DC: US Department of Justice, Bureau of Justice Statistics, 2012).

3. Centers for Disease Control and Prevention, Youth Risk Behaviors Surveillance System, online data analysis tool, https://nccd.cdc.gov/youthonline/App/Default.aspx, accessed July 5, 2019.

4. Pinker, *Enlightenment Now*, 229.

5. Howe and Strauss, *Millennials Rising*, 204.

6. Data for 2011 are from the Center for Behavioral Health Statistics and Quality, *Results from the National Survey on Drug Use and Health: Detailed Tables*, "Table 7.30B—Tobacco Product and Alcohol Use in the Past Month among Persons Aged 12 to 17, by Gender: Percentages, 2002–2011," https://www.samhsa.gov/data/sites/default/files/NSDUH-DetTabsPDFWHTML2011-web/NSDUH-DetTabsPDFWHTML2011/HTML/NSDUH-DetTabsSect7peTabs1to45-2011.htm, accessed July 5, 2019.

7. Howe and Strauss, *Millennials Rising*, 197–198.

8. Brady E. Hamilton and Stephanie J. Ventura, "Birth Rates for U.S. Teenagers Reach Historic Lows for All Age and Ethnic Groups," *NCHS Data Brief* No. 89 (Atlanta: National Center for Health Statistics, Centers for Disease Control and Prevention, 2012).

9. Howe and Strauss, *Millennials Rising*, 143–144.

10. National Center for Education Statistics, *Digest of Education Statistics: 2012* (Washington, DC: National Center for Education Statistics, US Department of Education, 2013), 242.

11. These are the dropout rates for ages sixteen to twenty-four. National Center for Education Statistics, *Digest of Education Statistics: 2013* (Washington, DC: National Center for Education Statistics, US Department of Education, 2015), 217.

12. Howe and Strauss, *Millennials Rising*, 216.

13. Mark Hugo Lopez and Karlo Barrios Marcelo, "Volunteering among Young People" (Medford, MA: Center for Information and Research on Civic Learning and Engagement, Tufts University, 2007), 5. Data showing increased volunteering among young people are also provided in Putnam, *Bowling Alone*, 130 and 265.

14. Center for Information and Research on Civic Learning and Engagement, "The Youth Vote in 2012" (Medford, MA: Center for Information and Research on Civic Learning and Engagement, Tufts University, 2013).

15. Some have also linked this upturn in civic involvement to the effects of 9/11 on young people's interest in politics, which seems plausible enough (see Thomas H. Sander and Robert D. Putnam, "Still Bowling Alone? The Post-9/11 Split," *Journal of Democracy* 21, no. 1 [2010]). But it's worth asking if this is really the right explanation, or the sole explanation, given how the civic engagement trends align so neatly with other wide-ranging changes in millennial attitudes and behavior that are unlikely to have been influenced by 9/11.

16. Jean Twenge, *Generation Me: Why Today's Young Americans Are More Confident, Assertive, Entitled—and More Miserable Than Ever Before*, rev. ed. (New York: Atria, 2014), 286.

17. Howe and Strauss, *Millennials Rising*, 17.

18. Howe and Strauss, *Millennials Rising*, 28.

19. Reginald W. Bibby with Sarah Russell and Ron Rolheiser, *The Emerging Millennials: How Canada's Newest Generation Is Responding to Change and Choice* (Lethbridge, AB: Project Canada Books, 2009), 199. Based on averaged results for male and female respondents.

20. Bibby, *Emerging Millennials*, 199.

21. Alexander McKay, "Trends in Canadian National and Provincial/Territorial Teen Pregnancy Rate: 2001–2010," *Canadian Journal of Human Sexuality* 21, no. 3–4 (2012): 161.

22. Public Safety Canada Portfolio Corrections Statistics Committee, "Corrections and Conditional Release Statistical Overview" (Ottawa: Public Works and Government Services Canada, 2009). The 2009 report provides data going back to 1989 (more recent reports track trends from 1998 on).

23. Jason Gilmore, "Trends in Dropout Rates and the Labour Market Outcomes of Young Dropouts," in *Education Matters: Insights on Education, Learning and Training in Canada* (Ottawa: Statistics Canada, 2010).

24. William Strauss and Neil Howe, "Will the Real Gen Y Please Stand Up," *Los Angeles Times*, March 2, 2007.

25. "The Most Sensible Generation in Years," *Maclean's*, April 13, 2009, 4.

26. Bibby, *Emerging Millennials*, 175. Researchers who have studied the connection between openness and paranormal belief have found that the two are closely connected. See Douglas A. MacDonald, "Spirituality: Description, Measurement and Relation to the Five Factor Model of Personality," *Journal of Personality* 68, no. 1 (2000): 186.

27. Kyung Hee Kim, "The Creativity Crisis: The Decrease in Creative Thinking Score on the Torrance Tests of Creative Thinking," *Creativity Research Journal* 23, no. 4 (2011).

28. Kim, "Creativity Crisis," 293.

29. Kim, "Creativity Crisis," 292. An earlier paper making the explicit link between creativity and openness is Robert McCrae, "Creativity, Divergent Thinking, and Openness to Experience," *Journal of Personality and Social Psychology* 52, no. 6 (1987).

30. Howe and Strauss, *Millennials Rising*, 28.

31. A number of studies have linked personality traits and choice of college major, finding that high levels of openness are common among those choosing to study in the arts and humanities, whereas those high in conscientiousness tend to opt for other majors—science, law, business, etc. A recent review of these studies appears in Anna Vedel, "Big Five Personality Group Differences across Academic Majors: A Systematic Review," *Personality and Individual Differences* 92 (2016).

32. Howe and Strauss, *Millennials Rising*, 32.

33. Howe and Strauss, *Millennials Rising*, 32.

34. Peter Gray, "As Children's Freedom Has Declined, So Has Their Creativity," *Psychology Today*, September 17, 2012.

35. Howe and Strauss, *Millennials Rising*, 134.

36. Lori Gottlieb, "How to Land Your Kid in Therapy," *Atlantic*, July/August 2011, 64–78.

37. See World Bank, "Fertility Rate, Total (Births per Woman)," https://data. worldbank.org/indicator/sp.dyn.tfrt.in.

38. Joyce A. Martin et al., "Births: Final Data for 2010," *National Vital Statistics Reports* 61, no. 1 (2012): 24.

39. Estimate from the Guttmacher Institute, https://www.guttmacher.org/fact-sheet/ induced-abortion-worldwide, accessed July 5, 2019.

40. Eric Kaufmann, *Shall the Religious Inherit the Earth? Demography and Politics in the Twenty-First Century* (London: Profile Books, 2010), xii.

41. Kaufmann, *Shall the Religious Inherit the Earth?*, 34.

42. Claude Belanger, Readings in Quebec History, "Birth Rate," http://faculty.mari anopolis.edu/c.belanger/quebechistory/events/birth8.htm. Last revised August 28, 2000.

43. Réal Bates, "Naissance d'une population. Les Française établis au Canada au XVIIᵉ siècle," *Population* 44, no. 1 (1989): 163.

44. Data from the Canadian census on common-law unions can be found at http:// www12.statcan.ca/census-recensement/2011/as-sa/98-312-x/2011001/tbl/tbl2-eng.cfm, accessed July 5, 2019. Research studies on abortion rates in Quebec are cited in Brian Daly, "Sky-High Quebec Abortion Rates Worry Researchers," *Toronto Sun*, May 15, 2014.

45. Results of public opinion polls on same-sex marriage have consistently found Que-becers to be more supportive than other Canadians. See Religious Tolerance, http://www. religioustolerance.org/hom_marz.htm.

46. Kenan Malik, "Shall the Religious Inherit the Earth? by Eric Kaufmann," *Guardian*, May 2, 2010.

47. Bibby, *Emerging Millennials*, 178.

48. My own calculations based on 1976, 1977, 2010, and 2011 Monitoring the Future data sets. For more detailed analysis confirming my conclusion see Jean M. Twenge et al., "Generational and Time Period Differences in American Adolescents' Religious Orienta-tion, 1966–2014," *PLoS ONE* 10, no. 5 (2015).

49. Kaufmann, *Shall the Religious Inherit the Earth?*, 99–100.

50. Phillip Longman, "The Liberal Baby Bust," *USA Today*, March 13, 2006. More detailed analysis of the connection between political preferences and fertility rates can be found in Ron J. Lesthaeghe and Lisa Neidert, "The Second Demographic Transition in the United States: Exception or Textbook Example?," *Population and Development Review* 32, no. 4 (2006).

51. Kaufmann, *Shall the Religious Inherit the Earth?*, 101.

52. For the 2008 election, it's estimated that among those under thirty, 66 percent voted for Obama, 32 percent for McCain. For the 2012 election, the estimates are 60 percent for Obama, 37 percent for Romney. See Paul Taylor and Scott Keeter, eds., *Millennials: A Portrait of Generation Next* (Washington, DC: Pew Research Center, February 2010), 63; and Center for Information and Research on Civic Learning and Engagement, "Youth Vote in 2012," 1.

53. For those in the thirty-five-to-fifty age band, for example, the average number of biological children is 2.07 (low openness) versus 1.65 (high openness). My own calcula-tions based on the original data for the study.

54. Average number of biological children for those sixty plus is 2.76 (low openness) versus 2.69 (high openness).

55. Howe and Strauss, *Millennials Rising*, 33.

56. Jean M. Twenge, Brittany Gentile, and W. Keith Campbell, "Birth Cohort Differ-ences in Personality," in *APA Handbook of Personality and Social Psychology*, vol. 4, *Per-sonality Processes and Individual Differences*, ed. Mario Mikulincer and Phillip R. Shaver (Washington, DC: American Psychological Association, 2015), 543.

57. Markus Jokela, "Birth-Cohort Effects in the Association between Personality and Fertility," *Psychological Science* 23, no. 8 (2012).

58. Markus Jokela et al., "Reproductive Behavior and Personality Traits of the Five Factor Model," *European Journal of Personality* 25, no. 6 (2011): 495.

59. Jokela et al., "Reproductive Behavior and Personality Traits of the Five Factor Model," 495.

60. M. Brent Donnellan, Rand D. Conger, and Chalandra M. Bryant, "The Big Five and Enduring Marriages," *Journal of Research in Personality* 38, no. 5 (2004): 499.

61. Twenge et al., "Birth Cohort Differences in Personality," 543.

62. Iris A. M. Smits et al., "Cohort Differences in Big Five Personality Traits over a Period of 25 Years," *Journal of Personality and Social Psychology* 100, no. 6 (2011).

63. Jokela, "Birth-Cohort Effects in the Association between Personality and Fertility," 839.

64. Brent W. Roberts and Timothy Bogg, "A Longitudinal Study of the Relationships between Conscientiousness and the Social-Environmental Factors and Substance-Use Behaviors That Influence Health," *Journal of Personality* 72, no. 2 (2004): 336.

65. Markus Jokela et al., "Adult Temperament and Child-Bearing over the Life Course," *European Journal of Personality* 24, no. 2 (2010): 160.

66. Smits et al., "Cohort Differences in Big Five Personality Traits over a Period of 25 Years," 1133–1134.

67. Miller and Lynam, "Structural Models of Personality and Their Relation to Antisocial Behavior." Some researchers actually conceptualize antisocial attitudes as personality markers in themselves rather than linking them to underlying Big Five traits. Like the Big Five personality traits, these antisocial dispositions have been found to have a strong genetic component. See Christopher J. Ferguson, "Genetic Contributions to Antisocial Personality and Behavior: A Meta-analytic Review from an Evolutionary Perspective," *Journal of Social Psychology* 150, no. 2 (2010).

68. All calculations in this paragraph are for the baby boom cohort, but only those who were twenty-five or older at the time of being surveyed—in order to focus on those at a stage of life where some of these questions would become more meaningful and relevant to respondents.

69. Again, all calculations in this paragraph are for baby boomers who were twenty-five or older at the time of being surveyed.

70. A recent paper describing the genetic underpinnings of parental nurturing is Augustine Kong et al., "The Nature of Nurture: Effects of Parental Genotypes," *Science* 359 (2018). Perhaps more common is the observation that genetic dispositions can lead individuals to seek out an environment that is consonant with their inherited inclinations and therefore has an amplifying effect on genetic expression. This point is discussed in John R. Hibbing, Kevin B. Smith, and John R. Alford, *Predisposed: Liberals, Conservatives, and the Biology of Political Differences* (New York: Routledge, 2014), 227–228.

CONCLUSION

1. Richard V. Reeves and Dimitrios Halikias, *The Liberal Case for Character in a Populist Age* (Washington, DC: Brookings Institution, 2017).

2. Paul Tough, "How Kids Really Succeed," *Atlantic*, June 2016.

3. On this point see Reeves and Halikias, *Liberal Case for Character in a Populist Age*, 9–11.

4. Tough, "How Kids Really Succeed."

5. The column was followed by a book: Lenore Skenazy, *Free-Range Kids: How to Raise Safe, Self-Reliant Children (without Going Nuts with Worry)* (San Francisco: Jossey-Bass, 2009).

6. John Dewey, "The School as Social Center," *Elementary School Teacher* 3, no. 2 (1902): 76.

7. Lee Benson, Ira Harakavy, and John Puckett, *Dewey's Dream: Universities and Democracies in an Age of Education Reform* (Philadelphia: Temple University Press, 2007), 27.

8. Dewey, "School as Social Center," 73.

9. Benson, Harakavy, and Puckett, *Dewey's Dream*, 71–73.

Bibliography

Alter, Charlotte. "The Young and the Relentless." *Time*, April 2, 2018, 25–31.

Alwin, Duane. "From Obedience to Autonomy: Changes in Traits Desired in Children, 1924–1978." *Public Opinion Quarterly* 52, no. 1 (1988): 33–52. https://doi.org/10.1086/269081.

American Psychiatric Association. *Diagnostic and Statistical Manual of Mental Disorders.* 5th ed. Arlington, VA: American Psychiatric Association, 2013.

Anderson, Lisa R., and Jennifer M. Mellor. "Predicting Health Behaviors with an Experimental Measure of Risk Preference." *Journal of Health Economics* 27, no. 5 (2008): 1260–1274. https://doi.org/10.1016/j.jhealeco.2008.05.011.

André, Malin, Lauren Lissner, Calle Bengtsson, Tore Hällström, Valter Sundh, and Cecilia Björkelund. "Cohort Differences in Personality in Middle-Aged Women during a 36-Year Period. Results from the Population Study of Women in Gothenburg." *Scandinavian Journal of Public Health* 38, no. 5 (2010): 457–464. https://doi.org/10.1177/1403494810371247.

Aristotle. *On Rhetoric: A Theory of Civic Discourse.* 2nd ed. Translated by George A. Kennedy. New York: Oxford University Press, 2007.

Arnett, Jeffrey Jensen. *Emerging Adulthood: The Winding Road from the Late Teens through the Twenties.* New York: Oxford University Press, 2004.

———. "Oh, Grow Up! Generational Grumbling and the New Life Stage of Emerging Adulthood—Commentary on Trzesniewski and Donnellan." *Perspectives on Psychological Science* 5, no. 1 (2010): 89–92. https://doi.org/10.1177/1745691609357016.

Ball, Kylie, and David Crawford. "Socioeconomic Status and Weight Change in Adults: A Review." *Social Science and Medicine* 60, no. 9 (2005): 1987–2010. https://doi.org/10.1016/j.socscimed.2004.08.056.

Barber, Benjamin. *Consumed: How Markets Corrupt Children, Infantilize Adults, and Swallow Citizens Whole.* New York: W. W. Norton, 2007.

Bartlett, Sharon and Marie Lerose, dir. *Generation Boomerang.* Vancouver: Dreamfilm Productions, 2011.

Bates, Réal. "Naissance d'une population. Les Français établis au Canada au XVIIᵉ siècle." *Population* 44, no. 1 (1989): 159–164. https://doi.org/10.2307/153333.

Bauerlein, Mark. *The Dumbest Generation: How the Digital Age Stupefies Young Americans and Jeopardizes Our Future.* New York: Penguin, 2009.

Belanger, Claude. Quebec History, "Birth Rate." Last revised August 28, 2000. http://faculty.marianopolis.edu/c.belanger/quebechistory/events/birth8.htm.

Bell, Daniel. *The Cultural Contradictions of Capitalism.* New York: Basic Books, 1976.

Benjamin, Oliver, and Dwayne Eutsey. *The Abide Guide: Living Like Lebowski.* Berkeley, CA: Ulysses, 2011.

Benson, Lee, Ira Harakavy, and John Puckett. *Dewey's Dream: Universities and Democracies in an Age of Education Reform.* Philadelphia: Temple University Press, 2007.

Bhatti, Yosef, and Kasper M. Hansen. "The Effect of Generation and Age on Turnout to the European Parliament—How Turnout Will Continue to Decline in the

Future." *Electoral Studies* 31, no. 2 (2012): 262–272. https://doi.org/10.1016/j.electstud.2011.11.004.

Bibby, Reginald W., with Sarah Russell and Ron Rolheiser. *The Emerging Millennials: How Canada's Newest Generation Is Responding to Change and Choice.* Lethbridge, AB: Project Canada Books, 2009.

Blais, André, Elisabeth Gidengil, Neil Nevitte, and Richard Nadeau. "Where Does Turnout Decline Come From?" *European Journal of Political Research* 43, no. 2 (2004): 221–236. https://doi.org/10.1111/j.1475-6765.2004.00152.x.

Bly, Robert. *Sibling Society: An Impassioned Plea for the Rediscovery of Adulthood.* New York: Vintage Books, 1997.

Borghans, Lex, Angela Lee Duckworth, James J. Heckman, and Bas ter Weel. "The Economics and Psychology of Personality Traits." *Journal of Human Resources* 43, no. 4 (2008): 972–1059. https://doi.org/10.3368/jhr.43.4.972.

Brandstätter, Hermann, and Karl-Dieter Opp. "Personality Traits ('Big Five') and the Propensity to Political Protest: Alternative Models." *Political Psychology* 35, no. 4 (2014): 515–537. https://doi.org/10.1111/pops.12043.

Brashears, Matthew E. "Small Networks and High Isolation? A Reexamination of American Discussion Networks." *Social Networks* 33, no. 4 (2011): 331–341. https://doi.org/10.1016/j.socnet.2011.10.003.

Bromnick, Rachel D., and Brian L. Swallow. "I Like Being Who I Am: A Study of Young People's Ideals." *Educational Studies* 25, no. 2 (1999): 117–128. https://doi.org/10.1080/03055699997855.

Brown, Sarah, Gaia Garino, and Karl Taylor. "Household Debt and Attitudes towards Risk." *Review of Income and Wealth* 59, no. 2 (2013): 283–304. https://doi.org/10.1111/j.1475-4991.2012.00506.x.

Brunell, Amy B., Sara Staats, Jamie Burden, and Julie M. Hupp. "Narcissism and Academic Dishonesty: The Exhibitionism Dimension and the Lack of Guilt." *Personality and Individual Differences* 50, no. 3 (2011): 323–328. https://doi.org/10.1016/j.paid.2010.10.006.

Buck, Walter. "A Measurement of Changes in Attitudes and Interests of University Students over a Ten-Year Period." *Journal of Abnormal and Social Psychology* 31, no. 1 (1936): 12–19. https://doi.org/10.1037/h0057733.

Burgo, Joseph. "How Aggressive Narcissism Explains Lance Armstrong." *Atlantic,* January 28, 2013. https://www.theatlantic.com/health/archive/2013/01/how-aggressive-narcissism-explains-lance-armstrong/272568/.

Cain, Susan. *Quiet: The Power of Introverts in a World That Can't Stop Talking.* New York: Crown, 2012.

Campbell, Colin. *The Romantic Ethic and the Spirit of Modern Consumerism.* Oxford: Basil Blackwell, 1987.

Carney, Dana R., John T. Jost, Samuel D. Gosling, and Jeff Potter. "The Secret Lives of Liberals and Conservatives: Personality Profiles, Interaction Styles, and the Things They Leave Behind." *Political Psychology* 29, no. 6 (2008): 807–840. https://doi.org/10.1111/j.1467-9221.2008.00668.x.

Carpenter, Christopher. "Narcissism on Facebook: Self-Promotional and Anti-social Behavior." *Personality and Individual Differences* 52, no. 4 (2012): 482–486. https://doi.org/10.1016/j.paid.2011.11.011.

Case, Anne, and Angus Deaton. "Rising Morbidity and Mortality in Midlife among White Non-Hispanic Americans in the 21st Century." *Proceedings of the National Academy of Sciences* 112, no. 49 (2015): 15078–15083. https://doi.org/10.1073/pnas.1518393112.

Center for Information and Research on Civic Learning and Engagement. "The Youth Vote in 2012." Medford, MA: Center for Information and Research on Civic Learning and Engagement, Tufts University, 2013. https://civicyouth.org/wp-content/uploads/2013/05/CIRCLE_2013FS_outhVoting2012FINAL.pdf.

Chance, Zoë, Michael I. Norton, Francesca Gino, and Dan Ariely. "Temporal View of the Costs and Benefits of Self-Deception." *Proceedings of the National Academy of Sciences* 108, Supplement 3 (2011): 15655–15659. https://doi.org/10.1073/pnas.1010658108.

Chein, Jason, Dustin Albert, Lia O'Brien, Kaitlyn Uckert, and Laurence Steinberg. "Peers Increase Adolescent Risk Taking by Enhancing Activity in the Brain's Reward Circuitry." *Developmental Science* 14, no. 2 (2011): F1–F10. https://doi.org/10.1111/j.1467-7687.2010.01035.x.

Chudacoff, Howard. *How Old Are You? Age Consciousness in American Culture.* Princeton, NJ: Princeton University Press, 1989.

Cohen, Taya R., A. T. Panter, and Nazli Turan. "Guilt Proneness and Moral Character." *Current Directions in Psychological Science* 21, no. 5 (2012): 355–359. https://doi.org/10.1177/0963721412454874.

Coleman, James. *The Adolescent Society: The Social Life of the Teenager and Its Impact on Education.* New York: Free Press, 1961.

Collins, W. Andrew, Eleanor E. Maccoby, Laurence Steinberg, E. Mavis Hetherington, and Marc H. Bornstein. "Contemporary Research on Parenting: The Case for Nature and Nurture." *American Psychologist* 55, no. 2 (2000): 218–232. https://doi.org/10.1037/0003-066X.55.2.218.

Comacchio, Cynthia. *The Dominion of Youth: Adolescence and the Making of Modern Canada, 1920 to 1950.* Waterloo, ON: Wilfrid Laurier University Press, 2006.

Costa, Paul, and Robert McCrae. *Revised NEO Personality Inventory (NEO PI-R) and NEO Five-Factor Inventory (NEO-FFI): Professional Manual.* Lutz, FL: Psychological Assessment Resources, 1992.

Côté, James. *Arrested Adulthood: The Changing Nature of Maturity and Identity.* New York: NYU Press, 2000.

Credé, Marcus. "Much Ado about Grit: A Meta-analytic Synthesis of the Grit Literature." *Journal of Personality and Social Psychology* 113, no. 3 (2017): 492–511. https://doi.org/10.1037/pspp0000102.

Crissman, Paul. "Temporal Change and Sexual Difference in Moral Judgments." *Journal of Social Psychology* 16, no. 1 (1942): 29–38. https://doi.org/10.1080/00224545.1942.9714102.

Cross, Gary. *Men to Boys: The Making of Modern Immaturity.* New York: Columbia University Press, 2008.

Csikszentmihalyi, Mihaly, and Reed Larson. *Being Adolescent: Conflict and Growth in the Teenage Years.* New York: Basic Books, 1984.

Cutler, David M., and Adriana Lleras-Muney. "Education and Health: Evaluating Theories and Evidence." Working Paper no. 12352, National Bureau of Economic Research, Cambridge, MA, 2006. https://doi.org/10.3386/w12352.

——. "Understanding Differences in Health Behaviors by Education." *Journal of Health Economics* 29, no. 1 (2010): 1–28. https://doi.org/10.1016/j.jhealeco.2009.10.003.

Dalton, Russell J., and Christian Welzel. *The Civic Culture Transformed: From Allegiant to Assertive Citizens.* Cambridge: Cambridge University Press, 2014.

Delli Carpini, Michael X., and Scott Keeter. *What Americans Know about Politics and Why It Matters.* New Haven, CT: Yale University Press, 1996.

Devaux, Marion, Franco Sassi, Jody Church, Michele Cecchini, and Francesca Borgonovi. "Exploring the Relationship between Education and Obesity." *OECD Journal: Economic Studies* 2011, no. 1 (2011): 121–159. http://dx.doi.org/10.1787/eco_studies-2011-5kg5825v1k23.

Dewey, John. "The School as Social Center." *Elementary School Teacher* 3, no. 2 (1902): 73–86. https://www.jstor.org/stable/992485.

Doidge, David. *The Brain That Changes Itself: Stories of Personal Triumph from the Frontiers of Brain Science.* New York: Penguin Books, 2007.

Donnellan, M. Brent, Rand D. Conger, and Chalandra M. Bryant. "The Big Five and Enduring Marriages." *Journal of Research in Personality* 38, no. 5 (2004): 481–504. https://doi.org/10.1016/j.jrp.2004.01.001.

Donnellan, M. Brent, and Kali H. Trzesniewski. "How Should We Study Generational 'Changes'—or Should We? A Critical Examination of the Evidence for 'Generation Me.'" *Social and Personality Psychology Compass* 3, no. 5 (2009): 775–784. https://doi.org/10.1111/j.1751-9004.2009.00204.x.

Donnellan, M. Brent, Kali H. Trzesniewski, and Richard W. Robins. "Personality and Self-Esteem Development in Adolescence." In *Handbook of Personality Development,* edited by Daniel K. Mroczek and Todd D. Little, 285–309. Mahwah, NJ: Lawrence Erlbaum Associates, 2006.

Dostie-Goulet, Eugénie, Isabelle Lacroix, Jean-François Allaire, Ginette Boyer, and Paule Simard. "The School as a City—Cities in the School." Paper presented at Seminar on Lowering the Age to Vote to Sixteen, Brussels, September 23–24, 2010.

Duckworth, Angela. *Grit: The Power of Passion and Perseverance.* New York: Scribner, 2016.

Elkind, David. "Egocentrism in Adolescence." *Child Development* 38, no. 4 (1967): 1025–1034. https://doi.org/10.2307/1127100.

Epstein, Robert. *The Case against Adolescence: Rediscovering the Adult in Every Teen.* Sanger, CA: Quill Driver Books, 2007.

Erikson, Erik. *Identity, Youth and Crisis.* New York: W. W. Norton, 1968.

Fass, Paula S. *The Damned and the Beautiful: American Youth in the 1920's.* Oxford: Oxford University Press, 1977.

Ferguson, Christopher J. "Genetic Contributions to Antisocial Personality and Behavior: A Meta-analytic Review from an Evolutionary Perspective." *Journal of Social Psychology* 150, no. 2 (2010): 160–180. https://doi.org/10.1080/00224540903366503.

Finkelstein, Eric A., Olga A. Khavjou, Hope Thompson, Justin G. Trogdon, Liping Pan, Bettylou Sherry, and William Dietz. "Obesity and Severe Obesity Forecasts through 2030." *American Journal of Preventive Medicine* 42, no. 6 (2012): 563–570. https://doi.org/10.1016/j.amepre.2011.10.026.

Florida, Richard. *The Rise of the Creative Class.* New York: Basic Books, 2002.

——. *Who's Your City? How the Creative Economy Is Making Where to Live the Most Important Decision of Your Life.* Canadian ed. Toronto: Vintage Canada, 2009.

Foa, Roberto Stefan, and Yascha Mounk. "Democratic Deconsolidation in Developed Democracies, 1995–2018." CES Open Forum Series, Minda de Gunzburg Center for European Studies, Harvard University. Accessed July 5, 2019. https://ces.fas.harvard.edu/uploads/art/Working-Paper-PDF-Democratic-Deconsolidation-in-Developed-Democracies-1995-2018.pdf.

——. "The Democratic Disconnect." *Journal of Democracy* 27, no. 3 (2016): 5–17. https://doi.org/10.1353/jod.2016.0049.

——. "The End of the Consolidation Paradigm: A Response to Our Critics." https://www.journalofdemocracy.org/wp-content/uploads/2018/12/Journal-of-Democracy-Web-Exchange-Foa-and-Mounk-reply-2_0.pdf.

——. "The Signs of Deconsolidation." *Journal of Democracy* 28, no. 1 (2017): 5–15. https://doi.org/10.1353/jod.2017.0000.

Forni, P. M. *Choosing Civility: The Twenty-Five Rules of Considerate Conduct.* New York: St. Martin's Griffin, 2002.

——. *The Civility Solution: What to Do When People Are Rude.* New York: St. Martin's Griffin, 2009.

Foster, Joshua D., W. Keith Campbell, and Jean M. Twenge. "Individual Differences in Narcissism: Inflated Self-Views across the Lifespan and around the World." *Journal of Research in Personality* 37, no. 6 (2003): 469–486. https://doi.org/10.1016/S0092-6566(03)00026-6.

Fowler, James, and Cindy Kam. "Delayed Gratification and Turnout: Patience as a Political Virtue." *Political Behavior* 28, no. 2 (2006): 113–128. https://doi.org/10.1007/s11109-006-9004-7.

Galambos, Nancy L., Giselle C. Kolaric, Heather A. Sears, and Jennifer L. Maggs. "Adolescents' Subjective Age: An Indicator of Perceived Maturity." *Journal of Research on Adolescence* 9, no. 3 (1999): 309–337. https://doi.org/10.1207/s15327795jra0903_4.

Galbo, Joseph J. "Adolescents' Perceptions of Significant Adults." *Adolescence* 18, no. 70 (1983): 417–427.

——. "Adolescents' Perceptions of Significant Adults: A Review of the Literature." *Adolescence* 19, no. 76 (1984): 951–970.

Gallego, Aina, and Daniel Oberski. "Personality and Political Participation: The Mediation Hypothesis." *Political Behavior* 34, no. 3 (2012): 425–451. https://doi.org/10.1007/s11109-011-9168-7.

Gerber, Alan S., Gregory A. Huber, David Doherty, and Conor M. Dowling. "The Big Five Personality Traits in the Political Arena." *Annual Review of Political Science* 14, no. 1 (2011): 265–287. https://doi.org/10.1146/annurev-polisci-051010-111659.

Gilmore, Jason. "Trends in Dropout Rates and the Labour Market Outcomes of Young Dropouts." In *Education Matters: Insights on Education, Learning and Training in Canada.* Ottawa: Statistics Canada, 2010. Accessed July 5, 2019. http://www.statcan.gc.ca/pub/81-004-x/81-004-x2010004-eng.htm.

Goldin, Claudia. "America's Graduation from High School: The Evolution and Spread of Secondary Schooling in the Twentieth Century." *Journal of Economic History* 58, no. 2 (1998): 345–374. https://www.jstor.org/stable/2566738.

Gottlieb, Lori. "How to Land Your Kid in Therapy." *Atlantic*, July/August 2011, 64–78.

Grasso, Maria. *Generations, Political Participation and Social Change in Western Europe.* Abingdon, UK: Routledge, 2016.

Gray, Peter. "As Children's Freedom Has Declined, So Has Their Creativity." *Psychology Today*, September 17, 2012. https://www.psychologytoday.com/intl/blog/freedom-learn/201209/children-s-freedom-has-declined-so-has-their-creativity.

Grund, Francis. *The Americans in Their Moral, Social and Political Relations.* 1837. Reprint, New York: Johnson Reprint, 1968.

Ha, Shang E., Seokho Kim, and Se Hee Jo. "Personality Traits and Political Participation: Evidence from South Korea." *Political Psychology* 34, no. 4 (2013): 511–532. https://doi.org/10.1111/pops.12008.

Hall, Stanley. *Adolescence: Its Psychology and Its Relation to Physiology, Anthropology, Sociology, Sex, Crime, Religion and Education.* London: S. Appleton, 1904.

Halpern, David. "Moral Values, Social Trust and Inequality: Can Values Explain Crime?" *British Journal of Criminology* 41, no. 2 (2001): 236–251. https://www.jstor.org/stable/23638820.

Hamilton, Brady E., and Stephanie J. Ventura. "Birth Rates for U.S. Teenagers Reach Historic Lows for All Age and Ethnic Groups." *NCHS Data Brief* no. 89. Atlanta: National Center for Health Statistics, Centers for Disease Control and Prevention, 2012. http://www.cdc.gov/nchs/data/databriefs/db89.pdf.

Harris, Judith Rich. *The Nurture Assumption: Why Children Turn Out the Way They Do.* Rev. ed. New York: Free Press, 2009.

Hart, Daniel, Robert Atkins, Patrick Markey, and James Youniss. "Youth Bulge." In *Youth Activism: An International Encyclopedia*, edited by Lonnie R. Sherrod, 688–690. Westport, CT: Greenwood, 2006.

Hedges, Chris. *Empire of Illusion: The End of Literacy and the Triumph of Spectacle.* Toronto: Alfred A. Knopf Canada, 2009.

Hermann, Silke, Sabine Rohrmann, Jakob Linseisen, Anne M. May, Anton Kunst, Herve Besson, Dora Romaguera, et al. "The Association of Education with Body Mass Index and Waist Circumference in the EPIC-PANACEA Study." *BMC Public Health* 11 (2011): 169–181. https://doi.org/10.1186/1471-2458-11-169.

Hibbing, John R., Kevin B. Smith, and John R. Alford. *Predisposed: Liberals, Conservatives, and the Biology of Political Differences.* New York: Routledge, 2014.

Hoffer, Eric. *The Passionate State of Mind and Other Aphorisms.* New York: Harper & Row, 1954.

Hollingshead, August B. *Elmtown's Youth: The Impact of Social Classes on Adolescents.* New York: John Wiley & Sons, 1949.

Howe, Neil, and William Strauss. *Millennials Rising: The Next Great Generation.* New York: Vintage Books, 2000.

Howe, Paul. *Citizens Adrift: The Democratic Disengagement of Young Canadians.* Vancouver: University of British Columbia Press, 2010.

——. "Eroding Norms and Democratic Deconsolidation." *Journal of Democracy* 28, no. 4 (2017): 15–29. https://doi.org/10.1353/jod.2017.0061.

Huang, Jian, Henriëtte Maassen van den Brink, and Wim Groot. "College Education and Social Trust: An Evidence-Based Study on the Causal Mechanisms." *Social Indicators Research* 104, no. 2 (2011): 287–310. https://doi.org/10.1007/s11205-010-9744-y.

Hugo Lopez, Mark, and Karlo Barrios Marcelo. "Volunteering among Young People." Medford, MA: Center for Information and Research on Civic Learning and Engagement, Tufts University, 2007. https://civicyouth.org/PopUps/FactSheets/FS07_Volunteering.pdf.

Inglehart, Ronald. "After Postmaterialism: An Essay on China, Russia and the United States: A Comment." *Canadian Journal of Sociology*, 41, no. 2 (2016): 213–222. https://doi.org/10.29173/cjs27993.

Inglehart, Ronald, and Christian Welzel. *Modernization, Cultural Change and Democracy: The Human Development Sequence.* Cambridge: Cambridge University Press, 2005.

Issacson, Walter. *Steve Jobs.* New York: Simon & Schuster, 2013.

Jensen, Frances E., with Amy Ellis Nutt. *The Teenage Brain: A Neuroscientist's Survival Guide to Raising Adolescents and Young Adults.* New York: HarperCollins, 2015.

Jokela, Markus. "Birth-Cohort Effects in the Association between Personality and Fertility." *Psychological Science* 23, no. 8 (2012): 835–841. https://doi.org/10.1177/0956797612439067.

Jokela, Markus, Alexandra Alvergne, Thomas V. Pollet, and Virpi Lummaa. "Reproductive Behavior and Personality Traits of the Five Factor Model." *European Journal of Personality* 25, no. 6 (2011): 487–500. https://doi.org/10.1002/per.822.

Jokela, Markus, Taina Hintsa, Mirka Hintsanen, and Liisa Keltikangas-Järvinen. "Adult Temperament and Child-Bearing over the Life Course." *European Journal of Personality* 24, no. 2 (2010): 151–166. https://doi.org/10.1002/per.749.

Kam, Cindy. "Risk Attitudes and Political Participation." *American Journal of Political Science* 56, no. 4 (2012): 817–836. https://doi.org/10.1111/j.1540-5907.2012.00605.x.

Kaufmann, Eric. *Shall the Religious Inherit the Earth? Demography and Politics in the Twenty-First Century*. London: Profile Books, 2010.

Keeter, Scott, Nick Hatley, Courtney Kennedy, and Arnold Lau. "What Low Response Rates Mean for Telephone Surveys." Washington, DC: Pew Research Center, 2017.

Kim, Kyung Hee. "The Creativity Crisis: The Decrease in Creative Thinking Scores on the Torrance Tests of Creative Thinking." *Creativity Research Journal* 23, no. 4 (2011): 285–295. https://doi.org/10.1080/10400419.2011.627805.

Kinney, David A. "From 'Headbangers' to 'Hippies': Delineating Adolescents' Active Attempts to Form an Alternative Peer Culture." *New Directions for Child and Adolescent Development*, no. 84 (1999): 21–35. https://doi.org/10.1002/cd.23219998404.

Kong, Augustine, Gudmar Thorleifsson, Michael L. Frigge, Bjarni J. Vilhjalmsson, Alexander I. Young, Thorgeir E. Thorgeirsson, Stefania Benonisdottir, et al. "The Nature of Nurture: Effects of Parental Genotypes." *Science* 359 (2018): 424–428. https://doi.org/10.1126/science.aan6877.

Konrath, Sarah. "The Empathy Paradox: Increasing Disconnection in the Age of Increasing Connection." In *Handbook of Research on Technoself: Identity in a Technological Society*, edited by Rocci Luppicini, 204–228. Hershey, PA: Information Science Reference, 2013.

Koritzky, Gilly, Eldad Yechiam, Irit Bukay, and Uzi Milman. "Obesity and Risk Taking: A Male Phenomenon." *Appetite* 59, no. 2 (2012): 289–297. https://doi.org/10.1016/j.appet.2012.05.020.

Kroger, Jane. *Identity Development: Adolescence through Adulthood*. 2nd ed. Thousand Oaks, CA: Sage, 2007.

Lapsley, Daniel K., Robert D. Enright, and Ronald C. Serlin. "Toward a Theoretical Perspective on the Legislation of Adolescence." *Journal of Early Adolescence* 5, no. 4 (1985): 441–446. https://doi.org/10.1177/0272431685054004.

Larsen, Christian Albrekt. "Why Social Cohesion Declines in Liberal Regimes, and Increases in Social Democratic Regimes." Paper presented at the International Sociological Association Research Committee 19 conference, Montreal, 2009. http://www.cccg.umontreal.ca/rc19/PDF/Albrekt%20Larsen-C_Rc192009.pdf.

Lesthaeghe, Ron J., and Lisa Neidert. "The Second Demographic Transition in the United States: Exception or Textbook Example?" *Population and Development Review* 32, no. 4 (2006): 669–698. https://doi.org/10.1111/j.1728-4457.2006.00146.x.

Levitsky, Steven, and Daniel Ziblatt. *How Democracies Die*. New York: Crown, 2018.

Lodi-Smith, Jennifer, and Brent Roberts. "Social Investment and Personality: A Meta-analysis of the Relationship of Personality Traits to Investment in Work, Family, Religion and Volunteerism." *Personality and Social Psychology Review* 11, no. 1 (2007): 68–86. https://doi.org/10.1177/1088868306294590.

Lynd, Robert S., and Helen Merrell Lynd. *Middletown: A Study in American Culture*. New York: Harcourt, Brace, 1929.

——. *Middletown in Transition*. New York: Harcourt, Brace, 1937.

MacDonald, Douglas A. "Spirituality: Description, Measurement and Relation to the Five Factor Model of Personality." *Journal of Personality* 68, no. 1 (2000): 153–197. https://doi.org/10.1111/1467-6494.t01-1-00094.

Marcus, George E., John L. Sullivan, Elizabeth Theiss-Morse, and Sandra L. Wood. *With Malice toward Some: How People Make Civil Liberties Judgments.* Cambridge: Cambridge University Press, 1995.

Martin, Joyce A., Brady E. Hamilton, Stephanie J. Ventura, Michelle J. K. Osterman, Elizabeth C. Wilson, and T. J. Mathews. "Births: Final Data for 2010." *National Vital Statistics Reports* 61, no. 1 (2012). https://www.cdc.gov/nchs/data/nvsr/nvsr61/nvsr61_01.pdf.

May, Elizabeth. *Losing Confidence: The Crisis in Canadian Democracy.* Toronto: McClelland & Stewart, 2009.

McAdams, Dan. "The Psychology of Life Stories." *Review of General Psychology* 5, no. 2 (2001): 100–122. https://doi.org/10.1037/1089-2680.5.2.100.

McCabe, Donald L., Linda Klebe Treviño, and Kenneth D. Butterfield. "Cheating in Academic Institutions: A Decade of Research." *Ethics and Behavior* 11, no. 3 (2001): 219–232. https://doi.org/10.1207/S15327019EB1103_2.

McCrae, Robert R. "Creativity, Divergent Thinking, and Openness to Experience." *Journal of Personality and Social Psychology* 52, no. 6 (1987): 1258–1265. https://doi.org/10.1037/0022-3514.52.6.1258.

——. "Social Consequences of Experiential Openness." *Psychological Bulletin* 120, no. 3 (1996): 323–337. https://doi.org/10.1037/0033-2909.120.3.323.

McCrae, Robert R., Paul T. Costa, Margarida Pedroso de Lima, António Simões, Fritz Ostendorf, Alois Angleitner, and Ralph L. Piedmont. "Age Differences in Personality across the Adult Life Span: Parallels in Five Cultures." *Developmental Psychology* 35, no. 2 (1999): 466–477. https://doi.org/10.1037/0012-1649.35.2.46.

McKay, Alexander. "Trends in Canadian National and Provincial/Territorial Teen Pregnancy Rate: 2001–2010." *Canadian Journal of Human Sexuality* 21, no. 3–4 (2012): 161–175.

McPherson, Miller, Lynn Smith-Lovin, and Matthew E. Brashears. "Social Isolation in America: Changes in Core Discussion Networks over Two Decades." *American Sociological Review* 71, no. 3 (2006): 353–375. https://www.jstor.org/stable/30038995.

Meyer, Dick. *Why We Hate Us: American Discontent in the New Millennium.* New York: Three Rivers, 2008.

Miller, Joshua D., and Donald Lynam. "Structural Models of Personality and Their Relation to Antisocial Behavior: A Meta-analytic Review." *Criminology* 39, no. 4 (2001): 765–798. https://doi.org/10.1111/j.1745-9125.2001.tb00940.x.

Milner, Henry. *Civic Literacy: How Informed Citizens Make Democracy Work.* Hanover, NH: University Press of New England, 2002.

Mondak, Jeffery J. *Personality and the Foundations of Political Behavior.* Cambridge: Cambridge University Press, 2010.

Mondak, Jeffery J., Matthew V. Hibbing, Damarys Canache, Mitchell A. Seligson, and Mary R. Anderson. "Personality and Civic Engagement: An Integrative Framework for the Study of Trait Effects on Political Behavior." *American Political Science Review* 104, no. 1 (2010): 85–110. https://doi.org/10.1017/S0003055409990359.

Montepare, Joann M., and Margie E. Lachman. " 'You're Only as Old as You Feel': Self-Perceptions of Age, Fears of Aging, and Life Satisfaction from Adolescence to Old Age." *Psychology and Aging* 4, no. 1 (1989): 73–78. https://doi.org/10.1037/0882-7974.4.1.73.

Murray, Charles. *Coming Apart: The State of White America, 1960–2010.* New York: Crown Forum, 2012.

Mutz, Diana C. *Hearing the Other Side: Deliberative versus Participatory Democracy.* New York: Cambridge University Press, 2006.

National Center for Education Statistics. *Digest of Education Statistics: 2012.* Washington, DC: National Center for Education Statistics, US Department of Education, 2013. https://nces.ed.gov/pubs2014/2014015.pdf.

——. *Digest of Education Statistics: 2013.* Washington, DC: National Center for Education Statistics, US Department of Education, 2015. https://nces.ed.gov/pubs2015/2015011.pdf.

Nettle, Daniel. *Personality: What Makes You the Way You Are.* New York: Oxford University Press, 2007.

Nicholson, Nigel, Emma Soane, Mark Fenton-O'Creevy, and Paul Willman. "Personality and Domain Specific Risk-Taking." *Journal of Risk Research* 8, no. 2 (2005): 157–176. https://doi.org/10.1080/1366987032000123856.

Nie, Norman H., Jane Junn, and Kenneth Stehlik-Berry. *Education and Democratic Citizenship in America.* Chicago: University of Chicago Press, 1996.

Ogden, Cynthia, Margaret D. Carroll, Brian K. Kit, and Katherine M. Flegal. "Prevalence of Childhood and Adult Obesity in the United States, 2011–2012." *Journal of the American Medical Association* 311, no. 8 (2014): 806–814. https://doi.org/10.1001/jama.2014.732.

Orth, Ulrich, Richard W. Robins, and Christopher J. Soto. "Tracking the Trajectory of Shame, Guilt, and Pride across the Life Span." *Journal of Personality and Social Psychology* 99, no. 6: 1061–1071. https://doi.org/10.1037/a0021342.

Ortiz-Ospina, Esteban, and Max Roser. "Trust." Our World in Data, 2017. Accessed July 5, 2019. https://ourworldindata.org/trust.

Palladino, Grace. *Teenagers: An American History.* New York: Basic Books, 1996.

Parmenter, K., J. Waller, and J. Wardle. "Demographic Variation in Nutrition Knowledge in England." *Health Education Research* 15, no. 2 (2000): 163–174. https://doi.org/10.1093/her/15.2.163.

Peterson, A. D. C. *A Hundred Years of Education.* London: Gerald Duckworth, 1952.

Pinker, Steven. *Enlightenment Now: The Case for Reason, Science, Humanism, and Progress.* New York: Viking, 2018.

Postman, Neil. *Amusing Ourselves to Death: Public Discourse in the Age of Show Business.* 20th anniversary ed. New York: Penguin Books, 2005.

Pressey, S. L. "Changes from 1923 to 1943 in the Attitudes of Public School and University Students." *Journal of Psychology* 21, no. 1 (1946): 173–188. https://doi.org/10.1080/00223980.1946.9917279.

Preston, Samuel H., and John McDonald. "The Incidence of Divorce within Cohorts of American Marriages Contracted since the Civil War." *Demography,* 16, no. 1 (1979): 1–25. https://doi.org/10.2307/2061075.

Provencher, Véronique, Catherine Bégin, Marie-Pierre Gagnon-Girouard, Angelo Tremblay, Sonia Boivin, and Simone Lemieux. "Personality Traits in Overweight and Obese Women: Associations with BMI and Eating Behaviors." *Eating Behaviors* 9, no. 3 (2008): 294–302. https://doi.org/10.1016/j.eatbeh.2007.10.004.

Public Safety Canada Portfolio Corrections Statistics Committee. "Corrections and Conditional Release Statistical Overview." Ottawa: Public Works and Government Services Canada, 2009. https://www.publicsafety.gc.ca/cnt/rsrcs/pblctns/ccrso-2009/2009-ccrs-eng.pdf.

Pugh, Mary Jo V., and Daniel Hart. "Identity Development and Peer Group Participation." *New Directions for Child and Adolescent Development,* no. 84 (1999): 55–70. https://doi.org/10.1002/cd.23219998406.

Putnam, Robert. *Bowling Alone: The Collapse and Revival of American Community*. New York: Touchstone, 2000.

——. *Our Kids: The American Dream in Crisis*. New York: Simon & Schuster, 2015.

R. A. Malatest & Associates. National Youth Survey Report. Ottawa: Elections Canada, 2011. http://www.elections.ca/content.aspx?section=res&dir=rec/part/nysr&document=index&lang=e.

Reeves, Richard V., and Dimitrios Halikias. *The Liberal Case for Character in a Populist Age*. Washington, DC: Brookings Institution, 2017. https://www.brookings.edu/wp-content/uploads/2017/04/ccf_20170421_liberal_case_for_character_reeves.pdf.

Riesman, David, with Nathan Glazer and Reuel Denney. *The Lonely Crowd: A Study of the Changing American Character*. New Haven, CT: Yale University Press, 1950.

Ringer, Fritz K. *Education and Society in Modern Europe*. Bloomington: Indiana University Press, 1979.

Roberts, Brent W., and Timothy Bogg. "A Longitudinal Study of the Relationships between Conscientiousness and the Social-Environmental Factors and Substance-Use Behaviors That Influence Health." *Journal of Personality* 72, no. 2 (2004): 325–354. https://doi.org/10.1111/j.0022-3506.2004.00264.x.

Roberts, Brent W., Nathan R. Kuncel, Rebecca Shiner, Avshalom Caspi, and Lewis R. Goldberg. "The Power of Personality: The Comparative Validity of Personality Traits, Socioeconomic Status, and Cognitive Ability for Predicting Important Life Outcomes." *Perspectives on Psychological Science* 2, no. 4 (2007): 313–345. https://doi.org/10.1111/j.1745-6916.2007.00047.x.

Roberts, Paul. *The Impulse Society: America in the Age of Instant Gratification*. New York: Bloomsbury, 2014.

Romano, Andrew. "How Ignorant Are Americans?" *Newsweek*, March 20, 2011. http://www.newsweek.com/how-ignorant-are-americans-66053.

Rosentiel, Tom. "Public Knows Basic Facts about Politics, Economics, but Struggles with Specifics," Pew Research Center, November 18, 2010, http://www.pewresearch.org/2010/11/18/public-knows-basic-facts-about-politics-economics-but-struggles-with-specifics/.

Rumbaut, Rubén G. "Children of Immigrants and Their Achievement: The Role of Family, Acculturation, Social Class, Gender, Ethnicity, and School Contexts." In *Addressing the Achievement Gap: Theory Informing Practice*, edited by Ronald D. Taylor, 23–59. Charlotte, NC: Information Age, 2005.

Sander, Thomas H., and Robert D. Putnam. "Still Bowling Alone? The Post-9/11 Split." *Journal of Democracy* 21, no. 1 (2010): 9–16. https://doi.org/10.1353/jod.0.0153.

Sasse, Ben. *The Vanishing American Adult: Our Coming-of-Age Crisis and How to Rebuild a Culture of Self-Reliance*. New York: St. Martin's, 2017.

Savage, Jon. *Teenage: The Creation of Youth Culture*. New York: Viking, 2007.

Schadwel, Philip, and Christopher R. H. Garneau. "The Diffusion of Tolerance: Birth Cohort Changes in the Effects of Education and Income on Political Tolerance." *Sociological Forum* 32, no. 4 (2017): 748–768. https://doi.org/10.1111/socf.12374.

Schegel, Alice, and Herbert Barry III. *Adolescence: An Anthropological Inquiry*. New York: Free Press, 1991.

Schrum, Kelly. *Some Wore Bobby Sox: The Emergence of Teenage Girls' Culture, 1920–1945*. New York: Palgrave, 2004.

Schudson, Michael. *The Good Citizen: A History of American Civic Life*. Cambridge, MA: Harvard University Press, 1998.

Sercombe, Howard, and Tomas Paus. "The 'Teen Brain' Research: An Introduction and Implications for Practitioners." *Youth & Policy*, no. 103 (2009): 25–37.

Skenazy, Lenore. *Free-Range Kids: How to Raise Safe, Self-Reliant Children (without Going Nuts with Worry)*. San Francisco: Jossey-Bass, 2009.

Smits, Iris A. M., C. V. Dolan, H. C. Vorst, J. M. Wicherts, and M. E. Timmerman. "Cohort Differences in Big Five Personality Traits over a Period of 25 Years." *Journal of Personality and Social Psychology* 100, no. 6 (2011): 1133–1134. https://doi.org/10.1037/a0022874.

Snyder, Howard N. "Arrest in the United States, 1990–2010." Washington, DC: US Department of Justice, Bureau of Justice Statistics, 2012. https://www.bjs.gov/content/pub/pdf/aus9010.pdf.

Snyder, Thomas D., ed. *120 Years of American Education: A Statistical Portrait*. Washington, DC: US Department of Education, National Center for Education Statistics, 1993.

Soto, Christopher J., Oliver P. John, Samuel D. Gosling, and Jeff Potter. "Age Differences in Personality Traits from 10 to 65: Big Five Domains and Facets in a Large Cross-Sectional Sample." *Journal of Personality and Social Psychology* 100, no. 2 (2011): 330–348. https://doi.org/10.1037/a0021717.

Steinberg, Laurence. *Age of Opportunity: Lessons from the New Science of Adolescence*. New York: Mariner Books, 2015.

Steinberg, Laurence, Grace Icenogle, Elizabeth P. Shulman, Kaitlyn Breiner, Jason Chein, Dario Bacchini, Lei Chang, et al. "Around the World Adolescence Is a Time of Heightened Sensation Seeking and Immature Self-Regulation." *Developmental Science* 21, no. 2 (2018): 1–13. https://doi.org/10.1111/desc.12532.

Stevenson, Betsey, and Justin Wolfers. "Marriage and Divorce: Changes and Their Driving Forces." *Journal of Economic Perspectives* 21, no. 2 (2007): 27–52. https://doi.org/10.1257/jep.21.2.27.

Stouffer, Samuel A. *Communism, Conformity, and Civil Liberties*. Garden City, NY: Doubleday, 1955.

Strauch, Barbara. *The Primal Teen: What the New Discoveries about the Teenage Brain Tell Us about Our Kids*. New York: Anchor Books, 2003.

Sullivan, John L., James Piereson, and George E. Marcus. *Political Tolerance and American Democracy*. Chicago: University of Chicago Press, 1982.

Sunstein, Cass R. *Going to Extremes: How Like Minds Unite and Divide*. Oxford: Oxford University Press, 2009.

Susman, Warren I. "'Personality' and the Making of Twentieth-Century Culture." In *Culture as History: The Transformation of American Society in the Twentieth Century*. New York: Pantheon, 1984.

Sutin, Angelina, Luigi Ferrucci, Alan B. Zonderman, and Antonio Terracciano. "Personality and Obesity across the Adult Life Span." *Journal of Personality and Social Psychology* 101, no. 3 (2011): 579–592. https://doi.org/10.1037/a0024286.

Swift, J. A., C. Glazebrook, and I. Macdonald. "Validation of a Brief, Reliable Scale to Measure Knowledge about the Health Risks Associated with Obesity." *International Journal of Obesity* 30, no. 4: 661–668. https://doi.org/10.1038/sj.ijo.0803165.

Taylor, Charles. *The Malaise of Modernity*. Toronto: House of Anansi, 1991.

Taylor, Paul, and Scott Keeter, eds. *Millennials: A Portrait of Generation Next*. Washington, DC: Pew Research Center, February 2010.

Teigen, Karl Halvor, Hanne-Trine Engdal Normann, Jan Ove Bjorkheim, and Sturla Helland. "Who Would You Most Like to Be Like? Adolescents' Ideals at the Beginning and the End of the Century." *Scandinavian Journal of Educational Research* 44, no. 1 (2000): 5–26. https://doi.org/10.1080/713696661.

Terracciano, Antonio, Angelina R. Sutin, Robert R. McCrae, Barbara Deiana, Luigi Ferrucci, David Schlessinger, Manuela Uda, and Paul T. Costa Jr. "Facets of Personality Linked to Underweight and Overweight." *Psychosomatic Medicine* 71, no. 6 (2009): 682–689. https://doi.org/10.1097/PSY.0b013e3181a2925b.

Tocqueville, Alexis de. *Democracy in America.* Edited by J. P. Mayer. 1835. Reprint, Garden City, NY: Anchor Books, 1969.

Tough, Paul. *How Children Succeed: Grit, Curiosity, and the Hidden Power of Character.* Boston: Houghton Mifflin Harcourt, 2012.

——. "How Kids Really Succeed." *Atlantic,* June 2016.

Turkle, Sherry. *Alone Together: Why We Expect More from Technology and Less from Each Other.* New York: Basic Books, 2011.

Twenge, Jean M. "Birth Cohort Changes in Extraversion: A Cross-Temporal Meta-analysis, 1966–1993." *Personality and Individual Differences* 30, no. 5 (2001): 735–748. https://doi.org/10.1016/S0191-8869(00)00066-0.

——. *Generation Me: Why Today's Young Americans Are More Confident, Assertive, Entitled—and More Miserable Than Ever Before.* New York: Free Press, 2006.

——. *Generation Me: Why Today's Young Americans Are More Confident, Assertive, Entitled—and More Miserable Than Ever Before.* Rev. ed. New York: Atria, 2014.

Twenge, Jean M., and W. Keith Campbell. *The Narcissism Epidemic: Living in the Age of Entitlement.* New York: Free Press, 2009.

Twenge, Jean M., Julie J. Exline, Joshua B. Grubbs, Ramya Sastry, and W. Keith Campbell. "Generational and Time Period Differences in American Adolescents' Religious Orientation, 1966–2014." *PLoS ONE* 10, no. 5 (2015): 1–17. https://doi.org/10.1371/journal.pone.0121454.

Twenge, Jean M., Brittany Gentile, and W. Keith Campbell. "Birth Cohort Differences in Personality." In *APA Handbook of Personality and Social Psychology,* vol. 4, *Personality Processes and Individual Differences,* edited by Mario Mikulincer and Phillip R. Shaver, 535–551. Washington DC: American Psychological Association, 2015.

Twenge, Jean M., and Charles Im. "Changes in the Need for Social Approval, 1958–2001." *Journal of Research in Personality* 41, no. 1 (2007): 171–189. https://doi.org/10.1016/j.jrp.2006.03.006.

Twenge, Jean M., Sara Konrath, Joshua D. Foster, W. Keith Campbell, and Brad J. Bushman. "Egos Inflating over Time: A Cross-Temporal Meta-analysis of the Narcissistic Personality Inventory." *Journal of Personality* 76, no. 4 (2008): 875–901. https://doi.org/10.1111/j.1467-6494.2008.00507.x.

Underwood, Nora. "The Teenage Brain: Why Adolescents Sleep In, Take Risks and Won't Listen to Reason." *Walrus,* November 2006. Accessed July 5, 2019. https://thewalrus.ca/the-teenage-brain/.

van der Linden, Dimitri, Jan te Nijenhuis, and Arnold B. Baker. "The General Factor of Personality: A Meta-analysis of Big Five Intercorrelations and a Criterion-Related Validity Study." *Journal of Research in Personality* 44, no. 3 (2010): 315–327. https://doi.org/doi:10.1016/j.jrp.2010.03.003.

Vazire, Simine, Laura P. Naumann, Peter J. Rentfrow, and Samuel D. Gosling. "Portrait of a Narcissist: Manifestations of Narcissism in Physical Appearance." *Journal of Research in Personality* 42, no. 6 (2008): 1439–1447. https://doi.org/10.1016/j.jrp.2008.06.007.

Vedel, Anna. "Big Five Personality Group Differences across Academic Majors: A Systematic Review." *Personality and Individual Differences* 92 (2016): 1–10. https://doi.org/10.1016/j.paid.2015.12.011.

Wallace, Meri. "Coping with an Angry Teenager." *Psychology Today*, February 25, 2018. https://www.psychologytoday.com/ca/blog/how-raise-happy-cooperative-child/201802/coping-angry-teenager.

Wattenberg, Martin. *Is Voting for Young People?* New York: Pearson Education, 2008.

Welzel, Christian. *Freedom Rising: Human Empowerment and the Quest for Emancipation.* Cambridge: Cambridge University Press, 2013.

Wilkinson, Richard, and Kate Pickett. *The Spirit Level: Why Greater Equality Makes Societies Stronger.* New York: Bloomsbury, 2009.

Wiseman, Rosalind. *Queen Bees and Wannabes: Helping Your Daughter Survive Cliques, Gossip, Boyfriends, and Other Realities of Adolescence.* New York: Crown, 2002.

Wolfe, Alan. *The Politics of Petulance: America in an Age of Immaturity.* Chicago: University of Chicago Press, 2018.

Wolfe, Tom. "The 'Me' Decade and the Third Great Awakening." *New York Magazine*, August 23, 1976.

Zangwill, Israel. *The Melting Pot.* Toronto: S. B. Gundy, 1915.

Zuckerman, Marvin. *Sensation Seeking and Risky Behavior.* Washington, DC: American Psychological Association, 2007.

Index

abortion, 173, 177–78, 187. *See also* reproductive choices

academic success, 141–42, 169. *See also* education; education levels

adolescence: brain development during, 25–29; crucible of, 33–34, 41–42, 54, 60, 70 (*see also* adolescent society); origin of term "teenager," 42, 149, 204n30; personal identity and, 48–51; personality traits (*see* character development; influences on personality; personality traits); research literature on, 73–74; social/economic/legal constraints during, 13; storm-and-stress behavior, 12–13, 33, 38, 112; subjective age and, 48–51; values and, 29–30, 51

adolescent society, 1–11; cliques, 46–47; democracy and (*see* civic engagement; political engagement; voter participation); education and, 8–9 (*see also* education; postsecondary education; secondary education); education gaps and, 162–65; emergence of, 12; future of, 192–97; group identity and, 42; millennials and, 168–75 (*see also* millennial generation); negative effects of, 5–8, 21, 73–88, 97–106, 164–65, 193–96; origins of, 34–42; positive and liberating aspects of, 6–7, 89–97, 108–9; social change and, 69–70 (*see also* social change); socialization process and, 4–5, 8, 29, 35; social segregation of, 14. *See also* youth culture

adulthood: adolescent qualities in (*see* adolescent society); arrested, 107–8; emerging, 107, 139, 182; milestones of, 106–7

adulting, concept of, 106

advancement, individual, 142, 161, 164. *See also* economic behavior

adventurousness, 74, 103–6, 133–34

advertising, 54–55, 134, 146, 159

aesthetics, 23–24

African Americans. *See* racial and ethnic minorities

age-based restrictions, 13

aggressive behavior, 21–22, 38

agreeableness: decline in, 57, 60, 74; defined, 14; ethical behavior and, 85–87; marriage and, 76; overview of, 21–22; protest politics and, 120; reproductive choices and, 183–84, 188; social approval and, 62; work/family life and, 107

alcohol use, 168

alpha teens, 46–47

anger, 21–22, 30

antisocial attitudes and behavior: genetics and, 220n67; measurement of, 209nn24–25; negative effects of, 193; by politicians, 113, 129; prevalence in US, 147; reproductive choices and, 185–88; rise in, 57, 79–87; social trust and, 156–57; undemocratic views and, 127–28. *See also* criminal behavior

antisocial personality disorder, 85

Apple (corporation), 140

Apprentice, The (television show), 74

Aristotle, 63

Armstrong, Lance, 87

army rule, support for, 123–28

Arnett, Jeffrey, 107, 139

Arrested Development (television show), 1

A-Team, The (television show), 102

authoritarian attitudes, 128

autonomy, personal, 31, 48, 145–47, 150, 165; development of, 195; employment and, 139–40

baby boomers, 67–70

Barber, Benjamin, 6–7, 100, 146–47

Bauerlein, Mark, 101

Bell, Daniel, 215n3

Bibby, Reginald, 170, 179

Big Brother (television show), 74

Big Lebowski, The (film), 17

birthrates: among teenagers, 168–70; decline in, 176–77, 190

bohemian index, 136–37

brain development, 25–29

bribery, 80–81, 84–85, 127, 185, 216n25. *See also* antisocial attitudes and behavior

Britain, 149
British Household Panel Study, 15–16, 18, 23, 199
Brokaw, Tom, 170
Bronfenbrenner, Urie, 88
Brookings Institution, 194
Brooks, David, 112
Bush, George W., 64, 151

Cain, Susan, 52–55, 58, 71
Callahan, David, 86–87
Campbell, Colin, 134
Campbell, W. Keith, 60, 62, 67–68, 70, 134, 207n47
Canada, 11, 108; high schools, 40; millennial generation, 170–71; politicians in, 110–12. *See also* Quebec
Canadian surveys, 19–21, 24–25, 79, 114–15, 139
capitalism, 7, 146–50, 215n3
Carnegie, Dale, 53
Carpool Karaoke (television show), 1
Catcher in the Rye, The (Salinger), 48
Catholicism, 178–80
character development: environmental influences on, 66–68, 195–96; importance of, 191; long-term trends in, 7–8; parental influence on, 42–45; personal social networks and, 66–70. *See also* genetic dispositions; personality traits
character education, 151–52, 174
charisma, 53–55, 102
cheating, 6, 80–81, 84–87, 185. *See also* antisocial attitudes and behavior; bribery; lying; tax evasion
Cheers (television show), 24
childbearing. *See* birthrates; parenting; reproductive choices
childhood: peers and, 47–48; transition to adulthood, 5. *See also* adolescence; parental influence on children
child labor, 38
Christakis, Nicholas, 66
Chudacoff, Howard, 35
cigarette use, 168
Citizens Assembly (Canada), 102
city-schools, 37
civic duty, 114–15, 118, 152–54
civic engagement, 7, 71–72, 174; millennials and, 169, 218n15. *See also* political engagement; voter participation
civic knowledge, 116–17, 205n47
civility: decline in, 6, 75–76, 87, 111–13; democracy and, 131; principles of, 75, 87, 111
Civility Initiative, 75

civil rights movement, 121
Clark, Dick, 1
class: adolescent society and, 41; education and, 36; social advancement and, 164; social problems and, 163. *See also* creative class
climate change, 135
Clinton, Bill, 64, 151
Clinton, Hillary, 164, 173
cliques, 46–47
Colbert, Stephen, 103
Coleman, James, 2–3, 5, 32, 34, 36–37, 39, 46, 63
college. *See* postsecondary education
Comacchio, Cynthia, 58
compliance, 21
conformity, 31–32
conscientiousness: academic success and, 142; achievement motivation and, 184; choice of college major and, 172–73, 218n31; cliques and, 46; decline in, 57, 60, 74; defined, 14; ethical behavior and, 85–87; impulsivity and, 99, 133; individualism and, 30; marriage and, 76; obesity and, 159; occupational success and, 140; overview of, 15–17; reproductive choices and, 184–85, 188; social approval and, 62; work/family life and, 107
Conservative Party (Canada), 111
conservatives, 69, 129–30, 173; family size, 179–80; millennials and, 180
consumerism, 54–55, 99, 133–35, 193; impulsivity and, 133, 146–47
cost-benefit calculation, in voting, 115
Côté, James, 7, 107–8, 151, 159
creative class, 136–40, 161
creativity, 6, 161–62; cultivation of, 195; decline in, 171–72, 174; employment and, 38, 136–38, 161; openness and, 136–38, 140; social change and, 9
criminal behavior, 85, 87, 163; decline in, 168, 170–71
Cronkite, Walter, 116
Cross, Gary, 7, 58–59
cultural anthropology, 209n24
cultural change, 72. *See also* social change
culture wars, 69
curiosity, 142

Dead Poets Society (film), 38
Dean, James, 42
deception. *See* lying
demagogic leaders, 123
democracy, 4, 6, 10, 71–72, 90–91, 110–22; deconsolidation and dysfunction, 123–31,